Praise for *Buddhist Masters of Modern China*

"*Buddhist Masters of Modern China* is a long-awaited book on the prominent monastics who revitalized Chinese Buddhism in the modern era. Through engaging portrayals of their lives and teachings, it shows the resilience and innovation that sustained their tradition during times of political and social upheaval. For those seeking a deeper understanding of Chinese Buddhism's legacy, this work illuminates influential figures largely unknown in the West, offering a fresh perspective on modern Buddhism."

HAEMIN SUNIM, author of *The Things You Can See Only When You Slow Down*

"Buddhism has been inseparable from Chinese culture for two thousand years. Introduced originally from India, it developed new philosophical systems and meditative practices in China. Political upheavals and social unrest created grave challenges to Buddhism in modern China. But they also provided opportunities of reform, renovation, and revival. This book is about eight Buddhist masters who contributed to this new phase of modern Chinese Buddhism. By telling us their life stories and translating their dharma talks, poems, and writings, the authors show us the vitality and diversity of the Buddhist tradition in modern China. This book is essential reading for anyone interested in learning about modern Chinese Buddhism."

CHUN-FANG YU, Emerita Shengyan Professor in Chinese Buddhism, Columbia University

"This book is like no other. It focuses on the lives and practices of Tiantai, Pure Land, Chan, and teachers from other schools of thought in China. The work of these eminent nuns and monks reveals how modern Chinese Buddhists persevered in the face of political purges, Christian missionary activity, warfare, and natural disasters. By looking at eminent Buddhist poets, ritualists, meditation masters, and activists, Benjamin Brose and other contributors offer the reader refreshing accounts of the dynamism of Buddhism in modern China."

JUSTIN McDANIEL, author of *Wayward Distractions: Ornament, Emotion, Zombies and the Study of Buddhism in Thailand*

"A persistent trope in the discourse of Western Buddhists, particularly Zen practitioners, centers on the supposed long decay of Chinese Buddhism culminating in its death during Mao's Cultural Revolution. The biographies and translated teachings collected here by Benjamin Brose go a long way toward remedying such false notions. The lives of these remarkable modern teachers reveal not only the incredible vibrancy and adaptability of Buddhism in Chinese culture but also point out how Buddhism throughout the world must also adapt in years to come. Those wishing for the survival of a relevant Buddhadharma that preserves the vital thread of awakening will find much here to instruct and inspire."

MEIDO MOORE, Abbot of Korinji monastery and author of *The Rinzai Zen Way: A Guide to Practice* and *Hidden Zen: Practices for Sudden Awakening and Embodied Realization*

"Modern Chinese Buddhism has not attracted the attention it deserves, since it was long thought to be in a decrepit state, with nothing more than a corrupt and uneducated clergy. A generation of scholars and general readers have been swayed in their thinking about its history by accounts that have largely depicted it as a tradition that fell into disrepute, along with China itself, as it devolved away from its glorious earlier days. This excellent volume helps to reset that narrative of decline by telling a different story that sees the period from the late-nineteenth to early-twentieth centuries as one of recovery, recommitment, reform, rebuilding, and revitalization. Many of the figures showcased in this collection are well known—like Xuyun, Taixu, and Hongyi—but the others—like Jichan, Chanxing, and the nun Benkong—are likely new names to most readers. Many of the figures who represent this modernization movement were cosmopolitan figures who traveled outside of China to Japan, Tibet, North America, and Europe. The eight scholars who have been assembled here in this well-designed volume focus on key figures who represent the diversity of this era. We learn about their fascinating lives and the lasting impact they had on the development of modern Chinese Buddhism, and we are given a taste of their thinking, doctrinal orientation, and ideas for practice by hearing their own voices in the translations of a sample of their writings that conclude each section. After reading the chapters in this volume, one can hardly think about modern Chinese Buddhism in the same way as our forebearers and one hopes it will inspire a new generation of scholars to add further to.

This volume succeeds admirably in rewriting the standard narrative about Chinese Buddhism's decline to reveal a history that is filled with lively, committed, and innovative monks and nuns who reformed and restructured the tradition and ushered this new form of Chinese Buddhism into the modern age."

JAMES ROBSON, James C. Kralik and Yunli Lou Professor of East Asian Languages and Civilizations, Harvard University

Buddhist Masters of Modern China

The Lives and Legacies of Eight Eminent Teachers

EDITED BY BENJAMIN BROSE

SHAMBHALA

Shambhala Publications, Inc.
2129 13th Street
Boulder, Colorado 80302
www.shambhala.com

Cover design: Daniel Urban-Brown and Meredith Jarrett
Interior design: Kat Ran Press

9 8 7 6 5 4 3 2 1

First Edition
Printed in the United States of America

Shambhala Publications makes every effort to print on
acid-free, recycled paper.

Shambhala Publications is distributed worldwide by
Penguin Random House, Inc., and its subsidiaries.

LIBRARY OF CONGRESS CATALOGING-IN-PUBLICATION DATA
Names: Brose, Benjamin, editor.
Title: Buddhist masters of modern China: the lives and legacies of eight eminent
    teachers / Benjamin Brose.
Description: First edition. | Boulder, Colorado: Shambhala Publications, Inc.,
    [2025] | Includes bibliographical references and index.
Identifiers: LCCN 2024029255 | ISBN 9781645472230 (trade paperback)
Subjects: LCSH: Buddhism—Study and teaching—China. | Buddhists—China.
Classification: LCC BQ162.C62 A3 2025 | DDC 294.3070951—dc23/eng/20240814
LC record available at https://lccn.loc.gov/2024029255

The authorized representative in the EU for product safety and
compliance is eucomply OÜ, Pärnu mnt 139b-14, 11317 Tallinn, Estonia,
hello@eucompliancepartner.com.

Contents

Buddhist Masters of Modern China

Introduction

Flowers in the Snow

For hundreds of years, China was at the center of the Buddhist world. Clerics from central Asia and India went there to teach, translate, and study. Monks from Korea, Japan, and Vietnam made long and arduous journeys to study under eminent Chinese masters at thriving monasteries. Those intrepid travelers went on to transmit the teachings and traditions of China to their homelands. The entire edifice of East Asian Buddhism rests on foundations laid in China, but you wouldn't necessarily know that today.

In the United States and Europe, the Buddhist traditions that have put down the deepest roots have all come from elsewhere. We know about Tibetan Buddhism, of course, through charismatic teachers like the Dalai Lama (b. 1935) and Chögyam Trungpa (1939-1987). Zen came to the United States via Japan, first through the writings of D. T. Suzuki (1870-1966) and later with the efforts of monks like Nyogen Senzaki (1876-1958) and Shunryu Suzuki (1904-1971); and by way of Vietnam and the pioneering work of Thich Nhat Hanh (1926-2022). The monks Seungsahn (1927-2004) and Samu Sunim (1941-2022) brought Korean Seon to North America in the 1970s. The *vipassana* techniques that underly the modern mindfulness movement originated with prominent Southeast Asian monks and laypeople, men like Mahasi Sayadaw (1904-1982) and S. N. Goenka (1924-2013). Their Western disciples continue to maintain, transmit, and adapt their teachings for larger and larger audiences today. While many Chinese monks have come to the West to offer instruction and establish places of practice, they have mainly addressed their teachings to Chinese-speaking disciples and devotees. None have attracted sizable numbers of Western disciples. Chinese monks and nuns rarely feature in the pages of popular Buddhist magazines in the United States, and their teachings are seldom published by mainstream presses. It is a conspicuous absence. I have been studying Chinese Buddhism for about thirty years now. When I tell people what I do, I am often met with the same incredulous response: "They have Buddhism in China?"

The confusion is understandable. At the first high-profile introduction of Buddhism to the United States—the World's Parliament of Religions in Chicago in 1893—Chinese Buddhists were absent. There were representatives of Japanese Zen and Pure Land traditions. The Sri Lankan monk Anagarika Dharmapala impressed the audience with his eloquent presentation of core Buddhist principles; he would go on to preside over the first Buddhist initiation conducted in the United States. Those in attendance at the Parliament debated the value and veracity of the then novel Buddhist teachings, but they would not hear from any Chinese monks. Discussions of Chinese Buddhism came instead from Confucian officials and Christian missionaries. The news was not good. Pung Kwang Yu, the official Chinese representative to the Parliament, informed his American audience that although Buddhism claimed the greatest numbers of "believers" in China, it was merely a heterodox sect whose superstitious practices were promoted by an uneducated clergy.[1] The Presbyterian minister William Alexander Parsons Martin (1827-1916) concurred. The Buddhist "priesthood [in China]," he announced, "has lapsed into such a state of ignorance and corruption that in Chinese Buddhism there appears to be no possibility of revival."[2] There were no representatives of the Chinese clergy in Chicago, in other words, because there were no serious Buddhists left in China.

Christians had a professional interest in disparaging the competition, and there is a long and lively tradition of missionaries in China denigrating Buddhist teachings in terms such as "the parasitic smut and worm dust of the East."[3] But even Japanese Buddhists seem to have given up hope on their counterparts in China. D. T. Suzuki visited mainland China in the 1930s. He would later report that although "there are still many Zen monasteries in China, it seems to have ceased to be a living spiritual force, as it once was, in the land of its birth. Apparently, Japan is the only place on earth where Zen is still kept alive."[4] The Japanese Zen tradition that Suzuki so effectively championed in the United States first developed in China, and from there it was introduced to Japan in the thirteenth century. According to Suzuki and many of his compatriots, once Chan was established as Zen in Japan, it was refined into a purer, more perfect form. Thereafter, they surmised, Chan began to ossify and lose its vigor in China, devolving into a weak and dissipated form. China was once a great Buddhist empire, according to a line of thought that would be inherited and embraced by Western Zen converts, but that was a very long time ago.

There is a certain amount of cultural chauvinism in such assessments, of course. Japan was laying the groundwork for an invasion of China at the time of Suzuki's visit, and reports of cultural stagnation helped to justify the coming occupation. And yet, people in China did not necessarily disagree with these critiques. The early twentieth century was a tumultuous time on the continent. The two-thousand-year-old imperial system had just collapsed, and a nascent Republican government was struggling to assert control and suppress a proliferation of powerful warlords. China's economic and political sovereignty was embattled on multiple fronts. After two devastating "Opium Wars," when England forced Chinese authorities to allow British merchants to flood the Chinese market with the drug, China had to not only pay humiliating reparations but also grant Western merchants and missionaries the right to travel, trade, and proselytize wherever they pleased. The flood of foreigners that followed brought new ideas—from Christianity to evolution, democracy, capitalism, Marxism, scientific atheism, public education, and pragmatic philosophy—and sparked urgent debates about China's future. Russia was annexing territory in the north. Japan occupied Korea, Taiwan, and Manchuria. The French were in Southeast Asia, and the British controlled India and Hong Kong. With the United States in the Philippines, China was essentially surrounded by colonial powers. (A cartoon from this period shows Queen Victoria of England, Wilhelm II of Germany, Nicholas II of Russia, the French Marianne, and the Meiji emperor hungrily slicing up China as if it were an apple pie.) The Chinese people were in a dangerously vulnerable position, and they knew it. They did not yet have the resources to compete economically or militarily with the West or Japan. Their age-old traditions, the very basis of their collective culture, seemed to be failing them. If they wanted to avoid colonization and subjugation, they would have to modernize as quicky as possible.

In these troubled times, Buddhism was seen by many as a root cause of the nation's most pressing problems rather than a source for solutions. What was the point of maintaining premodern—some would say archaic—traditions like monastic Buddhism in the modern era? China needed social services, political reform, new technologies, economic resources, industry, and defense capabilities. It didn't need legions of monks sitting in meditation and chanting dharani. In an age-old slate of critiques, reprised from past government repressions of the sangha, Buddhist clerics were deemed obstinate impediments to progress. They consumed resources but produced nothing of economic value. They were little more than "rice buckets" who owned extensive buildings and properties yet did not contribute to the material welfare of their communities. Monks were accordingly likened to viruses and parasites infecting the body politic. They taught their followers outmoded ideas about gods and ghosts. They emphasized future rewards—better, heavenly rebirths in far-off utopian pure lands—over practical solutions in the here and now. For many people in positions of power in China, Buddhist clerics and their teachings had become irrelevant at best, destructive at worst. They belonged to a bygone era and had no place in a modern nation.

In such a hostile and unforgiving environment, it is tempting to take Christian missionaries and Japanese observers at their word and conclude that Chinese Buddhism had entered a kind of death spiral. But that would be a mistake. It is often in times of extraordinary instability and tension that creativity and innovation come to the fore. So it was that during the first half of the twentieth century, a generation of monastics and laypeople were at the vanguard of a vigorous and transformative Buddhist movement in China. Often described as a great revival, it was a pivotal era for Buddhist thought and practice on the continent. Men and women, monastic and lay, worked diligently to both preserve the traditions they had inherited from their ancestors and ensure that those teachings would remain intact and accessible long into the future. Chinese Buddhism, far from being in its death throes, was in fact undergoing a kind of rebirth.

This book portrays the lives and teachings of some of the clerics at the forefront of this remarkable revitalization. Each came of age in uncertain, unstable times. The difficulties facing the empire were wide-ranging. Foreign militaries eroded the borders. The imperial court teetered and then fell. Famines, floods, and epidemics left millions of people dead. The suffering was devastating and indiscriminate, but Buddhists were often singled out for special persecution. In 1850, a man claiming to be the younger brother of Jesus Christ launched a massive armed rebellion with the aim of overthrowing the Qing dynasty (1644-1911) and replacing it with a Christian theocracy. Known as the Taiping Heavenly Kingdom, this independent, heavily militarized state controlled tens of thousands of miles of territory for roughly twenty years. Their battles and purges resulted in millions of deaths. The Taipings were based in the Buddhist heartland of southeastern China, and their loathing of Buddhist idolaters meant that countless Buddhist temples were burned to the ground, their resident monks either killed or exiled. When the rebellion was finally put down by the Qing army (with significant help from foreign forces), the road to recovery for Buddhist monks, nuns, and laypeople was long and strewn with obstacles.

Some of the challenges were practical. The cost of rebuilding would be enormous; the timber alone would consume entire forests. Even more daunting was the ideological opposition. Perhaps, some people suggested, there were better uses for the land, buildings, and labor that had previously sustained so many monasteries. Maybe all those images of buddhas and bodhisattvas would be more useful melted down for tools, weapons, or cash. At the end of the nineteenth century, the Qing emperor announced a new policy, "Requisitioning Temples for Promoting Education." Large monasteries and smaller temples were to be converted into schools or government offices. By the 1940s, it is estimated that well over half of China's temples had been destroyed or converted to other uses.[5] Monks and nuns, deprived of land and livelihood, saw their influence and their prospects wither. There is a recurring trope in the biographies of monks and nuns who ordained during this period: when they first try to enter a monastery, someone from their family chases them down and drags them back home. The monastic vocation was seen as a waste of potential.

In China's past, eminent clerics were thoroughly integrated into elite, aristocratic culture. They advised officials and accepted lavish, tax-exempt donations from affluent, well-connected families. Now, times had changed. Many among the patrician class—doctors, lawyers, engineers, civil servants—were converting to Christianity or embracing atheism. The tide of Marxist thought flowing in from Russia and Europe portrayed all religions as duplicitous instruments of oppression. As Chen Duxiu (1879-1942), the cofounder of the Chinese Communist Party, put it, "Amitābha is a cheat and a liar, Jehovah is a cheat and a liar, and so is the Jade Emperor. All the gods, buddhas, immortals, and ghosts that are revered by religionists are useless and cheating idols, and they should all be smashed."[6] For a truly prosperous future to be possible, "superstition" needed to be eradicated. The people should be taught to embrace evolution, revolution, and dialectical materialism. Buddhist doctrines and practices were perfect foils for a utilitarian rationalism. Clerics were accordingly dismissed as ignorant, exploitative, and corrupt. It would be better, many argued, to compel monks to return to lay life so that they could contribute their time and energy to the construction of a new nation. Some influential intellectuals went so far as to suggest a colder, more efficient solution for reducing the monastic population: execution.

These critiques, coming from all quarters, posed an immediate existential threat to the Buddhist order, which needed to respond if it wanted to survive. As the chapters in this book illustrate, those responses took a variety of forms. One thing they all had in common, however, was an admission of some culpability. They recognized that the state of the sangha was not what it ought to be. Snakes were mingling with dragons. Too many monks lacked proper training. Too many were ignorant of basic Buddhist doctrine. They lacked discipline. Monastic leaders thus shared many of the same concerns as their fiercest detractors. They agreed that there were serious problems that needed to be addressed. The solution, however, was not to weaken Buddhist institutions but to empower them. Buddhist texts needed to be studied more intensively and interpreted more creatively. Buddhist practices should be pursued more sincerely and with more tenacity. In short, prominent clerics argued that when Buddhist institutions were supported and permitted to function properly, communities, regions, and the entire nation would flourish. If people were accusing Buddhist monastics of having nothing to offer, it was up to those same monks and nuns to prove them wrong.

Many of the clerics who took up the task of revitalization were closely connected to one another. They studied together, trained in many of the same monasteries, belonged to the same organizations, frequently collaborated, and occasionally debated with one another. While they shared similar struggles and triumphs, their responses to the challenges they faced were by no means uniform.

Their visions of what constituted authentic Buddhist practice, likewise, were diverse and occasionally at odds. Some monastics sought a return to what they saw as the fundamentals of Buddhist training. The problem, according to these clerics, was not that the Buddhist tradition was outmoded but rather that too many monks and laypeople lacked the requisite rigor and self-control to attain results. A greater fidelity to the tradition was needed. Indeed, many Buddhists thought the problems facing China stemmed from a pervasive moral decline and the collective negative karma it generated.

In their efforts to purify themselves, it was common for eminent monks and nuns to focus on a single, relatively simple practice—investigating a "critical phrase" (huatou), reciting the Buddha's name (nianfo), studying a single sutra—and to encourage their disciples to similarly immerse themselves completely in one cultivation technique. This stripped-down, back-to-basics approach called for a return and recommitment to the essential principles—morality (śīla), meditation (samādhi), and wisdom (prajñā)—that had formed the core of Buddhist practice for millennia. One needed to first discipline one's body by adhering to the precepts. Only then could one's mind be tamed and brought to bear on objects of contemplation that generated the wisdom that led to liberation.

There were different opinions about how best to focus the mind and achieve awakening. Some recommended sutra study, others discouraged it. Some promoted social engagement, others went to great lengths to disengage from society. Clerics such as "the Eight-Fingered Ascetic," Jichan (chapter 8) and the brilliant scholar and poet Benkong (chapter 6) expressed their insights through verse, but at some of the stricter monasteries, writing poetry could get you punished or expelled.

For Pure Land masters like Yinguang (chapter 5), recitation of the Buddha's name was the most viable approach to salvation in an age as degenerate as the early twentieth century. Yinguang was committed to countering what he saw as a pervasive ethical malaise in China. People no longer believed in the consequences of karma and so were emboldened to act in ways that exacerbated their own suffering and the suffering of others. Holding out the prospect of rebirth in a heavenly pure land, Yinguang encouraged his legion of followers to cultivate the kind of moral fortitude that would ensure not only their future salvation but also, more broadly, the resolution of crises that were then convulsing the country.

Chan monks like Laiguo (chapter 2), by contrast, were completely convinced of the efficacy of huatou practice. They worried that merely reciting the Buddha's name and hoping for a better rebirth was a squandered opportunity for achieving full awakening in one's present life. Laiguo took the extreme step of discouraging his disciples from engaging in Pure Land practices, going so far as to forbid the recitation of Amitābha's name at his monastery. Instead, he created a rigorous (some might call it relentless) regime of training that focused exclusively on investigating the question "Who recites the Buddha's name?" The act of recitation alone was not enough for Laiguo; he urged his disciples to single-mindedly examine their own fundamental nature.

Laiguo's uncompromising commitment to the primacy of Chan was unusual. Most Buddhist masters in China, past and present, upheld a more eclectic approach. There were different methods suitable for different people—"different antidotes to different poisons," as Master Xuyun put it—but they all served the same goal of liberation. Xuyun (chapter 1) was one of the most prominent Chan masters of his generation, but he embraced an ecumenical approach. As he explained to his followers, "All the teachings of the Buddhadharma can be cultivated. Whichever teaching suits you, cultivate that teaching. One should not praise certain techniques and denigrate others. That would be delusion and attachment."[7] Xuyun upheld the widely accepted view that the great masters of the past had bequeathed a treasury of teachings for later generations. Modern Chinese Buddhists had inherited that rich legacy in its entirety. Tried and true, the tradition in its great diversity had served past generations. It was—all of it—no less effective in the present.

Differences in temperament and doctrinal orientation notwithstanding, all monks and nuns belonged to the same monastic order and were guided by the same sets of rules. Their lives, while unique in their particulars, followed similar rhythms. When they were ordained, monastics in China received the full precepts according to the Dharmaguptaka Vinaya (also known as the Four-Part Vinaya): monks vowed to abide by 250 rules, while nuns were required to follow 348.[8] Both also took the fifty-eight bodhisattva precepts. For some prominent clerics, like Master Hongyi (chapter 4), understanding and abiding by these regulations became a focal point of their practice.

After ordination, many monks and nuns spent their early years traveling, often on foot, to various monasteries throughout the continent. Likened to "clouds and water," wandering clerics followed well-trodden routes that linked both famous sites and obscure hermitages, seeking out prominent teachers and sampling the types of training on offer. Some major monasteries held ten-week-long intensive Chan retreats (described in chapter 2). Others hosted weeks-long buddha recitation or Lotus Samādhi retreats (discussed in chapter 6). Visiting monks and nuns could stay for the duration of a retreat or they might linger for a few months or years before setting off again. It was a formative stage of many monastics' education. They compared notes with fellow travelers, delved into different doctrines, and found affinities (or not) with particular masters and modes of practice.

Then as now, a network of Buddhist monasteries and temples crisscrossed a vast territory, from the alpine Mount Wutai in the northeast to subtropical Mount Jizu some seventeen hundred miles away to the southwest. There were affluent and opulent monasteries in urban centers that housed hundreds of resident clerics, but there were also countless small cloisters in villages and along mountain trails that might shelter just one or two monks or nuns. The southeastern provinces of Jiangsu, Zhejiang, and Fujian were especially dense with Buddhist institutions. This region had long served as the gravitational center of the Chinese Buddhist world, and in the early twentieth century it was home to a sizable population of pious laypeople whose support made monastic life possible. Most of the masters discussed in this book spent most, if not all, their lives in this southeastern "cradle" of Chinese Buddhism.

Large public monasteries in the southeast and elsewhere were the collective property of the entire sangha in the "ten directions." Any ordained monk or nun could expect to be lodged and fed free of charge. Once admitted, new residents were integrated into the daily schedule of the monastery. Temple upkeep and the support of large populations of monastics were secured, traditionally, through donations and the profits derived from various temple-owned businesses. Major monasteries had substantial land holdings that they rented out to tenant farmers. They also earned interest on loans, performed elaborate rituals for equally elaborate fees, and cultivated relationships with wealthy, politically connected patrons. It was an age-old arrangement that benefited certain well-endowed institutions, but it led to simmering resentment in some quarters. During the first half of the twentieth century, many large monasteries were accused of perpetuating a feudal system that exploited the common people. Monks lived like lords, some people fumed, and they treated hardworking people as their serfs or slaves. Some monastic lands were subsequently seized, and their sources of income were substantially curtailed. Without profit-generating properties, donations and rituals became ever more important sources of revenue. Whether on principle or of necessity, several monastic communities turned to subsistence farming on what little of their land remained.

Despite these challenges, a handful of public monasteries, places like Jinshan in the city of Zhenjiang and Mt. Lingyan in Suzhou, persevered and maintained their reputations for rigorous training and strict discipline. There were also smaller hereditary temples, which were owned and controlled by specific monastic lineages. Like a traditional Chinese family, the presiding master would anoint one of his senior tonsure disciples to inherit the temple after his death or retirement. Depending on the inclinations of the resident clerics, the daily schedule at such sites could be extremely demanding and regimented or it could be rather relaxed. Sampling all manner of sites during their travels, monks and nuns could find an environment and lifestyle that suited them.

After ordination, nearly all Buddhist clerics lived the remainder of their lives in monasteries and temples. This was a basic feature of Buddhist life, but several of the masters profiled in this book also spent extended periods of time outside of monastic institutions in solitary retreats. Distancing themselves from the distractions and responsibilities endemic to communal life in a monastery, these men and women sought out solitary places where they might engage in intensive practice without interruption. Some settled in simple huts or mountain caves. Others entered small chambers built on the outskirts of monastic complexes. Mountain hermitages ensured seclusion by their remote locations. There might be other recluses in the vicinity or the occasional passerby, but clerics could live a quieter, more spartan, and ideally more focused existence in these sequestered settings. Such solitude was harder to come by in heavily trafficked monasteries, and so clerics seeking prolonged periods of segregation would sometimes seal themselves inside rooms specially constructed for the purpose. The door would be bricked up or nailed shut, leaving only a small opening for receiving food and, on occasion, speaking with a visitor. There was no set formula for solitary retreats. Different masters kept different schedules and engaged in various kinds of practices. Some spent the bulk of their time in meditation. Others recited the Buddha's name and corresponded with disciples. Still others used the opportunity to study the scriptures and plan for the future. Sealed retreats typically lasted three years, but they could be extended or cut short as circumstances required.

While some monks and nuns devoted themselves to shoring up the foundations of traditional Buddhist institutions and practices, others worried that the old ways had not all aged well. Those ancient foundations, they felt, were not built to withstand the pressures of modern life. What was needed was not a renewed commitment to past precedents but a new vision better suited to the current reality. The most active and influential champion of this reform-oriented approach was the monk Taixu (chapter 3). For Taixu and his allies, Chinese Buddhism had reached an inflection point. The ideal of Buddhist clerics who focused only on self-cultivation and awakening without concern for the machinations of politics or the ever-shifting currents of cultural and social norms was no longer tenable. As members of communities and as citizens of the nation, monastics were obligated to take more active roles in society. Taixu thus proposed a radical restructuring of the sangha. Estimates place the monastic population of China in the early twentieth century at roughly half a million. Taixu proposed a 96 percent reduction to just twenty thousand clerics. These select few would form an elite corps of highly educated professionals trained in not only the entire range of Buddhist texts and traditions but also modern science, mathematics, psychology, political theory, and foreign languages. Rather than prioritizing liberation for themselves in a distant pure land, they would commit themselves to building a pure land here on earth for the emancipation of all people. The goal was not to transcend the world but to transform it.

For Taixu, the reinvigoration of the Chinese Buddhist tradition required a fresh infusion of Buddhist teachings. At his urging, for the first time in centuries, Chinese Buddhist monks ventured out of China in search of new texts, doctrines, and practices. Many traveled to Japan, where they found collections of Chinese Buddhist texts that were lost in China but preserved in Japanese monastic libraries. In addition to medieval commentaries and treatises, they also encountered the burgeoning academic discipline of Buddhist studies and its radical reconsideration of the tradition's history. Other Chinese monks went to Tibet to study the Tantric texts and rituals that had served the Tibetans and Mongols for hundreds of years but had never been translated into Chinese. As had happened on multiple occasions in the past, when Chinese Buddhists questioned the quality and comprehensiveness of their received tradition, they went abroad to gather and transmit a new cache of texts. The infusion of new ideas invigorated existing traditions.

Inspiration came from not only neighboring Buddhist countries but also the Christian missionaries who disparaged Buddhists as "black rot." Simultaneously inspired by and anxious about the growing influence of Protestants in China, Taixu and others took note. Adopting some of the missionaries' own strategies to better position Buddhism as a global religion on par with Christianity, they attempted, unsuccessfully, to unify disparate international Buddhist groups under a single hierarchical structure with Taixu at its head.[9] Emissaries were dispatched to India, Sri Lanka, Tibet, Southeast Asia, and Japan to forge global Buddhist alliances. In the same vein, the Young Men's Buddhist Association (YMBA) was established as the counterpart to the YMCA. The Red Swastika Society emerged in response to the Red Cross. Buddhist academies, like the Huayan universities set up by the monk Changxing (chapter 7), were modeled on Western institutions to better educate monks and nuns in Buddhist as well as secular topics. Dozens of new Buddhist journals were founded to circulate teachings, introduce novel ideas, and foster intellectual exchange. Social engagement—never particularly pronounced in the past—became a priority. Buddhist monks, nuns, and laypeople contributed to disaster relief, orphanages, prison ministry, humanitarian aid, and charitable organizations; they participated in military service and engaged in political advocacy. This was no wholesale adoption of Western European or North American values, which many viewed as irredeemably corrupted by materialism, narcissism, and violence. The goal of Buddhist activists was instead to selectively meld the strengths of native Chinese traditions with the most effective tools and techniques of the Christian West. The result would be a more vibrant, modern, and indispensable Chinese Buddhist tradition.

The diverging visions of prominent clerics inevitably led to heated debates and occasionally erupted into outright conflict, but, overall, the vast majority of monastics did not view different approaches as necessarily exclusive. Most struck a utilitarian balance between respect for tradition and embrace of innovation. The quintessential modernist Master Taixu, for example, was a serious student of the sutras and a devotee of buddhas and bodhisattvas. Master Yinguang, who is often portrayed as an archconservative, readily availed himself of new print technology to spread his teachings among the masses. For all their disagreements, these and other masters were united in their devotion to the Dharma and shared the same goal of protecting and preserving the Buddhist tradition in a time of extraordinary precarity.

Mao Zedong's People's Liberation Army marched on Beijing and established the People's Republic of China (PRC) in the fall of 1949. Controlled by the Chinese Communist Party (CCP), the new state brought an abrupt end to the revitalization efforts of monks, nuns, and laypeople. As several of the chapters in this book recount, many venerable elderly clerics were detained and beaten after the revolution. In the 1950s, the number of Buddhist monastics in China had dwindled to just one hundred thousand in a population of over five hundred million.[10] Farther afield, the CCP launched their invasion and occupation of Tibet, decimating that country's Buddhist traditions and institutions. That tragedy—which sent Tibetan monks into exile and spread Tibetan Buddhist teachings throughout the world—was followed in China by the Great Leap Forward and the ensuing famine that claimed tens of millions of lives. The Cultural Revolution further roiled mainland China from 1966 until Mao's death in 1976, leaving tens of thousands of temples in ruins and sending countless clerics into hiding or early graves. Many fled to Taiwan, Hong Kong, and Chinese diaspora communities in Southeast Asia. Most of the monks and nuns that remained were laicized and "reeducated" at labor camps. The practice of Buddhism—along with all other religions—was outlawed. All devotion was due to Mao alone. In a century of extreme hardship for Chinese Buddhists, these were perhaps the darkest days.

Conditions began to improve in the 1980s with the rise of the more moderate Deng Xiaoping (1904–1997). Restrictions on religious practices were eased. Sutras and statues were brought out from the backs of closets or dug up from underground. Former monks and nuns exchanged their Mao suits for monastic robes and got to work reclaiming and restoring temples. Young people, unmoored by the trauma of the Cultural Revolution, unmoved by the new "to get rich is glorious" culture of capitalism, and in search of some kind of spiritual sustenance in a ravaged religious landscape, started reading Buddhist texts, visiting monasteries, and asking questions. Some decided to shave their heads and take the precepts, replenishing the monastic ranks. And yet, the tradition had a generation-sized hole at its center. There were young novices eager to learn and old monks and nuns ready to pick up the pieces of their former lives, but there were precious few middle-aged clerics with both the energy to rebuild everything that had been destroyed and the experience to train a new generation of monastics. The critical work of revival fell to the disciples of masters like those profiled in this book. Most of the major Chan temples in contemporary China, for example, are now headed by the disciples and grand disciples of Master Xuyun. The Tiantai tradition—currently flourishing in Hong Kong—traces itself back to Master Dixian (1858–1932) and his heirs. The massive monastic institutions now championing "Humanistic Buddhism" in Taiwan were inspired by Taixu and his work. From mainland China, Taiwan, and Hong Kong, these traditions spread throughout the world, from Singapore to South Africa, London to Luxembourg, California to New York.

In North America and Europe, skepticism about the vitality of Chinese Buddhism stems from not just a lack of information about the past but an abundance of information about the present. Under the current president of China, Xi Jinping, Buddhist monks and monasteries have been enlisted to serve the CCP's social, economic, and diplomatic agendas. The Buddhist Association of China, which oversees all Buddhist activities in the PRC, answers to the United Front Work Department of the Central Committee of the Chinese

Communist Party. In a speech in 2023, the president of the Buddhist Association of China, the monk Yanjue, set forth his goals for the association: We "will unite and lead the entire national Buddhist community to reinforce the political leadership, deeply study and fully realize General Secretary Xi Jinping's major discussions related to religious work, and use the Party's innovative theories and policies to guide the construction of Buddhist thought in this new era."[11] Obligatory genuflection to the party line is now the price paid for survival. These kinds of official statements are by design the most visible indicators of the loyalties and commitments of Chinese Buddhist monastics. Anyone following the state-run media in China could be forgiven for dismissing Chinese Buddhists as mere ornaments of legitimacy for a repressive regime. But not all monks and nuns march in lockstep behind the politburo. There are still plenty of people—both in major monasteries in cosmopolitan cities and in small temples far from the thickets of power—who quietly go about the work of studying, embodying, and transmitting the teachings, biding their time until conditions change, as they always do.

Change is a perennial theme in classical Chinese painting and poetry, often evoked by the plum blossom. A harbinger of spring after bone-cold, monochrome winters, the flowering plum conveys the sight and scent of new life. No matter how bitter the weather or how dark the days, spring always returns. In fact, as many poets have pointed out, without ice and snow, there would be no bloom. Several of the masters portrayed in this book were poets, alert to the changing of the seasons and well versed in the allusions of China's rich poetic tradition. Master Benkong wrote movingly of the blossoms that appeared after the frost and snow. Master Jichan, who served as the first president of the newly formed Chinese Buddhist Association, was likewise drawn to the plum. As a child, he buried both his parents. As a young monk, he burned off two fingers in his zeal to awaken. As an adult, he watched as the Chinese empire disintegrated. He later died under mysterious circumstances, with many suspecting that he was murdered by government officials. Like most monks of his generation, Jichan was on intimate terms with suffering. He was also a devotee of the plum. He imagined the roots of gnarled trees coming alive under the frozen ground. In the depths of winter, he noted the buds swelling on bare branches. One of his poems begins:

> Though a chrysanthemum may brave frost,
> Only the plum blossom will burst through snow.

Further Reading

Aviv, Eyal. *Differentiating the Pearl from the Fish-Eye: Ouyang Jingwu and the Revival of Scholastic Buddhism*. Leiden: Brill, 2020.

Birnbaum, Raoul. "Buddhist China at the Century's Turn." *China Quarterly*, no. 174 (June 2003):428–50.

Chen-hua. *In Search of the Dharma: Memoirs of a Modern Chinese Buddhist Pilgrim*. Edited and with an introduction by Chun-fang Yu. Translation by Denis C. Mair. Albany: State University of New York Press, 1992.

Goossaert, Vincent, and David A Palmer. *The Religious Question in Modern China*. Chicago: University of Chicago Press, 2011.

Hammerstrom, Erik J. *The Science of Chinese Buddhism: Early Twentieth-Century Engagements*. New York: Columbia University Press, 2015.

Ji Zhe, Gareth Fisher, and André Laliberté, eds. *Buddhism after Mao: Negotiations, Continuities, and Reinventions*. Honolulu: University of Hawai'i Press, 2019.

Katz, Paul R., and Vincent Goossaert. *The Fifty Years That Changed Chinese Religion 1898-1948*. Ann Arbor, MI: Association for Asian Studies, 2021.

Kiely, Jan, and J. Brooks Jessup. *Recovering Buddhism in Modern China*. New York: Columbia University Press 2016.

Ownby, David, Vincent Goossaert, and Ji Zhe, eds. *Making Saints in Modern China*. New York: Oxford University Press, 2017.

Pittman, Don Alvin. *Toward a Modern Chinese Buddhism: Taixu's Reforms*. Honolulu: University of Hawai'i Press 2001.

Prip-Møller, Johannes. *Chinese Buddhist Monasteries: Their Plan and Its Function as a Setting for Buddhist Monastic Life*. Hong Kong: Hong Kong University Press, 1967.

Scott, Gregory Adam. *Building the Buddhist Revival: Reconstructing Monasteries in Modern China*. Oxford: Oxford University Press, 2020.

Shengyan. *Orthodox Chinese Buddhism: A Contemporary Chan Master's Answers to Common Questions*. Elmhurst, NY: Dharma Drum Publications; Berkeley, CA: North Atlantic Books 2007.

Welch, Holmes. *The Practice of Chinese Buddhism*. Cambridge, MA: Harvard University Press, 1967.

Yang, Mayfair Mei-hui. *Chinese Religiosities: Afflictions of Modernity and State Formation*. Berkeley: University of California Press 2008.

About This Book

For this book, eight scholars of Chinese Buddhism were invited to profile a prominent monk or nun who lived between the fall of the Qing dynasty in 1911 and the establishment of the People's Republic of China in 1949. Each chapter begins with a biographical sketch of the cleric, situating their life and teaching within broader cultural and historical contexts. This introductory section is then followed by translations selected to convey the substance and flavor of the master's teaching. For the most part, these teachings focus on issues of practice, though what "practice" entails varies from person to person. For some it meant sitting in meditation and focusing the mind on a word or phrase (*huatou*). For others it meant reciting the Buddha's name (*nianfo*) without interruption. For still others it entailed the composition of poetry or the explication of doctrine.

The figures represented here illustrate some of the diversity of Chinese Buddhism during this era. They specialized in a range of different traditions—Chan, Huayan, Pure Land, Tiantai, Vinaya—and expressed their teachings in a variety of styles. Most of these masters were major figures, well known in China to this day, but they are, to be sure, a small and selective sample of those responsible for preserving, invigorating, and transmitting the Dharma during this transformative and challenging era. This book provides only a glimpse of the broader Buddhist cultures in which these men and women were immersed. Many other accomplished masters—including monks from Tibet and Mongolia as well as from China—played pivotal leadership roles in the modern Chinese sangha. Not

Master Laiguo around the age of sixty.

only have many eminent monks and nuns been omitted but deeply influential laypeople—such as Yang Wenhui (1837-1911), Ouyang Jingwu (1871-1943), Ding Fubao (1874-1952), Wang Yiting (1867-1938), and Gao Henian (1872-1962)—are also not discussed in this book. One could produce a multivolume series focused on this formidable generation of Buddhists. (Indeed, a Taiwanese publisher has done just that; the series consists of over two hundred entries in five volumes spanning nearly two thousand pages.)[1] The figures profiled in the following pages are thus a substantial but small part of a vast and vibrant tradition.

The chapters are not arranged in any particular order, and the reader is encouraged to skip around and follow their interests. Many of these masters had connections—personal, intellectual, and practical—with one another. The nun Benkong, for example, was inspired by the teachings of Yinguang. Changxing collaborated with Taixu, and Taixu was a student of Jichan. Jichan, Xuyun, and Laiguo were all members the same Chan lineage and engaged in intensive *gong'an* (Japanese koan) practice. In tracing these connections and surveying the ideas and individuals that bound them together, the authors—all of whom are leading specialists in the scholarly study of Chinese Buddhism—have borne the nonspecialist in mind. Footnotes have been kept to a minimum, Chinese characters have been mostly omitted, and, whenever feasible, Chinese terms have been translated or glossed in English. For those interested in pursuing these figures and their teachings in more depth, a list of suggested readings is provided at the end of each chapter.

Master Xuyun in 1957 at Mount Yunju in Jiangxi province.

1 | The Modern Reviver of Chan

Xuyun

GUO GU (JIMMY YU)

Chan master Xuyun (1839-1959), or "Empty Cloud," is one of the two most illustrious Chinese Buddhist clerics in the modern period (the other being Laiguo, detailed in chapter 2). Known as a meditation master, Xuyun is also celebrated for many extraordinary accomplishments; he is renowned for maintaining long meditative absorptions, burning his fingers as an ascetic, performing miracles, and renovating several important Chan monasteries. Xuyun in many ways is a modern version of the great Buddhist saints enshrined in premodern hagiographies. For the purposes of this volume, I focus only on his Chan teachings on how to practice the method of "critical phrase," or huatou. At the end of this chapter is a translation of his essential instructions for this practice. But first a few words about Chan and Xuyun's biography, legacy, and the themes that emerge from his Chan instructions.

Chan Buddhism

Any explanation of Chan should begin with the historical Śākyamuni and his ultimate significance as the Buddha, which means "awakened one." This title embodies the core message of Buddhism. All the different traditions and teachings in Buddhism point to

| 25

awakening. Chan is one among many traditions of Buddhism that survives to the present day. It is the precursor to Japanese Zen, Korean Seon, and Vietnamese Thien. There are plenty of good historical studies of Chan, so I will not describe its development here. Instead, I will explain Chan as it was understood by Xuyun and other Chan practitioners at the time.

Chan is a tradition that focuses on the direct experiential embodiment of the Buddha's teachings. Over the centuries, it has developed distinct approaches to practice and awakening, one of which is the method of meditating on the "critical phrase," or huatou. There are two aspects of huatou practice. The first can be found in the meaning of the word itself. *Huatou* (pronounced hua-tow) literally means "the source (*tou*) of spoken words (*hua*)." Most of us are so conditioned by words and the stories we make with them that we seldom examine what lies beyond or before them. What is the source of words? Why do words matter so much to us? Why do we define ourselves with narrow concepts, constrained by the limited scope of mere words? How do thoughts, feelings, and ideas emerge anyway? Meditators are all too familiar with the coming and going, rising and ceasing of wandering thoughts and feelings; they recognize thoughts and feelings as the birth and death of each moment. But from where do thoughts come? To where do they recede? What is this source? What is it?

Huatou points to this, an abyss of what is unnamed. Some of the most popular critical phrases are: Who am I? Who is reciting the Buddha's name? (Reciting the Buddha's name is a popular method of Buddhist practice, and details of Chinese variants on this practice are given below.) Who's dragging this corpse around?—which is really asking, what is animating this body? Many huatou are connected to *gong'ans*, or public cases of awakening stories.[1] Something unfathomable is present in us, and it cannot be described through words. The site of awakening is where all the roads of rumination and story-making are severed and where the wondrous function of wisdom manifests. This wisdom is freedom from self-referentiality, which is none other than selfless compassion. Any of the technical names for awakening—buddha-nature, *tathagatagarbha* (matrix of the thus come one), *sunyata* (nature of emptiness), *nirvana*, *anātman* (no-self), and so on—are just dead words. What is that which lies before these notions? What is it? This is what huatou points to.

In terms of meditating on the critical-phrase method, the point is to evoke a fundamental sense of not knowing or wonderment concerning our own question of birth and death or the meaning of life. "Wonderment" is a rendering of the Chinese term *yiqing*, which is often translated literally as "doubt sensation." Yet, the literal translation carries with it the connotation of suspicion and distrust, which is misleading. Experientially, yiqing conveys the sense of not knowing and uncertainty, like in an existential crisis. Like Śākyamuni Buddha's great spiritual quest to resolve the meaning of life and the suffering of birth and death, one's practice of huatou directly confronts this uncertainty and wonderment of existence and search for a resolution within—not through words, discursive reasoning, or ruminations but by making the question itself the experiential center of practice. In fact, all the Buddhist saints and lineage masters of the past resolved their fundamental existential wonderment in this way. Chan masters realized that this energy of questioning—or wonderment—was more valuable than constructed explanations or answers. When this wonderment culminates and bursts, delusion and self-referential grasping burst as well, and one is freed, awakened.

Thus, when using huatou, one must cultivate a decisive "sense of wonderment," or yiqing. The key is never to rely on any intellectual understanding, personal experience, wit, reason, logic, or even Buddhist doctrine. Everything must be put down. Simply bring forth the sense of not knowing with regard to the critical phrase, or huatou, until the sense of wonderment shatters. This wonderment is the gateway to awakening. There are many huatous, or critical phrases, but they all point back to this not knowing. The greater the wonderment, the more potent and all-consuming it is. Master Xuyun's text, translated below, speaks of how to work with huatou and wonderment.

Xuyun's Life

Xuyun is known as a great reviver of the Chan tradition and specifically the huatou method. In the eighteenth and early nineteenth centuries, there are hardly any references in the Buddhist canon to this Chan method. In the text below, Xuyun talks of "great wonderment" as essential to awakening. In fact, since his youth, he was driven by a strong sense of wonderment about the meaning of life and death, which ultimately led him to renounce the household life and become a monk so he could investigate Chan.

Xuyun's life was filled with extraordinary events, including a miraculous birth. According to his autobiography, he was born into a well-off family that relocated to Fujian Province because his father was assigned to be a local magistrate there. His parents feared that they would have no descendants because they were both in their forties. We are told that his mother prayed for a child at a local Guanyin temple, and soon after she became pregnant. At that time, both parents had the same visionary dream of an old man sitting on a tiger and wearing a crown with Guanyin Bodhisattva on it. His mother died during childbirth, but not before she had expelled a "flesh ball," which may refer to an unbroken amniotic sac. When the physician cut open the sac, he discovered a healthy baby inside. Stories like this about Xuyun abound. These stories are what make up the hagiographic literature of eminent Buddhist monks of the past.[2]

These legends notwithstanding, what is more extraordinary about Xuyun was his earnestness and perseverance in Chan practice. For example, because Xuyun showed precocious signs of a religious vocation, his father arranged for Xuyun's marriage in Xuyun's late teens in an effort to preempt his son from taking up that vocation full-time. Just before his arranged marriage, Xuyun ran away to become a hermit, but he was caught on the way to Hunan Province and brought back home. He escaped again after marriage and was finally successful. In 1858 he received ordination by Master Miaolian (ca. 1824-1907) at Yongquan Monastery on Mount Gu in Fujian

Province and was given the Dharma name Guyan Yanche (Xuyun was a self-styled name he took on in later years). After ordination, Xuyun engaged in asceticism and lived in a cave behind Yongquan Monastery for three years. Subsequently he came out to support the monastery through manual labor. After four years of this, he again entered a solitary retreat in the mountains.

Sometime around 1866, he sojourned to various places and received the aforementioned huatou—"Who is dragging this corpse around?"—from a Tiantai master, Rongjing (n.d.). He stayed and studied Tiantai Buddhism with Rongjing for several years and took this huatou as his primary method of cultivation. After many years of practice, sojourning further to many monasteries, studying the *Lotus*, *Śuraṃgama*, and *Avataṃsaka* sutras with several prominent masters, and occasionally doing solitary retreats, he ended up doing a three-month retreat at Gaomin Monastery in Jiangsu Province. One evening, steeped in the experience of wonderment, someone accidentally spilled hot water on his hand and he dropped the teacup he was holding to the ground. Upon hearing the shattering of the teacup, Xuyun experienced a great awakening. Upon awakening, he uttered the following verse:

Teacup falls to the ground with the crisp shattering sound.
Smashing this vast emptiness to pieces—
This unruly mind is pacified.
With hand burned, and teacup shattered,
The family is also broken with all of its members dead.
Yet, as spring arrives, the flowers' scent spreads everywhere.
The mountains and the earth are all tathāgatas!

His awakening did not come easy. He practiced with utmost diligence for decades. He was awakened relatively late in life, at age 56. Fortunately, he supposedly lived for another sixty-four years to a ripe age of 120.

Prior to his decisive awakening, he traveled widely as part of his ascetic practice, including a pilgrimage by foot to Tibet, Bhutan,

India, and South and Southeast Asia. According to his autobiography, his pilgrimage took him to Tibet and Bhutan when he was forty-nine years old. Not understanding the cultural practices or the language of the Tibetans, he was dismayed by the meat-eating practice at Tibetan monasteries. Not staying long, he simply paid respect to what the locals referred to as "living buddhas," the Thirteenth Dalai Lama Thubten Gyatso (1876–1933) and the Eighth Panchen Lama Tenpai Wangchuk (1855–1882). He then traveled through the snowy mountains to Bhutan, and then south to India, visiting various holy sites connected with the Buddha. The only time he did not travel by foot was when he had to sail across the sea to Sri Lanka and then to Burma to visit famous monasteries. His pilgrimage took a total of two years. In his own words,

> I forded streams and climbed mountains braving rains, gales, frost and snow. The scenery changed every day, but my mind was pure like a bright and solitary moon hanging in the sky. My health grew more robust, and my steps became rapid. I felt no hardship on this march, but on the contrary, I realized the harmfulness of my former self-indulgence. An ancient rightly said that "after reading ten thousand books, one should travel ten thousand miles."[3]

After his awakening, he continued to spread Chan teachings and would often give talks on Mahāyāna scriptures to fundraise for the renovation of dilapidated monasteries or the printing of the Buddhist canon. On one occasion, he was invited to Thailand to give teachings. During his lecture on Avalokiteśvara, the Bodhisattva of Compassion, in the Lotus Sutra, he inadvertently entered a deep samādhi, or meditative absorption, lasting nine consecutive days. The news of this event immediately spread throughout the country. Soon thousands of Thai and Chinese citizens, including the Thai king, came to the monastery where he was lecturing to see the master in samādhi. Xuyun was subsequently invited to the royal palace to give teachings to the king, his family, and other royals, resulting in a large gift of money to bring back to China to finish his temple renovation work. Xuyun was sixty-eight years old at the time.[4]

Renovating monasteries was a major part of his post-awakening practice, ensuring that Chan institutions would be preserved for posterity. For example, in the 1940s, he renovated some of the main Chan monasteries, including Nanhua Monastery of Huineng (638–713), the sixth ancestor of Chan, and Yunmen Monastery of Chan master Yunmen Wenyan (864–949).

His intensive Chan retreats, open to both laypeople and monastics, were of different lengths, from seven days to forty-nine days. His perseverance revived the Chan tradition. During his time, very few Buddhist clerics offered intensive retreats at all, especially for the laity.

Xuyun's Legacy

The memory of Xuyun still resonates in the hearts and minds of Chinese Buddhists and longtime Western Zen (and even Theravāda) practitioners alike. In 2009, the Chinese television producer CCTV created a twenty-episode drama entitled "A Hundred Years of Xuyun" (*Bainian Xuyun*). The show aired in China in Mandarin and popularized Xuyun's legacy among Chinese-speaking Buddhists around the world. The program is notable for being the first one about a Chan master produced in modern China. In the West, his autobiography and teachings, translated by Charles Luk, appeared as early as 1960 and captured the imagination of spiritual seekers of the time.

Xuyun's Chan teachings come to us through several of his dharma descendants who had broad influence in the West. He was known as a lineage holder of the Linji school of Chan, but because of his authority in Chinese Buddhism, he "revived" the other four Chan lineages—the Weiyang, Yunmen, Fayan (these three lineages had died out by the early twelfth century), and Caodong schools—and also passed down dharma transmission in those lines. Most notable among his transmission recipients was Master Xuanhua Dulun, also known as Master Hsuan Hua (1918-1995), who received Xu-yun's Weiyang transmission and founded the City of Ten Thousand Buddhas, a large monastic complex in Ukiah, California. Most of the followers of Xuanhua are Chinese immigrants, although he did have several outstanding Western monastic disciples.

In the Yunmen line, Xuyun's transmission recipient was Master Miaoci Fayun (1933-2003), who resided in a small temple in New York City's Chinatown and stayed out of the limelight. He occasionally gave dharma talks on Sundays to the Chinese community at his temple.

Xuyun had two heirs in the Linji line. One was Master Benzong Jinghui (1933-2013), who became the abbot of Bailin Monastery in Hebei Province when, after China's Cultural Revolution (1966-1976), the Communist Party again allowed Buddhist monasteries to operate. For the last ten years of his life, Benzong Jinghui wielded great influence in the flourishing of Chan in China. His publications in Chinese have now been translated into English and are in circulation. The other Linji heir was Master Benmiao Zhiding (1917-2003), also known as Jy Din Śākya, who established the Zen Order of Hsu Xun in 1997 in Hawaii. His descendants are mostly Westerners, and they carry on his Chan approach to buddha-name recitation.

Xuyun also had a dharma heir named Lingyuan Hongmiao (1902-1988). Due to the conventions of giving dharma names in Chinese Buddhism, Xuyun ordained Lingyuan in the name of one of his deceased disciples, and thus even though Lingyuan was Xuyun's Linji dharma heir, he was technically a grand disciple of Xuyun. Lingyuan then transmitted the Linji line to Huikong Shengyan, or Chan Master Sheng Yen (1931-2009).[5] (The dharma name Huikong Shengyan was given by Master Dongchu Denglang [1907-1977] from another Chan lineage; his dharma name from Xuyun's lineage was Zhigang Weirou.) Out of all the descendants of Xuyun, perhaps Sheng Yen was the most widely known in Chan-Zen circles through his thirty years of teaching and publishing in the West. His "Dharma Drum lineage" unites Linji and Caodong approaches to Chan practice. His disciples continue his Chan teachings to this day.

Xuyun's Teachings

Xuyun's instructions in the text below are geared toward both beginners and seasoned Chan practitioners. However, some of the things he says, particularly regarding various states of meditative experiences, are applicable to all serious spiritual seekers. These instructions represent his essential teachings and provide a glimpse of the kind of concerns Chan practitioners had during this time.

The clarity of Xuyun's instructions on meditation is exceptional. He not only details the importance of harmonizing the body and mind—which, surprisingly, many contemporary Zen practitioners ignore—but also offers remedies to psychosomatic impediments. His instructions for beginners—to distinguish between host and guest, understand the method of huatou and wonderment, and develop perseverance and genuine practice—should be read and reread again and again, especially in different phases of our spiritual development. He identifies the signposts on the path, distinguishes different kinds of awakening, and identifies the difficulties for both beginners and seasoned practitioners. He presumably adopted this approach out of a concern that mirrors something we see today: with such great accessibility of information, including Chan and Zen awakening stories, and misinformation about practice, it is easy for people to think they have realized something extraordinary when in fact they're still wallowing in words and language, stewing in vexations and habitual tendencies.

A common misperception in Zen circles is that there is something "pure" about its practice or method distinct from the rest of the Buddhist traditions. In this text, Xuyun discusses the method of reciting Amitābha Buddha's name as a Chan method. Readers who are used to Japanese Zen texts may find this focus on recitation and Amitābha strange, thinking it to be a degenerate syncretic form of the Pure Land method that creeped into Chan. In Japan, Buddhist schools exist independently from one another as separate and competing institutions—each with its own centrally organized canon, system of doctrine and practice, and historical lineage traceable to a founder. Such an exclusionary approach was never a widespread nor widely accepted position in China. It only gained support and became cemented in Japan in the late nineteenth to early twentieth centuries. In China, there was never an independent Pure Land school. The teachings and practices related to the Pure Land of Amitābha Buddha only reached intermittent and minimal institutional organization in premodern times. These institutional centers were regional and short-lived, lasting no longer than a few generations. However, because of the decentralization, Pure Land sentiments and practices—specifically those related to recitation of Amitābha in order to be reborn in Sukhāvatī, or the Land of Bliss—were integrated into all traditions of Chinese Buddhism. Thus, it was quite natural for Chan practitioners to engage in reciting Amitābha's name as a practice. But this is not to say that all Chan teachers taught it this way. For example, Laiguo appears to have forbidden this as a practice.

In recent decades, scholars have conclusively shown the historical inaccuracy of the received rhetoric of "degeneration" from the idealized "pure" form of Chan practiced in the Tang dynasty (618–907) that flowered only in Japan, as well as the view that Chan Buddhist teachings in China have been dead for centuries, let alone in modern times. Surprisingly, such erroneous views still linger in popular Western Zen circles today. There never was any "pure" form of Chan. Chan teachings have always been fluid, adapting to and in connection with other Buddhist practices throughout history. In fact, if we examine the lives of important past Chan masters, many were scriptural commentators, steeped in Huayan and Tiantai Buddhist thought. (As discussed in chapters 6 and 7, Huayan Buddhism stems from the *Avataṃsaka Sutra*, and Tiantai thought stems from the Indian Madhyamaka, or Middle Way, school and the *Lotus Sutra*.) The views of Chan masters were therefore very flexible, and they adopted a wide range of practices, focusing not on rigid doctrinal boundaries but rather on the underlying principles that informed those practices. Naturally, some of the Chan masters taught the method of reciting the Buddha's name as early as the seventh century, and it became particularly widespread in late imperial times. Hence, Xuyun inherited and perpetuated this way of teaching Chan. The Chan twist to this method is that instead of reciting the Buddha's name to be reborn in the Pure Land after death, Xuyun encouraged those who have reached a state of deep concentration to ask, "Who is reciting the Buddha's name?" In this fashion, the Buddha's name recitation method was turned into a critical phrase of inquiry: huatou.

The Translation

The tract translated here is an excerpt from an abbreviated version of Xuyun's "Essentials of Chan Practice" given during an intensive Chan meditation retreat (*chanqi*) in 1953, in Shanghai. This version of the text was prepared by the late Venerable Sheng Yen, a third-generation holder of Xuyun's Chan lineage, for his book *Chanmen xiuzheng zhiyao* (Essentials of Practice and Awakening in the Chan Gate).[6] The text provides a window into Xuyun's teaching style during intensive Chan retreats, but it also reveals the major impediments to Chan practice and awakening.

I have translated Xuyun's text with a broad readership in mind, making the text as accessible as possible. While I try to stay true to the text, I took the liberty to render some terms and ideas in ways that would resonate with Western readers. I hope this proves useful.

XUYUN

Talks on the Methods of Practice in the Chan Hall

Introduction

Many people come to ask me for guidance. I feel humbled. Everyone works so hard—splitting firewood, hoeing the fields, carrying soil, moving bricks—and yet from morning to night not putting down the thought of practicing the Way. Such determination for the Way is moving. I, Xuyun, repent for my inadequacy and lack of virtue. I am unable to instruct you and can use only a few sayings from the ancients in response to your concerns. As for practicing the Way, there are four prerequisites: (1) deep conviction in cause and effect; (2) strict observance of precepts and virtue; (3) steadfast conviction; (4) decisive determination to stick to a dharma practice.

Essentials of Chan Practice

Your everyday activities must be carried out as the Way. Is there anywhere that is not a place for practicing the Way? Originally, a "Chan Hall" should not even be necessary, and Chan practice is not limited to sitting meditation. The Chan Hall was designed for us pitiable sentient beings with deep karmic obstructions and shallow wisdom.

When you sit in meditation, you must first know how to harmonize your body and mind. If they are not well harmonized, then small issues will turn into illnesses and larger issues will lead to pathological disorders, which would be most unfortunate. Walking and sitting meditation in the Chan Hall are for harmonizing your body and mind. There are, of course, many other ways to harmonize the body and mind, but I will briefly speak about sitting meditation.

When you sit in the lotus position, you should sit erect naturally. Do not purposefully stiffen your waist and arc your lumbar area. Doing so will raise your inner heat, which later could result in having rheum in the corner of your eyes, bad breath, constricted breathing, loss of appetite, and in the worst scenario, hematemesis. If dullness or sleepiness occurs, open your eyes wide, straighten your back, and gently rock your buttocks from side to side. Dullness will naturally vanish. If you practice with an anxious attitude, you will give rise to agitation. At that time, you should put everything down, including your efforts to practice. Rest for a few minutes. Gradually, after you recuperate, continue to practice. If you don't do this, as time goes on you will develop a hot-tempered character, or, in the worst case, you could go insane or fall prey to psychological maladies.

There are many experiences you may encounter when sitting in meditation, too many to speak of. However, if you do not attach to any of them, they will not interfere with you. This is why the saying goes: "Seeing an anomaly but think nothing of it, and the anomaly will subside of its own accord." If you encounter or perceive an adversity, don't bother with it and have no fear. If you experience something extraordinary, don't make a thing out of it and don't give rise to fondness. The *Śūraṃgama Sutra* says, "There is nothing to any state unless one thinks that one has now realized something holy. If one does think one has realized something holy, one would be open to a host of deviant influences."[7]

How to Start the Practice:
Distinction between Host and Guest

How should one begin to practice? In the *Śūraṃgama Sutra* congregation, Kauṇḍinya the Honored One (i.e., one of Śākyamuni's first five disciples), mentioned these words: "guest" and "dust."[8] This is precisely where beginners should begin discerning in their practice. He said, "A traveler who stops at an inn may stay overnight or get something to eat. When he is finished or rested, he packs his bags and continues his journey, for he does not have time to stay longer. If he were the host, he would have no place to go. Thus, considering this, he who does not stay is called a 'guest' because not staying is the essence of being a guest. He who stays is called a 'host.' Moreover, on a clear day, when the sun rises and the sunlight enters a dark room through an opening, one can see dust in empty space. The 'dust' is moving but the space is still. That which is clear and still is called space; that which is moving is called dust because moving is the essence of being dust."[9] "Guest" and "dust" refer to illusory thoughts, whereas "host" and "space" refer to self-nature. That the permanent host does not follow the guest in his comings and goings illustrates that permanent self-nature does not follow illusory thoughts in their fleeting rise and fall. Therefore, it was said, "If one is unaffected by all things, then there will be no obstructions even when one is constantly surrounded by things." The moving dust does not block the clear, still, empty space; illusory thoughts, which rise and fall by themselves, do not hinder the self-nature of suchness. Thus, "If my mind does not arise, all things are blameless." In such a state of mind, even the guest does not drift with illusory thoughts. If he understands space and dust, illusory thoughts will no longer be hindrances. It is said that when one recognizes what truly is "an adversary," there will be no more adversaries in your mind. If one can investigate and understand all this before starting to practice, it is unlikely that one will make serious mistakes.

Huatou and Wonderment

The ancient ancestors pointed directly at the mind to see self-nature and realize buddhahood. This was the case when Bodhidharma pacified the mind of his disciple and when the sixth ancestral master only discussed the matter of seeing self-nature. All that was necessary was the decisive apprehension and relinquishing [of self-attachment]—nothing else. There was no such thing as observing the huatou. More recent ancestors, however, saw that practitioners could not throw themselves into practice with total dedication and could not instantaneously see their self-nature. Instead, people played games and imitated words of wisdom, counting other people's treasure as their own. For this reason, later ancestors were compelled to set up schools and devise specific ways to help practitioners, hence the method of observing the huatou.

There are many huatous, such as "All dharmas return to one, where does this one return to?" "What was my original face before I was born?" and so on. The most common one, however, is "Who is reciting the Buddha's name?"

What is huatou? *Hua* means "the spoken words"; *tou* means "head" or "before the spoken words." So *huatou* means that which is before spoken words. For example, to recite the name "Amitābha Buddha" is a hua, and the huatou is before you utter the Buddha's name. Thus, a huatou is that moment before a thought arises. Once a thought arises, it is already the "tail," or *wei* (i.e., not the "head" of the hua). That moment before a thought has arisen is called the "non-arising." When your mind is not distracted, not dull, not attached to quiescence, and not in a state of nothingness, it is called "nonperishing." Single-mindedly and uninterruptedly, turning inward and illuminating the state of this non-arising and nonperishing is called observing the huatou, or taking care of the huatou.

To investigate the huatou, one must first generate wonderment. This wonderment is like a walking cane for the method of huatou. What is meant by wonderment? For example, you may ask, "Who is reciting the Buddha's name?" Everyone knows that it is oneself who is reciting the name, but am I using my mouth or mind [to recite it]? If it is my mouth, then after I die and my mouth is still there, how come I am unable to recite Buddha's name? If it is my mind, then what is this mind? It is simply unfathomable! I cannot understand it. From here, the question of "Who?" gives rise to a subtle wonderment. This wonderment should never be coarse. The subtler it is the better. At all times and in all places, single-mindedly observe and keep this not knowing, and keep it going like a fine stream of water. Do not get distracted by any other thought. When the wonder is there, do not disturb it. When the wonder is no longer there, gently pick it up again. Beginners will find that it is more effective to use this method in stillness rather than in motion. You should not have a discriminating attitude. Regardless of whether your practice is effective or not, or whether you are stationary or moving, just single-mindedly engage with this practice.

In the huatou, "Who is reciting the Buddha's name?" the emphasis should be on the word *who*. The other words serve to provide a general context, just like in asking, "Who is dressing?" "Who is eating?" "Who is moving their bowels?" "Who is urinating?" "Who is ignorantly selfing and othering?" "Who is knowing and being wakeful?" Regardless of whether you are walking, standing, sitting, or reclining, it is this word, *who*, that can easily generate the sense of wonderment. It is easy to give rise to a sense of wonderment if you don't rely on discursive thinking, conjecture, or contrivance. Hence, this "Who?" huatou is just a wonderful method for investigating Chan. But don't just repeat "Who is reciting Buddha's name?" like any recitation practice. Nor should you use reasoning to seek an answer to the question, taking this as "wonderment." There are some people who uninterruptedly repeat the phrase, "Who is reciting the Buddha's name?" They would accumulate more merit and virtue if they repeatedly recited Amitābha Buddha's name instead. There are others who let their minds wander, thinking that is the meaning of having doubt, and they end up more involved in illusory thoughts. This is like trying to ascend but descending instead. Be aware of this.

The wonderment that is generated by a beginning practitioner tends to be coarse, intermittent, and sometimes strong, other times weak, all of which do not truly qualify as the sense of wonderment. This phenomenon can only be called "thoughts." Gradually, only after the wild thoughts have settled and you have more control can the process be considered an "investigation" (*can*) of Chan. As your practice becomes ripe, the wonderment naturally arises and abides of its own accord. At this point you won't be aware of where you are sitting when you sit. Nor will you be aware of the existence of a body or mind or environment. Only the wonderment is present. This is a true state of the "sense of wonderment."

Realistically speaking, the beginning states cannot be considered "cultivation." You are merely engaging in wandering thoughts. Only when genuine wonderment arises by itself can it be called true cultivation. This moment is a crucial juncture, and it is easy for the practitioner to deviate from the right path: (1) At this stage, there is just clarity and purity, with an unlimited sense of lightness and peace. However, if you fail to fully maintain your wakefulness and illumination (wakefulness is prajñā, not delusion; illumination is samādhi, undisturbed), you may fall into a subtle state of haziness. If there is a clear-eyed person around, he will be able to tell right away that the practitioner is in this mental state and hit him with the "incense board,"[10] dispersing all clouds and fog. Many people become enlightened this way. (2) It is also possible that at this stage, there is just clarity and purity, empty and vacuous. If you lose the wonderment, then you may fall into the state of stupor. This is what is meant by "sitting like a dried log, at the edge of the cliff" or "a rock soaking in cold water." In this situation, you must "pick up" your wakefulness and illumination. Don't pick up or bring forth the wonderment like someone in the beginning stages of practice, where it is coarse. Instead, the wonderment must be extremely refined—just this single present thought [of wonderment]—still and quiet, quiescent and luminous. It should be unmoving, potent, clear; and such wakefulness should be continuous and ever present, like the smoke from a fire that is about to go out, a narrow stream without interruption. When your cultivation reaches this point, it is necessary to have a diamond eye in the sense that you should not try to "pick up" [the wonderment] anymore. To pick it up at this point would be like putting a head on top of a head.

A monk once asked Chan Master Zhaozhou (778–897), "What should one do when not a single thing comes?" Zhaozhou replied,

"Put it down!" The monk asked, "If nothing comes up, what is there to put down?" Zhaozhou replied, "If you can't put it down, then pick it up." This dialogue refers precisely to this kind of situation. The true flavor of this state [of wonderment] cannot be described. Like someone drinking water, only he knows how cool or warm it is. If you reach this state, you will naturally understand. If you are not in this state, no explanation will suffice. This is what is meant by "To a sword master you should offer a sword; do not bother showing your poetry to someone who is not a poet."

Taking Care of the Huatou and Turning Inward to Hear One's Self-Nature

Someone might ask, "How is Bodhisattva Avalokiteśvara's method of turning inward to perceive self-nature considered investigating Chan?" I have elsewhere explained that taking care of huatou is being with only a single thought, moment after moment, reversing the light inward to illuminate "that which is not born and not destroyed." To reverse the light of your awareness to illuminate your self-nature is to, at all times and places, turn the single arising of thought around to perceive your self-nature. To turn it around is what is meant by "reverse"—that which is "not born or destroyed" *is* your self-nature. When "perceiving" and "illuminating" follow sound and form in the worldly stream, perceiving does not go beyond sound and seeing does not go beyond form. However, when you turn inward and contemplate your self-nature, against the flow of the worldly stream, then you won't pursue sound and form. This principle is clear. At that time, "perceiving" and "illuminating" are not two different things.

Thus, we should know that taking care of your huatou and turning inward to perceive self-nature does not mean using your eyes to see and your ears to hear. If you use your ears to hear or your eyes to see, then you are chasing after sound and form. As a result, you will be affected by them. This is to succumb to the worldly stream. If you practice with one thought only, single-mindedly abiding in that which is not born and not destroyed, not chasing after sound and form, with no wandering thoughts, then you are going against the stream. This is also called taking care of the huatou or turning inward to perceive your self-nature. This is not to say you should shut your eyes tightly or plug up your ears. Just do not stir up your thoughts to seek after sound and form.

The Mind of Birth and Death and Perseverance

In Chan training, the most important thing is to develop an earnestness to leave birth and death and to generate a persevering mind. If there is no earnestness to leave birth and death, then you cannot generate wonderment and your practice will be ineffective. If there is no perseverance in your mind, the result will be like a man who practices for one day and rests for ten. Your practice will not be a continuous whole. If you have perseverance, when genuine wonderment arises, then the dustlike afflictions will cease of their own accord. When the time comes, the melon will naturally ripen and drop from the vine.

I will tell you a story. During the Qing dynasty in 1900 when the Eight-Nation Alliance sent their armies to Beijing, Emperor Guangxu fled westward from Beijing to Shaanxi Province. Every day he walked tens of miles. For several days he had no food to eat. On the road, a peasant offered him sweet potato stems. After he ate them, he asked the peasant what they were because they tasted so good. Think about the emperor's usual awe-inspiring demeanor and his arrogance. How long do you think he could continue to maintain his imperial attitude after so long a journey on foot? Do you think he had ever gone hungry? Do you think he ever had to eat sweet potato stems? At that time, he gave up all his airs. After all, he had walked quite a distance and had eaten stems to keep from starving. Why was he able to put down everything at that time? Because the allied armies wanted his life, and his only thought was to save himself. But when peace prevailed and he returned to Beijing, once again he became proud and arrogant. He didn't have to run anymore. He no longer had to eat any food that might displease him. Why was he unable to put down everything at that time? Because the allied armies no longer wanted his life. If the emperor always had an attitude of running for his life, and if he could turn such an attitude toward the path of Chan practice, there would be nothing he could not accomplish! It's a pity he did not have perseverance. When favorable circumstances returned, so did his former habits.

Fellow practitioners! Time is passing, never to return. It is constantly looking for our lives. It is more frightening than the allied armies. Time will never compromise or make peace with us. Let us generate a mind of perseverance immediately in order to escape from birth and death! Chan ancestor Gaofeng Yuanmiao (1238-1295) once said, "Concerning practice, perseverance should be like a stone dropping into the deepest part of the pool—ten thousand feet deep—continuously and persistently sinking down without interruption toward the bottom. If you can practice like this without stopping, continuously for seven days and still be unable to cut off your wandering, illusory thoughts, and vexations, I, Gaofeng, will have my tongue pulled out for cows to plow on forever."[11] He continued by saying, "When you practice Chan, you should set out a certain time for success, like a man who has fallen into a pit a thousand feet deep. All his tens of thousands of thoughts are reduced to one—to escape from the pit. If you can really practice from dawn to dusk, from night to day, without a second thought, and not attain complete awakening within three, five, or seven days, I would be committing a great lie for which I shall have my tongue pulled out for cows to plow on forever." This old master had great compassion. Knowing that we would probably be unable to generate such a persevering mind, he made two great vows to guarantee our success.

Awakening and Cultivating the Path

The ancestor Hanshan (1546-1623) once said,

> There are practitioners who realize awakening first and then start their cultivation, and those who engage in cultivation first and then realize awakening. However, there are two kinds of awakening: awakening through understanding and through

actualization. If a person realizes mind by following the teach-ings of the Buddha and the ancestral masters, it is considered awakening through understanding. Many with such an expe-rience will only have a conceptual grasp [of truth]. In all cir-cumstances they will still be powerless. Their minds and the environment are separated, not integrated, and [their under-standing remains] stagnated. Therefore, in most scenarios they will feel obstructed. It may be a simulated prajñā but it is not something from real practice. On the other hand, those who are awakened through actualization would concretely, in a down-to-earth fashion, start with their minds. They stick to their methods in a straightforward manner until the mountains are toppled and rivers are dried up—until the last thought suddenly van-ishes and they thoroughly relinquish their [deluded] minds. This would be like seeing your own father at a crossroads—there is no doubt about it. Or it is like drinking water—only the person drinking knows if it is warm or cold. Inexpressible to others. Such is the process of genuine practice and solid awakening. Afterward, from this awakening, they integrate everything into their realization to purify and eradicate the karmic retributions of the present life, their wandering thoughts, and their emotional afflictions—leaving only the single flavor of the true mind. This is awakening through actualization.

Awakening through actualization can also be deep or shallow. If one puts effort in following the fundamental principle and destroys the nest of the eighth consciousness[12] and overturns the dark caves of ignorance, then one transcends [delusion and] heads directly for awakening without recourse. Those who achieve this have extremely sharp karmic roots and experience deep awakening.

Those who practice gradually experience shallow awakening. The worst case is when people attain little but are self-satisfied—taking appearances, like shadows created by light, at the sense doors as awakening. Why? Because the eighth consciousness, the root of vexations, has not been dismantled; whatever they experience would be conditioned by it and hence would be matters that belong to the peripheral. Believing such peripheral things to be authentic realizations would be like mistaking a thief for one's son. An ancient has said, "Because cultivators take the activities of their consciousness as real, they do not recognize what is genuine. The basis for the countless transmigrations of birth and death is that which the ignorant takes as their true self." This is an impasse that all must go through.

As there are those who experience sudden awakening and cultivate gradually, although their awakening is thorough, they still cannot suddenly purify their habitual tendencies. So, through the power of their illumination, they meet all their [habitual tendencies] in life's situational conditions through the substance of their awakening. They utilize situational conditions to train their minds—melting away a portion of these conditions to regain a portion of their dharmakaya; dissolving a portion of their deluded thinking to manifest a portion of their original wisdom—all of which depends on the consistency and subtlety of their cultivation, deriving further power from situational conditions of life.

We can see that irrespective of whether someone is awakened or not, or whether such awakening is from understanding or from actualization, we have to genuinely sustain and continue our practice and cultivation. The difference is that those who are awakened first, followed by cultivation, are like old horses that are familiar with the road; they would not go astray, which would be easier than those who cultivate first and then realize awakening. Those who are awakened are grounded, unlike those who are awakened through understanding, whose understanding is shaky and superficial. Those who are awakened through actualization are more likely to derive power from their practice. Even at the age of eighty, the elder master Zhaozhou still traveled [to visit different masters]. For forty years, the master used his mind without any wandering; he only investigated the word *Wu*, or "No."[13] He is a true exemplar for us all. Do you doubt that this elder has yet realized awakening? His conduct reminds us all not to be self-satisfied with little and not to be arrogant or haughty.

There are indeed those who, after reading a few sutras or discourse collections of Chan masters, start blabbering things like, "The mind is buddha!" or "Vertically, it extends through the three periods and, horizontally, it pervades the ten directions! [referring to their awakening]." Meanwhile, these words are incongruent with their fundamental way of being. Some even consider themselves to be reincarnates of ancient buddhas or brag to people that they have realized thorough awakening. Their blind followers will even brag for them. This is like mistaking fisheyes for pearls; they do not know the difference between what is real and false. People like this end up messing things up, making people lose faith, or, worse, slandering [buddhadharma]. The reason why the Chan school is not flourishing these days is mainly due to the actions of these unruly practitioners.

I sincerely hope you all can be diligent in your practice. Do not be pretentious. Do not speak about Chan with empty words. You must engage in true investigation and realize genuine awakening so that in the future you can propagate and revive Chan as a dragon elephant in the dharma gate.

Investigating Chan and Reciting Buddha's Name

Those who recite the Buddha's name usually criticize those who investigate Chan, and those who investigate Chan usually slander those who recite the Buddha's name. They seem to oppose each other like enemies. Some of them even wish that the others would perish. This is something terrible in Buddhism. There is a saying that goes something like this: "A family in harmony will succeed in everything; a family in decline stems from arguments." Fighting among siblings is something that outsiders laugh at and look down upon. Investigating Chan, reciting the Buddha's name, and other methods are all teachings of Śākyamuni Buddha. The Way is originally not two. It is only because of the different karmic roots and mentalities of sentient beings that different methods are taught. It is like giving different antidotes for different poisons. Subsequent masters made distinct different teachings and schools because they needed to respond to the changing times. If you practice a method that fits your character, then regardless of which dharma gate you use, that would be the wonderous dharma gate that allows you to enter the path. Actually, there are no superior and inferior dharma gates. Furthermore, dharma gates are interconnected. All are perfect and without obstruction. For example, when one recites the Buddha's name to the point of single-mindedness, is this not investigating Chan? When one investigates Chan to the point of no separation between the investigator and that which is being investigated, is this not reciting the real characteristic of Buddha? Chan is none other than the Chan within the Pure Land, and Pure Land is none other than the Pure Land within Chan. Chan and Pure Land are mutually enriching, and they go together.

However, there are people who favor one over another out of biases, and they become defensive to guard their own views by praising oneself while slandering others like [the incompatibility of] fire and water that cannot coexist. They have misunderstood the profound intentions of the great masters of the past who developed different schools. Unintentionally, these people have committed the offense of damaging, slandering, and endangering Buddhism. Is this not sad and pitiable?

I hope that all of us, no matter which dharma gate we practice, understand the Buddha's and our ancestors' principle of harmony and stop wielding a halberd within the same household to fight with one another. We must help one another so that we may together steer this ship amid dangerous and violent waves.

The Two Kinds of Difficulty and Ease among Practitioners

There are two kinds of difficulty and ease, according to the depth of the practice, for practitioners: (1) the difficulty and ease for beginners; (2) the difficulty and ease for seasoned practitioners.

The common symptoms of beginner's disease are incapability of putting down wandering thoughts, habitual tendencies, ignorance, arrogance, jealousy, greed, anger, stupidity, desire, laziness, gluttony, and discriminations between self and other. All these fill their big bellies. How can this be in accordance with the Way?

There are people who were born into wealthy and privileged families. Not being able to forget their habits, they cannot endure one bit of difficulty or withstand any hardship. How can these people practice the Way? They have not considered the status of our original teacher, Śākyamuni Buddha, when he decided to become a monk.

There are other people who have some secular learnings but do not understand the context of the discourse records of the ancients, many of which were aimed at evaluating practitioners' levels of understanding. These people think they are smart; every day they scrutinize the discourse records and speak of "mind" and "buddha." They engage in interpreting the teachings of the ancients, but it is like talking about food and not eating it or counting the treasure of others and not owning it. They think of themselves as extraordinary and become incredibly arrogant. But when these people become seriously ill, they will cry out to heaven for help, and at the end of their lives they panic in bewilderment. At that time, whatever they have learned and understood will be useless, and it will be too late to regret. For example, some misunderstand the saying "Originally we are buddhas," which is not a teaching for practice and realization, and say that "[the Way] is originally replete; there is no need for practice or any realization." All day long they hang around with nothing to do, following their emotions, wasting time. These people praise themselves as eminent and therefore simply flow with causes and conditions freely. In the future, they will surely suffer greatly.

Then there are people who have the mind for the Way, but who do not know where to begin their endeavor or who are afraid of wandering thoughts. Unable to get rid of their thoughts, they vex themselves all day, disheartened and mourning their heavy karmic obstructions. Because of this, their mind for the Way regresses or dissipates.

There are also those people who want to battle till death with their wandering thoughts. Furiously they tense up their fists and push out their chests and eyes, as if they are involved in something big. Ready to die in battle against their wandering thoughts, they do not realize that wandering thoughts cannot be defeated. These people end up vomiting blood or going insane.

There are people who fear falling into so-called emptiness. Little do they know that demons have arisen in their minds [in thinking this way]. They can neither empty their minds nor get awakened. And there are those who strongly seek awakening, not understanding that seeking awakening and craving buddhahood is all just big, deluded thinking. One cannot cook sand hoping to eat rice. They can seek until the Year of the Donkey [in the Chinese calendar there is no "Year of the Donkey"!], and they still won't get awakened. Sometimes people become excited and joyful when occasionally they sit through a couple of peaceful sittings. These situations are like a blind turtle whose head happens to pass through a small hole in a piece of wood floating in the middle of the ocean. It is not the result of genuine practice. In their excitement, these people have just added an "excitement obstruction" on top of the ones they already have.

There are those who enjoy peace and purity and pass their time in this state. Since they cannot maintain it in activity, they avoid noisy places and spend their days soaking—like soaking in stale water. There are numerous examples of this. For beginners, it is very difficult to find an entry to the Way. If they are wakeful but have no illumination, then their minds tend to scatter and they cannot get their practice going; if they have illumination but no wakefulness, then their practice is like soaking in stale water waiting to die.

Even though practice may seem hard, once you find an entrance to the Way it becomes easier. What is the easiest way for beginners? There is nothing special other than being able to "put it down." Put what down? Put down all afflictions arising from ignorance. Fellow practitioners! Once this body of yours stops breathing, it becomes a corpse. The main reason you cannot put it down is because you place too much importance in it. Because of this, you give rise to the idea of self and other, right and wrong, love and hate, gain and loss. If you can have a firm belief that this body is basically a corpse, then you would not cherish it or look upon it as being yourself. Then, what is there that you cannot put down? You must learn to put it down anywhere, anytime, whether walking, standing, sitting, or sleeping, whether in motion or still, whether resting or active. If you would only have this single thought of wonderment about your huatou, internally and externally, cold and still, keeping it up peacefully and steadily without a moment of extraneous thoughts, then like a long sword extending into the sky—whatever comes in contact with its sharp edge is simply cut down without a trace or sound—then why would you be afraid of deluded thinking? What could harm or disturb you? Who would distinguish between motion and stillness, existence or emptiness? If you fear deluded thinking, then you have already added another layer of delusion. If you feel you have realized "purity," then you are already defiled. If you are afraid of falling into "emptiness," then you are already dwelling in existence. If you want to become a buddha, then you have already deviated onto the demonic path. Therefore, as long as you know how to enter the Way, carrying water and gathering firewood are all inseparable from the sublime way. Hoeing and planting fields are all opportunities for Chan (*chanji*); the Way is not limited to sitting cross-legged all day.

What difficulties are encountered by seasoned practitioners? Although some have practiced until the emergence of genuine wonderment and possess both wakefulness and illumination, they are still bound by birth and death. Those who have neither wakefulness nor illumination fall into false emptiness. To arrive at either of these situations is actually hard. After reaching this point, many cannot further free themselves. They stand at the top of a ten-thousand-foot pole unable to advance. Some people, having progressed to this stage and being skilled in practice, and having sidestepped situations they cannot solve, think that they have already eradicated fundamental ignorance. They think their practice has "arrived home." Actually, they are living in a cave of ignorance and do not even know it. When these people encounter a situation that they cannot solve—where they cannot be their own master—they just give up. This is a pity.

There are others who reach genuine wonderment, even gain a little wisdom from experiencing emptiness, and understand a few ancient gong'ans, but then they put down their wonderment, thinking that they are completely awakened. They may even compose poems and *gāthās*, act arrogantly, and call themselves virtuous friends of the Way. Not only do they fool themselves but they also mislead others—creating inexhaustible bad karma. In other cases, some mistake the words of Bodhidharma: "Extinguishing the myriad external conditions; stilling the mind internally with mind like a wall—such is the way to enter the Way"; and those of the sixth ancestor Huineng: "Not thinking of good or bad, at this time what is your original face, Venerable Ming?" They take sitting like a withered log or a large boulder at the edge of a cliff as the ultimate way. These people take the illusory city as their treasured palace or the temporary guesthouse as their hometown. This is exactly the point of the gong'an about the old woman who burned down the hut.[14] She was reprimanding the practitioners who act like a living corpse.

What is the easy way for these seasoned practitioners? Do not be proud and do not quit in the middle of cultivation. In the midst of continuous subtle practice, you have to be even subtler. When the time comes, the "bottom of the barrel" [i.e., ignorance] will naturally drop off on its own accord. If you cannot do this on your own, then find a virtuous teacher to pry off the nails of the barrel and pull out the joints. Master Hanshan [i.e., Cold Mountain] once chanted,

> On the peak of the highest mountain,
> the four directions expand to infinity.
> Sitting in silence, no one knows.
> The solitary moon reflected on cold springs.
> In the springs, there is no moon;
> the moon is in the sky.
> Just so, in humming this song,
> this song has no Chan.

The first two lines of this song reveal that the real does not belong to anything, pervading the whole world, filling it with bright luminosity without any obstructions. The third line speaks of the sublime essence of Suchness, which is not something that can be perceived by ordinary people. Even the buddhas of the three periods do not know where I abide. Therefore, the song says, "No one knows." The three lines beginning with "The solitary moon reflected on cold springs" are Hanshan's similes for this state. The last two lines are mentioned because he is afraid that people may "mistake the finger for the moon." Thus, he especially warns us that words and language are not Chan.

Conclusion

All the words I have spoken here are just ways to pull down the entangling vines—just distractions. Whatever words that can be said have no real meaning. For this reason, the ancient masters received students through either sticks or shouts. They weren't so wordy and long-winded. However, the present times cannot be compared with the past. One has no choice but to put up signposts to point at the moon. But who's pointing anyway? What is the moon?

Investigate!

Further Reading

Campo, Daniela. "Chan Master Xuyun: The Embodiment of an Ideal, the Transmission of a Model." In *Making Saints in Modern China*, edited by David Ownby, Vincent Goossaert, and Ji Zhe, 99–136. New York: Oxford University Press, 2016.

Guo Gu. *The Essence of Chan: A Guide to Life and Practice according to the Teachings of Bodhidharma*. Boulder, CO: Shambhala Publications, 2020.

———. *Passing through the Gateless Barrier: Koan Practice for Real Life*. Boulder, CO: Shambhala Publications, 2016.

———. "The Practice of Wonderment." *Buddhadharma Magazine*, 2021. Accessible through https://www.lionsroar.com/the-practice-of-wonderment.

Hsuan Hua. *The Chan Handbook: Talks about Meditation*. Ukiah, CA: Buddhist Text Translation Society, 2011.

Jing Hui. *The Gates of Chan Buddhism*. Buddha Dharma Education Association, 2004.

Luk, Charles. *Empty Cloud: The Autobiography of the Chinese Zen Master Xu Yun*. Shaftsbury, UK: Element Books, 1988.

Sheng Yen. *Attaining the Way: A Guide to the Practice of Chan Buddhism*. Boston: Shambhala Publications, 2006.

———. *Shattering the Great Doubt: The Chan Practice of Huatou*. Boston: Shambhala Publications, 2009.

Yu, Jimmy. *Readings of the Gateless Barrier*. New York: Columbia University Press, 2024.

———. *Reimagining Chan Buddhism: Sheng Yen and the Creation of the Dharma Drum Lineage of Chan*. Abingdon, UK: Routledge, 2021.

2 | A Formidable Chan Master

Laiguo

BENJAMIN BROSE

Laiguo Miaoshu (1881–1953), one of the most revered Chan monks in modern history, was sixty-one years old when he delivered the talks translated in this chapter. Together with Master Xuyun (introduced in the previous chapter), Laiguo worked tirelessly to reinvigorate the Chan tradition in China.

His base of operations was Gaomin Monastery, one of the country's preeminent sites of Chan training. Perched on the north bank of the Yangzi River in Jiangsu Province, Gaomin had been a site of Chan practice for centuries—it was in Gaomin's Meditation Hall that Xuyun was awakened by the sound of a shattering teacup—but the monastery had fallen into disrepair by the time Laiguo took up residence there. The iron on the temple's front gate was rusted through. Crumbling stone and broken tiles littered the weed-choked courtyard. For Laiguo, Gaomin's dilapidated condition, diminished resources, and general remoteness made it an ideal place for practice: there would be fewer distractions. He quickly set about reforming the rules and routines at the monastery. During his tenure as abbot, the focus of training at Gaomin would be entirely on Chan training. Unlike most other Buddhist monasteries in China at the time, the regulations at Gaomin forbade any sutra study, recitation of Amitābha Buddha's name, or funerary rites.

As his talks make clear, Laiguo was a strict and uncompromising teacher. He expected complete dedication and discipline from the monks in his monastery. Resident monks could not read the canon, engage in recitation retreats, or participate in rituals outside the monastery. Ceremonies sponsored by wealthy donors were a major source of income for most monasteries, but the economic consequences did not trouble Laiguo. "It would be better to beg for food from door to door," he told his students, "than be responsible for destroying the Chan tradition."

Laiguo's Early Life and Practice

Laiguo had risen to the position of abbot at Gaomin through years of single-minded and often severe practice. Born in 1881 in the twilight of the Qing dynasty, Laiguo (then known by his lay name of Liu Yongli) seemed to display all the hallmarks of a nascent buddha. Even as an infant, according to his own account, he refused to eat meat. He would make little buddha statues out of mud and then venerate them. When, at the age of seven, he happened to hear someone chant the *Heart Sutra*, he immediately grasped its meaning and resolved to become a Buddhist monk. While still a child, Laiguo attempted to run away and live at a temple, but his family tracked him down and dragged him back home. He could have no meaningful concept of what Buddhist practice entailed at that young age, but he got his first real taste when he was fifteen years old. Laiguo had "taken refuge" with a monk named Dazhi (Great Wisdom). Dazhi initially instructed Laiguo to recite Amitābha Buddha's name—the most common form of Buddhist practice at the time. This proved easy for Laiguo. In short order, he was able to do it even in his sleep. But then Dazhi asked him, "Who recites the Buddha's name?" This rendered Laiguo speechless. Who was saying these words? Who was he? Confronted with the realization that he did not in fact know, the ensuing shock, he said, was like "drinking a mouthful of icy water in a single gulp." The search for an answer to this question would occupy Laiguo for the next two decades.

Despite his early affinities with monastic life, Laiguo continued to follow the path of a householder. At nineteen, his parents arranged for him to be married. (He would later report that he never consummated the union.) Shortly thereafter, he found work as a minor government official. But at the age of twenty-four, he had already had enough. Leaving his family and his job, Laiguo traveled to the sacred Buddhist island of Putuo in the East China Sea. Although initially discouraged by the decadent and undisciplined clerics he encountered there, he eventually happened upon a group of ascetic monks—dressed in patched robes, walking barefoot, traveling light—and was inspired to follow their example. Laiguo cut off his hair, discarded his shoes and lay clothing, and returned to the mainland wearing a tattered robe. He carried only a bowl, a pair of chopsticks, a staff, a rush cushion, and a gourd for water. In this unorthodox fashion, he had essentially tonsured himself.

What followed was several years of hardship and deprivation. Often unsuccessful in his begging rounds, Laiguo was regularly on the verge of starvation. He lacked the proper paperwork and basic training required to gain entry to most monasteries. To make matters worse, his disheveled and dirty appearance put people on guard. Many suspected that he was merely a vagrant in search of free food and lodging. Hungry, demoralized, and out of options, Laiguo even contemplated suicide so that he might be reborn in a time and place where it was not so difficult to study the Dharma.

After two years of wandering, Laiguo finally gained entry into the prestigious monastic center of Jinshan. There he was able to formally take the precepts and receive a proper ordination. Jinshan was famous for its strict discipline, and Laiguo diligently studied the detailed regulations for resident monks. Rather than chafe at the rigidity of the rules as many other monks did, Laiguo embraced them as fundamental to his training.

Some months after his ordination, he left Jinshan and set out on a long and ill-advised pilgrimage to India. It was a journey of roughly four thousand miles, and he meant to do it all walking barefoot, sleeping outside, and scavenging for food, all while maintaining focus on the question "Who recites the Buddha's name?" Such a journey—in the midst of a crippling famine, political instability, and militarized borders—was doomed to fail. Laiguo made it as far as Inner Mongolia before turning back. He eventually returned to Jinshan where he redoubled his efforts in the Meditation Hall. Like the Buddha taking his seat under the bodhi tree, Laiguo vowed to achieve awakening or die trying.

His efforts culminated one autumn evening with the sound of a mallet striking a wooden board. As he reported in his autobiography,

> On the twenty-sixth day of the ninth month of the thirty-fourth year of the Guangxu era (1908), during the evening's sixth stick of incense, when the board was struck [to end the period of meditation] suddenly everything split [open and] dropped away. It was like dropping a thousand-pound burden or losing the nostrils one was born with. I wept continuously, filled with sorrow. I thought to myself, I have been blind until today, mired in samsara and suffering needlessly. So pitiful! So painful! My sadness was boundless, my grief beyond measure. The next day I went to see the instructor and asked for his teaching. All the words that had previously hindered me I could now understand. The instructor said, "You have awakened to words." He then asked, "Who recites the Buddha's name?" My response came flowing forth. He then asked me where I was before I was born, where I will go after I die, and other such questions. I was able to answer them all. My understanding was unobstructed.[1]

It was a joyous moment, the fulfillment of a long and arduous quest. But in many ways, it marked the beginning rather than the end of Laiguo's work. He would spend another decade deepening his realization, training at other monasteries under other masters and spending two years in a cave-hermitage deep in the Zhongnan mountains. When the call came for him to take over the abbacy of either Jinshan or Gaomin, he hesitated. Reluctant to give up the freedom his life as a "cloud and water" monk entailed, Laiguo also felt a deep responsibility to uphold and preserve the Chan tradition. He accepted the abbacy of Gaomin in 1919.

Laiguo's Abbacy at Gaomin

The training regimen at Gaomin had always been exacting, but the rigor was ratcheted up during Laiguo's tenure. He compiled a lengthy and detailed monastic code, outlining every rule and procedure at the monastery.[2] All resident monks were expected to know and abide by these regulations; they were required to recite the five-hundred-page code no fewer than four times a year. There was little tolerance for breaches in conduct. According to a sign Laiguo posted in the monk's quarters, "If two or three people seek out a quiet corner and talk in a low voice, they will be immediately expelled. Visiting monks may not go outside the gates, nor intrude into the apartments of the monastery, nor wander about in the gardens or fields. Anyone detected will be severely punished and expelled. Daily devotions, meals, and chores are not to be missed, and those who break this rule once shall be immediately expelled."[3] Laiguo had been discouraged by what he perceived as a lack of dedication and discipline among monks he encountered elsewhere in China. There would be no such laxity at Gaomin.

On average, the monks who lived in Gaomin's Mediation Hall engaged in seven periods of seated meditation each day. During periods of intensive retreat (known as "meditation weeks," or chanqi), however, the amount of meditation was dramatically increased. The days began at 3:00 a.m. and concluded twenty-two hours later at 1 00 a.m.[4] During this time, participants were expected to maintain both physical and mental composure. Laiguo instructed his disciples to follow the same deceptively simple method of meditation that he himself had employed: contemplation of the huatou (critical phrase) "Who recites the Buddha's name?" Emphasis was to be placed on the word *who*. The practitioner should constantly investigate this word and its implications. Who was doing this practice? Who was asking this question? Like Laiguo, they would quickly be confronted with their inability to resolve this fundamental matter. Their lack of understanding would arouse a feeling of great doubt (what Guo Gu described in the last chapter as "wonderment"), and this nagging uncertainty would become the fuel that fired their efforts. Ideally, a person would be completely consumed by this doubt and all their energy would be brought to bear on its resolution. As the great twelfth-century Chan Master Dahui Zonggao (1089–1163) once said, "Great awakening inevitably comes from great doubt."[5]

Laiguo viewed huatou practice as the most expedient path to awakening. It was superior, in his view, to more common practices like studying sutras, reciting dharani, and chanting Amitābha's name. His pointed rejection of basic Pure Land practices set Laiguo apart from other prominent clerics of his generation. The revered master Yinguang, for example, taught the recitation of Amitābha's name exclusively (see chapter 5). For Laiguo, constant repetition of the Buddha's name risked becoming a rote and meaningless exercise. He therefore urged monks, nuns, and laypeople to take up what he considered the more essential matter of their own identity: Who was it that called on Amitābha and sought rebirth in his Pure Land? This was all that really mattered. According to the eminent Ming dynasty Chan master Yunqi Zhuhong (1535–1615), "When you penetrate reciting the Buddha's name, you penetrate everything in the world."[6] Unlike the use of extensive koan curricula in Japanese Rinzai training halls, most Chinese Chan masters held that to resolve a single huatou was to resolve them all.

In Laiguo's talks, he lambasted those monks who limited their efforts to periods of intensive training. For him, Chan practice had to be all-pervading to produce results. It should be done not only during seated meditation but also when walking, eating the morning gruel, going to the bathroom, and slipping off one's shoes. It should infuse every activity. In other talks delivered during this same retreat, Laiguo recounted his own experiences of utter absorption in his huatou. He describes how he lost track of the monastic schedule and had to be reminded where to go and what to do.

In the refectory, he would raise his bowl but forget to eat. Walking down the corridors, he didn't look where he was going and careened into other monks When anyone spoke to him, he would only respond with, "Who recites the Buddha's name?" Such erratic and disruptive behavior earned him scoldings and beatings, but Laiguo viewed even these punishments as opportunities to test the strength of his concentration. If he could maintain focus on his huatou even while suffering blows, it was a sign that he was making real progress.

The celebrated Yuan dynasty Chan master Zhongfeng Mingben (1263-1323) once likened huatou practice to using an iron broom. "The more you sweep, the more [thoughts] remain; the more [thoughts] remain, the more you sweep. If you are unable to sweep, forfeit your life in the name of sweeping."[7] The progress of such sweeping is imperceptible, but with each pass of the broom the ground is slowly worn away. And then, one day, with a single sweep the ground breaks open and one drops into the great void. Intensive retreats, Laiguo reminded his disciples, were only effective if the ground had already been properly prepared. There was no time to relax or grow complacent. The task at hand was urgent and the tension was accordingly kept high. Participants were constantly reminded of the debts they owed to those who made it possible for them to take part in the retreat. They must not fail them. They must not fail themselves. They owed it to everyone to exert themselves to the utmost.

In his talks, Laiguo goads his disciples to abandon themselves completely to the practice, but his fierce exterior was tempered by a sense of compassion for those who were so clearly struggling with the immense difficulties of this task. He regularly reminds those in attendance that his sole purpose is to help them attain awakening. He holds them to the highest standards only because he recognizes their potential. He occasionally comforts them, telling them not to worry; even when things seem to be going poorly, real progress is actually being made. But just as often, Laiguo returns to the role of drill sergeant, castigating those in attendance as pitiful and unworthy. No matter one's status, no matter one's accomplishments, no one was ever allowed to let their guard down.

Laiguo's Later Years

Laiguo's three decades in the abbacy of Gaomin Monastery coincided with a time of tumultuous changes and extraordinary challenges in China. When he first assumed control of the derelict monastery, China's two-thousand-year-old imperial system had recently collapsed. Major political, economic, and educational reforms were transforming the unsteady republic, and Buddhist monasteries like Gaomin were coming under attack as moribund institutions that had no place in a modern society. Land reform programs instituted by the new Nationalist government resulted in the loss of many of the fields and tenant households that had previously supplied Gaomin with a steady stream of produce and income. The monastery's finances ran so low that they could only afford enough food for nine months out of every year. The sangha depended on donations to make up the shortfall.

The situation only grew more dire over time. By the early 1940s, when Laiguo delivered the talks translated below, the city of Yangzhou was occupied by Japanese forces. The infamous Nanjing Massacre had occurred just five years earlier. Over a hundred thousand Chinese soldiers and civilians died during the Japanese onslaught and its aftermath; tens of thousands more were assaulted and raped. Japanese troops marched on Yangzhou, fifty miles to the southwest of Nanjing, just days later. Interment camps and "comfort stations" (brothels where Chinese women were kept captive and forced to have sex with Japanese soldiers) were set up in the city. Some Buddhist monasteries became barracks for Japanese troops, but Gaomin, perhaps because of the monastery's Chan orientation and its reputation for strict discipline, was spared. Laiguo never mentions any of this in his talks, but everyone attending the retreat would have been acutely aware of the precarity of their situation.

   With Japan's surrender and withdrawal from China in 1945, Laiguo and the monks at Gaomin must have breathed a sigh of relief. They could not have known that even greater troubles lay ahead. The civil war pitting Nationalist forces against Communist insurgents brought widespread death and destruction. The Yangzi River, where Gaomin was located, often served as a front line. The Communist victory in 1949 put an end to the war, but the problems for Buddhist monastics only intensified. In the purges that followed, the seventy-year-old Laiguo was denounced as a feudal landlord. A stage was erected for his struggle session and the execution preordained to follow. Fortunately, Zhao Puchu (1907–2000), the secretary general of the Buddhist Association of China, intervened at the last minute and Laiguo was spared.[8] But it was all too much. Shortly thereafter, Laiguo fell ill. His disciples brought him to Shanghai, where he passed away in the winter of 1953.

   In one of his last recorded talks in Shanghai before his death, Laiguo took his place at the head of the meditation hall and addressed

Master Laiguo (left) and Master Xuyun (right) in Shanghai, 1952.

his disciples. "I see that everyone is working diligently to navigate this muddy road," he said. "Every step forward is an accomplishment. To create a life of farming and Chan, we must first find stability. Be that as it may, today I've ascended this seat to say a few words. Why?" Leaning on his staff, Laiguo went on, "Quick! Hang up your cloth bags. We have much to do before the end. No one can waste any time. There is not a moment to spare!" With that, he threw down his staff and descended his seat.[9]

The Translation

The talks translated below were delivered during a meditation retreat (*chanqi*) at Gaomin Monastery that began on November 22, 1942, and concluded seventy days later on February 1, 1943. Over these ten weeks, Laiguo gave a short talk nearly every day. These instructions were unscripted and thus have an informal, unpolished, and intimate tone. They offer a rare glimpse of a modern Chan master instructing and encouraging his disciples in the context of intense, extended training. All the talks Laiguo gave during this retreat were transcribed and published in a volume entitled *Laiguo chanshi chanqi kaishi lu* (Record of the Meditation Retreat Instructions of Chan Master Laiguo). I have translated four talks in their entirety: the opening address of the retreat, the instructions from the third day of the first week, the first day of the second week, and the seventh day of the third week.

LAIGUO

Instructions for an Intensive Meditation Retreat

Today, the residents of this monastery are supporting you so that you can sit this retreat. Many people are busy. Inside the Chan Hall and in the outer buildings, monastic leaders, rank-and-file monks, and even people beyond the monastery—they are all quite busy so that you can sit this retreat. Not only are people inside and outside the monastery busy, all the buddhas in the ten directions, and all great bodhisattvas, dharma protectors, and heavenly dragons are also busy. So busy they cannot rest! Just so that you can sit this retreat.

I ask you, what is it to sit retreat? Why make demands on so many people? As if that were not enough, all the buddhas in the ten directions, all the great bodhisattvas, dharma protectors, and heavenly dragons are even busier than we are. Why are they so busy? Do any of you know? What is it to sit retreat? There are probably some of you who still do not understand. You're thinking to yourself, "Ordinary suffering is unbearable, but I still want to sit retreat! What you say sounds good. The buddhas of the ten directions, the great bodhisattvas, ancestral masters, dharma protectors, and heavenly dragons are all working on our behalf. What are they busy doing? What is it to sit retreat? It is only to endure a little suffering, nothing more. Could there be anything else?" Right! Truly pitiful! Unspeakably pitiful! Even though you are so naïve, I still need to inform you of this monastery's rules.

You need to understand that the rules for this retreat are strict. They are different from our ordinary rules. How are they different? Today, you go before the all the ancestors and ask for leave from life and death. You also come to me to ask for leave from life and death. When I grant you leave from life and death, your life and death are in my hands. If I want you to live, you live. If I want you to die, you die—right where you are standing, you die. Ordinarily, your body belongs to the monastery and your life is entrusted to heavenly dragons. During retreat, it is not like this. Your body and your life are both in my hands.

What is so strict about the rules? Let me explain. From now on, during the retreat, members of the assembly do not bow to the rector. They also should not ask the [monastic] officers any questions. They should not bow to me or ask me any questions either. During retreat, you will not be venerating the Buddha or burning incense, so what need is there for bowing or asking questions? Let me say this up front. The worst thing that could happen is that you get severely ill. If the worst doesn't come to pass, you'll just be sick. If you have an illness, shouldn't you go to the rector to ask to be excused? The rector would not dare to excuse you. Then should you go and bow before one of the officers? That won't work either. Would the officers dare to excuse you? Not only sick leave but also leave from sitting, leave from walking—any kind of leave—the rector and the officers probably won't have the nerve to permit it. What is the reason for this? When you ask for leave from life and death, you don't ask the rector or the officers; you ask me. Would they dare grant such leave on my behalf?

If you're sick, what should you do? There is nothing to be done. When alive, you sit. When dead, you sit. When healthy, you sit. When sick, you sit. You sit until the end. If your illness is so severe that you cannot stand, how can you walk? If you truly get to the point where you cannot walk, we will throw your body beneath the sitting platform. If you're sick, fine. Alive, fine. Dead, fine. At the end of the retreat, we'll send you off to your next birth. But during the retreat, you will not be sent anywhere. Three or five people tossed beneath the sitting platform—this is our cure for illnesses.

Moreover, during retreat when you are walking, sitting, eating, or going to the bathroom, if you drop your head or laugh, I'm telling you, you have no future! What will happen? When you enter the hall, the officers and rector will all be holding up their incense boards.[10] Whether with one incense board or twenty, you will be beat on your head, face, and ears. If you haven't been beaten to death, you may continue the retreat. What should you do if you've been wounded by the beating? Just throw yourself beneath the sitting platform. At the end of the retreat, we'll send everyone off to their next birth together. Ordinarily, if someone is beaten to death, we quickly send them off to their next birth. If someone is injured, we send them to the infirmary. Retreats are not like this. So, at Gaomin Monastery, beating people to death isn't considered a big deal? In past retreats, there have always been a few. It's a common occurrence, nothing special.

Let me say it again: the rules are just as I have explained them. There will be no favoritism, and there can be no mistakes. I'll sum it up: If you're sick and want to die, you will not be excused. If you die, we'll toss you beneath the sitting platform. If you break the rules, you'll be beaten to death and then thrown beneath the sitting platform. My instructions are crystal clear. There cannot be the slightest error.

Furthermore, ordinarily during meditation, if you want to go to the bathroom, you ask the rector to be excused. After the rector strikes you six times with the incense board, you can open the door and leave. During retreat, this is not allowed. This is because in one day there are twelve periods of walking meditation, so there are twenty-four chances to go to the bathroom. Even if you have diarrhea, how many times do you need to go? It does not matter which period it is, opening the door is not allowed. If you shit in your pants or on your cushion, I won't blame you. You can shit on your cushion, but you cannot open the door. You should take care! What is it to sit retreat? Everyone should be clear. Aside from practicing Chan, awakening to the Way, understanding life, and escaping death, there is nothing else. If you want to practice Chan, it cannot be done without practicing "Who recites the Buddha's name?" If you want to understand life and death, it can be done by means of "Who recites the Buddha's name?"

Everyone arouse your minds! Investigate!

Serious practice lasts a thousand days; awakening occurs in an instant. Even if you train for a thousand days, awakening occurs in an instant. Suppose you train for one thousand days without interruption. In that case, I can guarantee your awakening. If, however, your training has not yet reached such a place, I would not dare offer any guarantees. In this assembly there are people who have been living here for three or five years. There are also those who have been at Jinshan for three or five years. Among those who have been practicing austerities at Jinshan and Gaomin for ten or twelve years, is it possible that there are none who have trained for a thousand days? If they already have trained for a thousand days, aren't they assured of awakening during this retreat? This retreat is specially focused on the practice that leads to awakening. So, why aren't you awakened? It is because you are too pitiful. Although you say you have five, ten, or twenty years of training, you don't yet have a thousand days of practice! If you don't have a thousand days of practice, you will not be able to awaken. When I talk like this, you are thinking, "In the summer it's so hot! We also must go to the Dharma Hall and refectory. It is not conducive to practice. Waiting for the time to pass, we are terribly busy following all the major regulations and minor rules. Then there are the additional periods of meditation. None of this leaves time for serious practice. Intensive retreats are for serious practice. We won't let this opportunity pass us by!" Right! You are probably all thinking this.

I see that you are thinking that over the course of a year you will do serious practice only during intensive retreat. Summer after summer, from one period to the next, you meditate but still have to go to the Dharma Hall and the refectory. During retreat is when you do serious practice. This type of person is of the lowest grade, the most confused. Why? Intensive retreat is a time set aside for attaining realization. It is called the season of a thousand awakenings. Is this when serious practice happens? Serious practice must occur during ordinary times. If one doesn't do serious practice during ordinary times and waits to begin during an intensive retreat, when will they awaken? This one word, *awakening*, do you have a stake in it? I'll give you an analogy: It's like someone during the Qing dynasty who has spent ten years reading. If an exam is held, wouldn't they go to be tested?[11] But if someone arrives at the examination site without being able to write or understand characters and then begins to make a serious effort, how would that turn out? Can they wear the cap of a scholar? They had ten years to study but did not read anything; they only gave themselves the title of scholar. During ordinary times, they did not study, but then they went to the exam and thought to put on a scholar's cap. I'm afraid that won't do.

This retreat is the same as an examination site. If you have spent three years making strenuous effort, you are already at a high level. When you arrive at this monastery and sit retreat, you will immediately awaken. It's true! But if during ordinary times you only take on the name of a serious practitioner yet do not engage in serious practice, when you come to this retreat, how will you be able to awaken? It's the same as someone who has not studied trying to take the civil service exam. This mistake you're making goes back a long way. It's not just today's mistake. Considering this, do you still want to sit retreat? If not, is not sitting an option? Since none of you has the qualifications to sit retreat, you have all really failed the monks of this monastery. The resident monks have prepared everything on your behalf. If anything was amiss, they quickly rectified it. If there was something that might distract you, they quickly took care of it. In this way, I dare to say that the resident monks have done right by everyone. You have let these monks down, but they have not let you down in the slightest.

If there is a person who has done serious training for three or five years—wearing their robe; eating food; visiting the Dharma Hall, refectory, bathroom; and going to sleep—they have already scaled the peaks of practice and released their hold from the precipice.

Today they have arrived at Gaomin prepared to sit retreat and attain realization. If the resident monks unexpectedly stopped supporting your retreat, they would be letting you down. I ask you, is there such a person? I ask you again. Do not say that you let the past three or five years slip past without engaging in serious practice. During the summer you did not raise "Who recites the Buddha's name?" but then you enter the Meditation Hall and do not know how to raise [the huatou] so it is not raised. Now, in this retreat, period after period, week after week, while sitting and walking, can you raise "Who recites the Buddha's name?"

You should calm your mind and ask yourselves, "Am I doing right by everyone?" In any kind of study, everyone wants to talk about progress. Do you know what constitutes progress for disciples of our tradition? Going to the Dharma Hall is progress; going to refectory is progress; going to the bathroom is progress. Every place is [an opportunity to make] progress. Do you understand how going to the Dharma Hall is progress? When you are standing in the hall and your head does not drop and your body does not move, that is progress. How so? When you practice to the point where you acquire some power, how could your head drop? How could your body move? When your head drops, if you're not seeing forms, you're hearing sounds. When your body moves, if you're not feeling sore, you're feeling itchy. So, can you really practice in the refectory, in the Dharma Hall, and in every other place? When you go to the toilet, the lid makes no sound. Raising your eyebrows, blinking your eyes, moving, standing, sitting, lying down—these are all opportunities for serious practice. You should understand that in our tradition these ordinary experiences are precious opportunities for intensive retreat.

Everyone arouse your mind!

For understanding life, escaping death, illuminating the mind, and seeing your nature, the one method of Chan practice is most effective. You could also say that it works for everyone. I truly believe in this method. Among the eighty-four thousand dharma gates, there are none that compare with this method. However, there are some among you who do not accept this, who wonder how "Who recites the Buddha's name?" could surpass eighty-four thousand other dharma gates. If you don't believe what I'm saying, that's okay. Let's set aside "Who recites the Buddha's name?" Can you tell me which method resolves life and death the most directly and quickly? Is it possible that there is a method that doesn't involve practice, doesn't entail serious effort but once encountered can illuminate the mind and [allow one to] see their nature? Think about it. If there were truly a quicker method than Chan practice, I would study it with you. Because your self-regard runs so deep, and your good roots are so shallow, I want to eliminate your biases and bring you back to this one great road. For that reason, I will give you some direction. Think about this carefully. Can reading the scriptures resolve life and death? Can reciting the Buddha's name or chanting dharani resolve life and death?

You have all come here because of life and death, so of course you want to investigate these things. It is no small matter. Consider this: Reading sutras only allows you to plant a few good roots and understand some ideas. It cannot resolve life and death. Reciting the Buddha's name, reciting "Amitābha Buddha" can resolve life and death, but it cannot lead one to the peak of nirvana. Chanting dharani, purifying the body and mind—these can convey some minor powers, but they cannot resolve life and death. Reading sutras, reciting the Buddha's name, and chanting all seek [something] outside. Each person's life and death are not obtained from the outside. They don't depend on others; they come from within one's own home. If you turn outward, the more you run, the farther away you are. You should know: to practice "Who recites the Buddha's name?" is to turn toward home. What does this mean? I'll give you an analogy. If a child is reading the *Book of Hundreds of Surnames*, they read straight through from the name Zhao to the names Qian, Sun, Li, Zhou, Wu, Zheng, and Wang.[12] After just a few days the child will learn them all by heart. But if you ask them what the words Zhao, Qian, Sun, and Li mean, what can they say? If you ask them any question, they'll be brought up short. One need only look into Zhao, Qian, Sun, and Li to know that Zhou, Wu, Zheng, and Wang also cannot be understood. When you investigate deeply, you'll realize that you cannot comprehend Zhao, Qian, Sun, and Li. Think about it. Reciting the Buddha's name, aren't you reciting "Amitābha Buddha, Amitābha Buddha" over and over again? Now I'm asking you: Which one is reciting the Buddha's name? Standing there, is it starting to dawn on you? It's the same as reciting "Zhao, Qian, Sun, and Li." Consider this carefully. Isn't it true? Isn't "Who recites the Buddha's name?" a way to return home? What is it to return home? Without life there is no death. We speak of illuminating the mind and seeing our nature, but this is just a lot of talk. Arriving home, the mind needs no illuminating. It has always been luminous. Nature doesn't need to be seen. It is already perfectly apparent. This "Who recites the Buddha's name?" sends you home with a single step. With only a single phrase, you can return home and sit steadfast. You know that this phrase "Who recites the Buddha's name?" is so effective! But you are thinking, "From morning until night, we raise 'Who recites the Buddha's name?' but random thoughts keep coming and we can't keep [our minds] still for long. Given this, how can you say practicing 'Who recites the Buddha's name?' will lead us home? What you teach is really hard to comprehend!"

Right! You need to understand, knowing that you are having random thoughts is a sign that your practice is progressing. If you raise [the phrase] but cannot maintain it for long, that is also progress. You should know, every dharma gate exists in the midst of random thoughts. Where else could you become aware of such thoughts? Being aware of random thoughts and knowing that you cannot maintain [concentration] for long—these are both good signs.

[And yet,] your cultivation of the Way is truly pitiful. All of you standing here are adults. You say that you cannot bear life and death and so you want to cultivate the Way. You start to investigate the phrase "Who recites the Buddha's name?" but are unable to penetrate it. After three or five years, it is still impenetrable. In this condition, what is this talk about cultivating the Way or finding life and death unbearable? It's a complete muddle! If you are unable to penetrate "Who recites the Buddha's name?" can you still be considered a person? Everywhere, people are concerned about their reputations. If you cannot penetrate "Who recites the Buddha's name?" you have no reputation. If you have a little bit of understanding, can you see how to do right by yourself? Are some of you weeping? Pitiful! Pathetic! You are all in the haze of a black cave. Day after day, I instruct you to close your eyes, and so you all close your eyes. I ask you, when you open your eyes, do you see me? When your eyes are closed, can you see yourself? Even when your eyes are not closed, inside the black cave nothing can be seen. I ask you again, when your eyes are closed and you take a step forward, where are you going? Do you have a clear understanding? Do you know where this step is taking you?

Investigate!

Under ordinary circumstances, when serious practitioners engage in training, everything is fine. When they want to eradicate random thoughts, they raise "Who recites the Buddha's name?" and the random thoughts vanish. Their work is effective. They can do it when still; they can do it while moving. It seems as though no thought is wasted. But now [you're thinking], "In this retreat, everything is turned around! Nothing is right! I cannot raise 'Who recites the Buddha's name.' I cannot eradicate random thoughts. It's so peaceful here, but I try to raise 'Who recites the Buddha's name?' and can't do it. I try a second, third, or fifth time; I try so hard that my head hurts, but I still can't do it. It seems like the retreat is ruined. Ordinarily everything is fine. Why is it that during retreat I can't seem to apply myself? It's exhausting! I want to give up!"

There are other people who reach this point and think, "This is great! It's peaceful here. Even though I'm not doing the practice,

I don't have any random thoughts. Since that's the case, I don't need to engage in serious practice. Wouldn't that just disrupt [my tranquil state]? I'll just rest awhile in this peaceful and orderly place." But there are a few of you with some mind for the Way. While practicing, you grope around and have inevitably encountered this problem. Why? This is a place that your practice must pass through. If you want to make progress, you will have to walk this road. When walking this road, don't be concerned with strange occurrences. Those who engage in serious practice must take this path. In so doing, there are two types of mistakes that people make. The first is that when they cannot raise [their huatou], they try a second, third, or fifth time and then give up. The other mistake is to not try at all, considering oneself already an expert. These paths will take you far from where you need to be! You will be as distant as heaven and earth! Both approaches are wrong! Why? Not being able to raise [your huatou] and not attempting to raise it both stem from an inability to penetrate the principle of this practice. If you can get to the bottom of it, you will naturally resolve the problems of not raising and not bothering to raise [the huatou].

Why do serious practitioners need to take this path? You should understand: Ordinarily when you are practicing, it is amid sounds and sights. If your eyes are not seeing forms, then your ears are hearing sounds. In such situations, although you raise "Who recites the Buddha's name?" you are still doing so with a coarse mind that is seeing forms and hearing sounds. This coarse mind is constantly producing random thoughts, muddled states, and karmic hindrances. That's just the way that coarse minds work. During this intensive retreat, all external sounds and forms cannot reach you, so you do not need to eliminate them. Sounds and forms are naturally absent. Because there are no external sounds or forms within, there are no discriminating thoughts. Your consciousness does not clamor after any external sounds and forms. Sounds and forms trigger consciousness to make distinctions. Sounds, forms, and consciousness come together in the coarse mind. Today, there are no sounds or forms. What can the consciousness clamor after?

When this clamoring consciousness, sounds, and forms are all gone, the coarse mind also vanishes. When the coarse mind is gone, everything comes to rest. When you try to raise [the huatou] but cannot, when you try to apply yourself but cannot, when you cannot eliminate random thoughts, when things feel peaceful and orderly, you have arrived at this place. Your coarse mind has come to rest.

This is how we talk in our lineage. We don't teach about the five prior consciousnesses or about what is seen, thought, or felt.[13] Our lineage teaches about sounds, forms, and the coarse mind. When the coarse mind comes to rest, it's not that nothing happens. You still must move forward and face things. If you can't raise "Who recites the Buddha's name?" how can you move forward? Is there a method for this? There is! It is a method that can be used by those who can't raise [the huatou] and want to give up and those who don't want to raise it because they feel like they are already experts. What is this method? When you come to the place where you cannot raise [the huatou], remember this technique: "Who recites the Buddha's name?" Do it! Don't say, "I already told you I can't raise it, so what am I supposed to do?" In that case, forget about raising it. Just recite this one sentence: "Who recites the Buddha's name?" Anybody can recite this! As you recite, engage in the recitation. Illuminate it in this way. When you arrive at another place where you cannot raise [the huatou] or do not want to raise it, recite "Who recites the Buddha's name?" With that recitation, start to engage again. This process will summon a feeling of doubt.[14] I'm telling you, if you don't want to engage, [the doubt] cannot help you. If the doubts come pouring forth, that is excellent! But, in the end, this is all just talk about my own [experience]. I want you to arrive at this place. Then you will understand that what I'm saying is true.

When I was at Jinshan, my practice reached this place. It was similar to what you are experiencing now. I would try to raise [my huatou] but couldn't do it. Let's not even talk about random thoughts. Of course I couldn't eradicate them! But my training was different from yours. At that time, I was just beginning to apply myself. During each stick of incense, I would investigate. After the bell signaling the end of the period, I would immediately interrogate myself. How was my work that period? Is my mind still murky? Do I still have random thoughts? If there was the slightest murkiness or any random thoughts, I would strike myself on my ears and mouth. The next period I would try harder to eliminate murkiness and random thoughts until there was just one thing: "Who recites the Buddha's name?" Once that was perfectly clear, I could it let go. At this point, even though there were still times when I could not raise [the huatou], I was different from others. I did not dwell in this place. I knew it was not a good realm. Even if it was a good realm, I would not dwell there. One must always penetrate completely. When there seemed to be no way forward, I looked for the ripest random thought and eliminated it. Then I would immediately look again. If there was nothing left to eliminate, then there was nothing left. Shanghai theater is really good? Eliminate that random thought! But I couldn't. I couldn't eliminate such thoughts. Later, I slowly recited the phrase "Who recites the Buddha's name?" I thought about and recited this phrase. Where does it come from? If I could recite it, why couldn't I practice it? I started at this place and the next day I tried again. It seemed like by the third day I was not eating. I'd see food but like a dead man had no appetite. Then I realized that I was using [the huatou] well and I kept going forward. That kind of thing happens all the time. I want you to reach this place and then we can talk some more.

Investigate!

Further Reading

Brose, Benjamin. "A New Kind of Missionary." *Tricycle: The Buddhist Review* (Summer 2023): 78–83, 107–10.

———. "Laiguo Miaoshu: The Making of a Modern Chan Master." In *Inner Worlds: Individuals and Interiority in Chinese Religious Life*, edited by Benjamin Brose and James A. Benn. Leiden: Brill, 2025.

Broughton, Jeffrey. *The Recorded Sayings of Chan Master Zhongfeng Mingben.* New York: Oxford University Press, 2023.

Campo, Daniela. "Disclosing the Self: Buddhist Instructions (*Kaishi*) and Religious Autobiography in Twentieth-Century China." In *Inner Worlds: Individuals and Interiority in Chinese Religious Life*, edited by Benjamin Brose and James A. Benn. Leiden: Brill, 2025.

Schlütter, Morten. "'Who Is Reciting the Name of the Buddha?' as Gongan in Chinese Chan Buddhism." *Frontiers of History in China* 8, no. 3 (2013): 366–88.

Welch, Holmes. *The Buddhist Revival in China.* Cambridge, MA: Harvard University Press, 1968.

———. *The Practice of Chinese Buddhism 1900–1950.* Cambridge, MA: Harvard University Press, 1967.

Master Taixu in the 1930s.

3 | The Great Reformer

Taixu

JUSTIN RITZINGER

No other figure is as closely associated with Chinese Buddhism's modernization as Master Taixu (1890-1947). A passionate and indefatigable advocate for reform of Buddhist institutions and engagement with the forces of modernity, he was compared by supporters and foreign observers of the day with Martin Luther. A more apt comparison, however, might be Martin Luther King. Although central to the movement to reform Chinese Buddhism, he, like King, was but the most prominent leader of many. And like King, he was significantly more complex in life than he has become in popular memory. The selections translated below were chosen to highlight the idea he is best known for—that Buddhist practice should be focused on action in the world—and to add some nuance to our understanding of Taixu as a leader, activist, and religious figure.

Taixu's Early Life and Politics

Born Lü Gansen on January 8, 1890, in northern Zhejiang Province, the man who would become Taixu was raised by his grandmother following the death of his father, a bricklayer, and the subsequent remarriage of his mother. She ensured that he received an education and exposed him to Buddhism with visits to temples and pilgrimage sites. After a short time as a shop apprentice, he left home to pursue the monastic life, ordaining at Tiantong Monastery in 1904. There he was singled out for his talent to receive the finest education the monastic system had to offer, practicing Chan and studying the sutras under prominent masters. He appeared quite successful. Yet he was unsatisfied. He felt he was simply aping the Chan masters of old and repeating profound doctrines like a parrot, while authentic insight eluded him. That insight at last came when he immersed himself in the canon.

One day, after reading the *Greater Perfection of Wisdom Sutra*, Taixu wrote in his *Autobiography*, "body, mind, and world suddenly disappeared. In the midst of empty quiescence, there was brilliant tranquility and numberless worlds gloriously manifested like mirages in the sky, illuminating endlessly." In the days that followed, he found that the ball of doubt he experienced practicing Chan had dissolved and the meaning of the profound doctrines he had studied was laid bare. He had "cast off the dust of the world like a cicada discarding its shell and begun a new life in the Dharma."

Not long after, his life took a turn that would define his subsequent career. In 1908 he met two young monks who exposed him to the reformist and radical ideas that were circulating in the dying days of the Qing dynasty. Taixu, just eighteen years old, then experienced a second awakening, this time political in nature. For the next several years, he would pursue an activist career with the goal of both Buddhist and political revolution. In Buddhist circles, he promoted a "threefold revolution" in doctrine, monastic rule, and temple property through a series of short-lived organizations. At the same time, he was running with revolutionaries and radicals, ultimately becoming one of the most prominent anarchists in China in the years following the 1911 revolution. His efforts in both areas failed. His hotheaded approach to Buddhist reform alienated many prominent figures. Most famously, he and his associate Renshan attempted to forcibly turn Jinshan, one of the most prominent Chan monasteries of the day, into a modern seminary. They did so by stacking a meeting with their supporters in what amounted to a democratic coup, only to have their faction expelled a few days later when the deposed abbot returned with armed toughs. Meanwhile, the moment of political openness inaugurated by the revolution proved to be brief. Yuan Shikai, a general who negotiated the Qing emperor's abdication in return for the presidency, sought to concentrate power in his own hands, sparking a second revolution in 1913 that ended with his forces crushing revolutionary groups, including the anarchists.

Taixu entered a period of solitary retreat in 1914 to lie low and regroup. During this period, he read extensively in both the Buddhist canon and the secular press, emerging in 1917 a more mature and measured leader and thinker. In the years that followed, he worked to build a movement to modernize and reform Buddhism. Circumstances were far from ideal. The general who took over the government died shortly thereafter, inaugurating a period of warlordism that fractured the country until 1927, when the Nationalist Party unified it. Besides political instability, Taixu faced exclusion from many of the powerful Buddhist institutions of the day due to the excesses of his youth. This was exacerbated by the actions of his students who sometimes engaged in the kinds of direct attacks on prominent figures like Yinguang (discussed in chapter 5) that Taixu himself had learned to avoid.[1] Largely cut off from the elite monastic networks in which he had been trained, he did not serve as abbot of a major monastery until late in his career when he was invited to head Xuedou Monastery near Ningbo by Chiang Kai-shek in 1932.

Without a firm institutional and economic base, Taixu was forever dependent on lay patrons, leaving him vulnerable to changing interests and fashions. Nevertheless, he managed to found the most important Buddhist periodical of the time, *The Sound of the Sea Tide*. This served as a platform for the dissemination of his ideas across the country, creating a community of readers and shared sense of identity among reform-minded monastics and laity while also featuring pieces by more conservative figures like Yinguang and Dixian. He also oversaw a series of seminaries to promote modern education for monks, beginning with the Wuchang Buddhist Seminary in 1922. Where traditional education focused on ritualized oral commentaries on the sutras by a monastic, typically in a Dharma Hall filled with reverent but passive listeners, these institutions employed lay as well as monastic lecturers who spoke in classrooms equipped with blackboards and would ask students questions that they were to answer in their own words and assign essays based on the material. Subjects included Buddhist texts and history but also secular fields such as science and languages. These seminaries were plagued with instability and never matched Taixu's lofty pedagogic goals, but they were nevertheless the anchors for a network of young monks who dreamed of a new Buddhism for a new China.

Taixu also pioneered the model of eminent monk as public intellectual that we see today in leaders such as the Dalai Lama. He would tour the country lecturing to crowds of hundreds or more and meet with political leaders and other prominent figures. Many of his "writings" are actually transcriptions of his talks made by his students.

Taixu's teachings were broad-ranging. He was deeply convinced of Buddhism's relevance to the modern world and regularly addressed the latest currents of social, political, and scientific thought circulating in China. He discussed relativity, evolution, anarchism, socialism, and more. He must have read voraciously. He also lectured widely on Buddhist texts and themes. He was convinced of the equality of the various Buddhist schools and believed Buddhism required all of them in order to thrive in China. Where other Buddhist teachers often specialized in a particular set of texts or school of thought, he delivered commentaries on nearly all the major sutras of Chinese Buddhism and a number of minor ones. He gave lectures on teachings from Chan, Pure Land, Tiantai, Huayan, and Esoteric teachings. While he might critique particular forms of practice that had developed, he universally praised the various texts and schools of thought themselves. All were part of a wonderful dharmic heritage that only needed to be understood and applied properly.

Some have suggested that all this breadth came at the expense of depth. Certainly Taixu was not a systemic thinker. It is best to think of him as an activist rather than a philosopher, a Martin Luther King rather than a Thomas Aquinas. The problems of his day were often the starting point for his thought and the focal point to which they returned. But he was more than a problem solver. He was a man of broad interests and genuine intellectual enthusiasm, both for the Buddhist tradition and for the new ideas, local and foreign, that were sweeping the country. This was, I believe, a key source of his appeal: the palpable conviction that modernity, for all its problems, offered much that was good and that Buddhism had much to offer the modern world.

Taixu's Death and Legacy

For a long time, Taixu's legacy appeared to be very limited. The Japanese invasion of China in 1937 threw the country into turmoil. Taixu followed the central government in its retreat to the country's interior, but he spent the next several years preoccupied by the war, with limited resources to pursue his own projects. While the war's end seemed to usher in a new moment of opportunity, his causes and conditions were almost exhausted. On March 12, 1947, Taixu suffered a fatal stroke. He took his last breath on March 17 surrounded by monastic and lay followers chanting the name of Maitreya to aid his ascent to the Inner Court, the bodhisattva's palace in Tuṣita heaven. The fulfillment of Taixu's dreams would have to fall to others.

At the same time, the political situation in China was deteriorating. The civil war between the Nationalists and the Communists that had been suspended to fight the Japanese reignited in 1946. In 1949 the Nationalists were routed, and Mao Zedong declared the establishment of the People's Republic. At first it was not clear that Communist regulation of religion would be much more restrictive than that of the Nationalists, but from the mid-1950s to the mid-1960s the state gradually dismantled the physical and human infrastructure of the religion. As monastics were forced to engage in productive labor and political study, their numbers dwindled and monasteries were consolidated, allowing the excess to be turned over to factories and offices. When the Cultural Revolution began in 1966, promising to sweep away the "four olds"—old ideas, old culture, old customs, and old habits—it seemed that Buddhism in China had truly perished.

The situation in Taiwan was better but still tenuous for decades. The Nationalists retreated to the island following their defeat, drawing in their wake their army and many refugees, including some of the most prominent clergy of the day. Chinese Buddhism thus continued on the island but under significant restraint. The Republic of China on Taiwan was impoverished in the 1950s and 1960s, and the Nationalists imposed martial law to guard against Communist subversion and subjugate the local populace. This left Buddhist leaders with little room to maneuver. A few prominent followers of Taixu made it to Taiwan but died or were sidelined, leaving more conservative figures in key positions of influence.

Nevertheless, seeds were being planted. Yinshun, an associate of Taixu considered by many the most brilliant scholar-monk in centuries, made Taiwan his base of operations. He would devote his life to education and scholarship, putting Taixu's vision of a Buddhism engaged with ordinary life in society, which Yinshun preferred to call Human Realm Buddhism, on firmer intellectual footing. Institutionally, in the 1970s two advocates of this approach, Master Cheng Yen and Master Hsing Yun, found loopholes in the restrictive regulation of social organizations that allowed them to expand. These organizations, the Tzu Chi Foundation and Buddha's Light International Association, exploded in size and influence as Taiwan began its transition to democracy in the 1980s. Joined shortly thereafter by Master Sheng Yen's Dharma Drum Mountain, these three organizations represent the fulfillment of Taixu's aspirations in many ways. Incorporating millions of people and organized along rational lines, they have brought the message of Human Realm Buddhism around the world.

But Taixu's legacy is not limited to Chinese forms of Buddhism. His publishing efforts had transnational reach, with copies of his journal *The Sound of the Sea Tide* reaching other East Asian countries, most consequentially Vietnam, where they informed the revival that took place in the 1920s. The message of Human Realm Buddhism, or *Nhat Gian Phat Giao* in Vietnamese, eventually inspired a young monk named Thich Nhat Hanh, who translated it into English as "Engaged Buddhism" and made it his own.

Despite a lifetime of frustrated ambitions, then, Taixu's vision of Buddhist practice as action in everyday life has had a major impact on Buddhism in the modern world.

The Translations

The three short pieces translated here represent a small sampling of Taixu's thought. In different ways, each of them addresses one of his central convictions: that Buddhism must be applied to ordinary life in society and that ethical action to make the world a better place is in fact the work of the bodhisattva and the very heart of the path.

The first, "My Aspiration and Practice," dates to 1924, toward the end of the warlord period. The absence of a strong central state preserved an atmosphere of revolution, and intellectuals and students of the time dreamed of transforming China's culture in order to break with the past and set the country on a course to utopia. Taixu and his associates represented the Buddhist wing of these developments. This piece provides the most direct and explicit statement of how he saw his mission at that time. Framed around a quote from Confucius, it briefly alludes to his aspiration to reform the monastic sangha in a new national framework and organize the laity through a new type of institution known as Right Faith Societies, referring readers to his major work *On Reforming the Sangha System* for details. Taixu would make several such proposals over the years with varying details but consistent themes. All iterations would have organized monasteries into a nationwide hierarchy, which would have broken the connection between Dharma and tonsure transmission and control of monastic property. Taixu saw this move as an antidote for factionalism, but others saw it as a threat to an already embattled monastic system. He also wanted to reduce the size of the sangha, laicizing monks and nuns who could not keep the precepts while raising the quality of those who remained through education and engaging them with society.

Though not restricted to monastics, the bodhisattva precepts that Taixu identifies as his practice also address the question of how to be a monk in the modern world. Where the bodhisattva precepts typically taken by monastics in China derive from the *Sutra on Brahma's Net*, he chose instead those abstracted from the *Yogācārabhūmi-śāstra* in a text entitled the *Yoga Bodhisattva Pratimokṣa*, translated below for simplicity as "The Yoga Bodhisattva Precepts." He felt that these precepts offered a mode of ethical practice that was better suited to beginner bodhisattvas in the modern world because they provided demanding yet flexible guidance that not only could accommodate work in the world but actively enjoined it. Indeed, he saw it as embodying a revolutionary ethic that could support dismantling unjust structures. After the Nationalists unified China in 1927 and Taixu moved away from a revolutionary left that was coming to be dominated by Communism, he began to downplay the revolutionary implications of the text but never disavowed them. Also interesting is the pride of place Taixu gives to precepts. Whereas they are typically seen as coequal with or preparatory to concentration and wisdom, Taixu presents them here as the essence of all Buddhist practice, to which concentration and wisdom are mere ancillary aids. While it might be a mistake to take this too literally—Taixu often effusively praises the text he is talking or writing about—we should nevertheless take it seriously as a remarkable inversion that highlights the central importance of *action* to his vision of the Buddhist path.

Published in 1945, the second piece, "The Goals of Human Life Buddhism," is a late explication of one of Taixu's signature ideas: Human Life Buddhism or Buddhism for Human Life. This idea became the hallmark of the reform movement, although ultimately

Human Realm Buddhism (sometimes misleadingly translated "Humanistic Buddhism") would come to be the preferred term. It is often described as simply the application of Buddhism to ordinary life in society, but here Taixu places it in a larger context, framing it with an exposition of the four goals that he sees as comprising the entirety of Buddhist teachings: improving the human world, achieving a better rebirth, escaping samsara, and attaining buddhahood. The last is the ultimate goal, while the other three are merely provisional.

The problem that Buddhism faced in modern China was that the three provisional goals had become imbalanced in a way that was not suitable for the age. Buddhist practice, in Taixu's view, had come to be dominated by the pursuit of rebirth in the paradisical pure land of Amitābha and world-rejecting meditation in monasteries secluded from society. Human Life Buddhism would adapt to the modern world by emphasizing the first goal: improving the human world. Practicing the bodhisattva path in the here and now, individuals would purify their own character advancing toward buddhahood in the midst of society rather than waiting for rebirth with Amitābha or absconding to the mountains. At the same time, they would purify this world, creating a utopia he elsewhere calls the Pure Land on Earth[2] by bringing Buddhism to all aspects of social existence. Contrary to those of his day who claimed that Buddhism was a relic of the past, Taixu thus argues here that it has universal relevance. It is comparable to science in its ability to improve human life, but it goes beyond science. As such, in his worldview, science is a useful ancillary to the Dharma but cannot replace it.

Such ideas have often led Taixu to be seen by Western observers as a modernizer in a secularizing vein. His Buddhism, in this view, rejected worship of unseen celestial bodhisattvas in favor of acting as a bodhisattva oneself. It dismissed rebirth in the otherworldly pure land of Amitābha after death in favor of building a pure land in this world now. Taixu, however, was inclusivist in orientation. There was a place for everything in his Buddhism. Teachings such as Pure Land or Esoteric Buddhism were neither illegitimate nor unreal, simply overemphasized and a bit unsuitable to the current age. They are not rejected but "enfolded" within Human Life Buddhism. Taixu himself engaged in certain esoteric practices and lectured on the sutras of Amitābha Pure Land. This inclusivism has been important to his continuing appeal in the Chinese-speaking world. Practitioners of any teaching or method can take up his ideas without a sense of contradiction.

The final selection places the emphasis on action in the world in a more cosmic context. Entitled "A Comparison of Tuṣita Pure Land and the Pure Lands of the Ten Directions," it records prefatory remarks Taixu made in 1936 when lecturing on the *Sutra of Maitreya's Ascent*. In 1924 Taixu had grouped this sutra together with two texts abstracted from a treatise believed to have been preached by Maitreya himself, the *Yogācārabhūmi*—the *Yoga Bodhisattva Precepts* discussed in our first selection and the "Chapter on Knowing Reality"[3]—as the Three Essentials of the Maitreya School, a new school of Buddhist practice formulated by Taixu. The "Chapter on Knowing Reality" described a Yogācāra method of meditation; the *Yoga Bodhisattva Precepts*, as we have seen, offers a set of precepts to guide behavior; and the *Ascent Sutra* promised rebirth in the future buddha Maitreya's pure land in the Inner Court of Tuṣita Heaven. The school was an important focus of Taixu's career and personal practice thereafter. He would go on to lecture on Maitreyan texts and themes more than any other topic.

Yogācāra texts were enjoying a wave of renewed popularity in Taixu's day. His interest in the *Ascent Sutra* and its promise of rebirth in the Inner Court was more unusual, even controversial. Rebirth with Maitreya had been a common goal in the early days of Buddhism in China but was completely eclipsed by the pure land of Amitābha by the Tang dynasty (618–907). In this essay, Taixu places Tuṣita Pure Land within the larger universe of buddha fields and makes a case for rebirth there. There are many pure lands, he reminds his audience, ranking them within Yogācāra and Tiantai frameworks from the ultimate pure lands experienced by Buddhas themselves to expedient pure lands created for the benefit of deluded beings. In this last category he places both Amitābha's Western Pure Land and the Tuṣita Pure Land. As in the previous piece, he then proceeds to argue for emphasizing a different expedient than has been stressed in the past. Maitreya's pure land in Tuṣita is uniquely suited to this world in this time. Rebirth can be attained through ethical action as human beings—that is, through the practice of Human Life Buddhism. Moreover, this ethical action will not only secure rebirth by Maitreya's side but also eventually purify this world in the distant future, creating the conditions for Maitreya's descent and attainment of buddhahood.

What we see here, then, is an enchantment of progress in which the pure land on earth is not simply an improved society but a purified world crowned by the presence of a Buddha. This allows practitioners to devote themselves to making the world a better place without having to worry that they will backslide and lose progress on the path. Nor need they worry that they are sacrificing themselves for a utopia they will never see, for all who are reborn in the Inner Court will also descend and be reborn with Maitreya and practice with him in his earthly pure land.

TAIXU

My Aspiration and Practice

Spring 1924

In recent years, with the aid of students of Buddhism in this country, I have been involved directly and indirectly in assorted activities to revive and reform Buddhism, but I fear I have not yet explained the aspiration and practice to which I have dedicated this body of retribution as sustenance for the long eons of the bodhisattva path. Now inaugurating the fifth year of *Sound of the Sea Tide*, I take this opportunity to offer the sea of believers a thorough explanation. Formerly, Confucius [said that] his aspiration lay in the *Spring and Autumn Annals* and his practice in the *Classic of Filial Piety*. So I say, "My aspiration lies in organizing and revitalizing the Buddhist sangha (the presiding monastics) and societies (lay right faith societies) and my practice lies in the *Yoga Bodhisattva Precepts*." I resolved upon this aspiration and practice in the winter of 1915 and have maintained it unwaveringly since. Below I shall try to elaborate.

As for the aspiration to organize and revitalize the Buddhist sangha and societies, aside from a few proposals that have appeared elsewhere, everything can be found in my work *On Reforming the Sangha System*. This discourse also touches on my basic proposals for Buddhist Right Faith Societies....For details, one can seek out the original essay....

As for my practice of the *Yoga Bodhisattva Precepts*, the Buddha-dharma can be gathered under teachings, principles, practice, and fruits, but practice alone is essential. The function of believing the teachings and understanding the principles lies in driving practice. If one believes and understands but does not practice, then the teachings and principles are all useless. Fruits are accomplished by practicing fully. If one doesn't practice or does not practice fully, the fruit is not accomplished. If the fruit were accomplished anyway, then it would simply be fate and one would have nothing to do with it. Therefore, that which has force and necessity is only practice. Practices are measureless but can be gathered under the ten perfections and further gathered under the three studies; distilled to its essence, practice lies in the precepts alone.

What are the precepts? Stopping evil and doing good are called the precepts. Now, if one stops all evil without exception, one leaves behind all defilements. If one does all good without exception, then one accomplishes all purity. Is this not the unsurpassed bodhi of the Tathāgatha? Only the precepts can accomplish this, thus I say practice lies in the precepts alone. Concentration and wisdom are then supplements to the precepts. They are not really coequal with the precepts like the three legs of a tripod. Thus, concentration is using the power of fixed concentration to stop [evil] and do [good]. Wisdom is using the power of judgment to stop [evil] and do [good]. If not for precepts' stopping [evil] and doing [good], then even if one had the power of concentration and wisdom, it would be useless. Know, then, that the Dharma lies in practice, and practice lies in the precepts, and precepts must take the bodhisattva precepts as their basis.

There are three groups of bodhisattva precepts. First, there are precepts of restraint that focus on stopping evil and are mostly shared with the Hinayāna. Second, there are precepts of virtue that focus on gathering self-regarding virtues and are seldom shared with the Hinayāna. Third, there are precepts benefiting living beings that focus on altruistically benefiting others and are not shared with the Hinayāna. Bodhisattvas mingling with ordinary people and buddhas manifesting in the world are both done to altruistically benefit others. Thus, the superiority of the bodhisattva precepts truly lies in the precepts that benefit sentient beings. [Among the sets of bodhisattva precepts,] those from the *Sutra of Brahma's Net* and the *Sutra on the Garland of the Bodhisattva's Original Deeds* differ in what they include and omit. Some of their lofty [precepts] are not for those who have just given rise to bodhi-mind. Moreover, they skew to the shared precepts of discipline and virtue.

The old translation of the Maitreyan precept text also seems to have some errors and omissions. Only the bodhisattva precept text taken from Xuanzang's hundred-fascicle translation of the *Yogācārabhūmi-śāstra* is truly the great standard for the bodhisattva's multifarious twofold benefiting [of self and other] and broad cultivation of myriad practices. (There have recently been those who practiced the *Yoga Bodhisattva Precepts* by itself, but I collected and published [it with] the *Three Essentials of Maitreya*: one, the *Yogācārabhūmi's* "Chapter on Knowing Reality," which illuminates the objects of cognition; two, the *Yoga Bodhisattva Precepts*, which regulate practice; and three, the *Sutra of Maitreya's Ascent*, which promises the fruit). These precepts distinguish item by item what should and should not be done and are moreover appropriate for the daily practice of those who have just given rise to bodhi-mind. I humbly hope that we who are starting to practice the bodhisattva path will all carefully read and reread them, deeply pondering their meaning, and vigorously practice them by implementing them in our own lives. Thus, I say that my practice lies in the *Yoga Bodhisattva Precepts*.

Today I will briefly take up a few points to illustrate where its superior spirit lies and give a general idea of its character.

First, of the ten weighty precepts of the *Sutra on Brahma's Net*, etc., the first—do not kill—to the sixth—do not speak of the faults of the four assemblies—are all shared precepts of restraint, whereas the *Yoga Bodhisattva Precepts* only takes the latter four, unshared precepts as its four weighty precepts, which it calls the four abodes of defeat: (1) the precept against praising oneself and slandering others out of desire for fame and advantage; (2) the precept against not practicing generosity out of miserliness with regard to property and the Dharma; (3) the precept against harming and afflicting others out of hatred and enmity; (4) the precept against slandering the true [Dharma] and delighting in a counterfeit [Dharma] out of attachment to wrong views. These are precepts of the Mahāyāna, unshared [with the Hinayāna]. The four abodes of defeat are the *parajikas*.[4] A bodhisattva who dwells in the pure precepts and disciplines of the bodhisattva dwells in victory. To break these precepts is to give up the abode of victory where the bodhisattva resides and fall into the abodes of defeat by non-bodhisattva others—devas, humans, devils, brahmas, Hinayāna disciples—and be overcome by the non-bodhisattva dharmas. In this way, they lose their bodhisattva life.

Second, the four abodes of defeat above are also first-degree offenses resulting in losing the pure bodhisattva precepts. If one loses the pure bodhisattva precepts, it is possible to receive them again in the present life. This is also completely different from the Hinayāna discipline.

Third, those [things] collected under "doing evil," such as the first, prohibiting not worshiping or making offerings; the second, prohibiting not respecting elders and worthies; and so on up to prohibiting not assisting sentient beings in doing things that they ought to do, all actively enjoin the good rather than merely stop evil.

Fourth, there are precepts such as these: the third and fourth prohibit not accepting the offerings of the faithful, the fifth prohibits not preaching the Dharma, and the sixth prohibits abandoning violent and evil sentient beings rather than reforming them. The seventh enjoins one to study with the Hinayāna disciples the prohibitions that protect the faith of others,[5] and the eighth enjoins one not to study with Hinayāna disciples the precepts enjoining one to do little, to accumulate little, and to dwell wishing for little but rather, [for the good of others] in accordance with the Dharma, seek to do more, accumulate more, and wish for more. The ninth through the sixteenth permit in rare circumstances the three natural sins of the body—killing, stealing, and fornicating—or the four natural sins of speech—lying, etc.—to do such things as depose cruel and tyrannical leaders—emperors, kings, ministers, and officials. Thus, these precepts incorporate without exception the appropriate and reasonable points of Tang of the Shang and Wu of the Zhou's rising up against a tyrant for the sake of the people and the Duke of Zhou and Confucius's approach to justice and governance,[6] on down to the political and class revolutions of today. The twentieth [precept] prohibiting not guarding against and clearing up slander of the Dharma and the twenty-first prohibiting not punishing those deserving of punishment, and so on up to the precept prohibiting not comforting the troubled and afflicted are all practices benefiting sentient beings, and to fail to do them is to break the precept.

Only if one is able to practice these bodhisattva precepts can one reorganize and restore the Buddhist sangha and [lay] societies. Only if one reorganizes and restores the Buddhist sangha and [lay] societies can the spirit of these bodhisattva precepts manifest. Such is my aspiration and practice. If there are others of the same aspiration and practice, what a joy that would be!

The Goals of Human Life Buddhism

The goals and results of Buddhism in its entirety can be divided into four:

Improvement of the Human World

[Buddhism] uses virtuous dharmas such as the five precepts of the Shared Dharma of the Five Vehicles[7] to purify the human world. If [worldly activities] from familial ethics to society's economic, educational, legal, and political practices, even a just international order, can be based on the spirit of the Dharma, they can attain perfection, reducing the regrets and sufferings of life. Thus, ordinary life can be based on Buddhism and thereby improved and purified. Buddhism shares this with forms of learning such as science, philosophy, and Confucianism, but it has a distinctive approach and unique character. Grounded in its own unique character, it can incorporate the strengths of the others. In this way, Buddhism has limitless potential to improve human life.

Progress in the Next Life

We course endlessly through samsara, receiving retribution in accordance with our karma. Having been born, we die; having died, we are born. From this realm we depart for another, revolving without cease. Therefore, we should not only improve the present life but also seek progress in the next. Through the cultivation of the ten virtuous activities and various meditative absorptions, one can be reborn in the heavenly realms. By upholding a buddha's name and relying on his power, one can be reborn in a purified buddha land in another world. Although one has not put an end to samsara, one can gain birth with a superior body and environment, avoiding evil paths and even the human path. This is a goal and result that can be attained through the Dharma. It is a focus of Pure Land and Esoteric teachings. Higher worldly religions, such as Christianity which seeks rebirth in heaven, also share this goal.

Liberation from Samsara

Progress in the next life is not a bad thing, but all conditioned things are impermanent, all tainted things are suffering, all that is born cannot but die, all that now abides cannot but perish. We never reach the end of it. How, then, can suffering be cut off at the root and the taints extinguished? That which is born must die, therefore we must transcend birth. That which now abides must perish, therefore we must not abide among existent things. Sever the flow of birth and death, pass over the sea of suffering, and alight upon the further shore of quiescent nirvana. This life is exhausted, pure conduct is established, what was to be done has been accomplished, there will be no further becoming—what are Mara's armies of samsara now? This is a further, more advanced goal of the Dharma: transcending the world. It is the shared result of the Three Vehicles,[8] not reached through worldly learning.

Perfect Illumination of Reality

The liberation of nirvana is wonderful as far as it goes but doesn't completely remove karmic impressions or cut off noetic obstructions or attain omniscience or perfectly illuminate all reality. Moreover, all sentient beings have been my closest relations over the course of beginningless time. How could one simply seek cessation for oneself with no regard for others? For this reason, bodhisattva-*mahasattvas*, taking all beings as their own body and feeling their pain as though it were the slicing of their own flesh, are filled with great compassion and vow to save them all. Through the eons, they broadly seek limitless merit and wisdom, they completely eliminate the karmic impressions of the two hindrances,[9] and finally they perfectly illuminate reality, fusing with all things without obstruction. This is the supreme result of the Mahāyāna and the ultimate goal of the Dharma.

These four goals encompass the entirety of the Dharma. Yet in absolute terms, only buddhahood's perfect illumination of reality is ultimate—that is, it is the true goal of all Buddhism; the first three levels are provisional. Earlier Buddhism has wearily rejected the immediacies of ordinary life, consistently emphasizing progress in the next life or the quiescence of birthlessness. Pure Land and Esoteric teachings are provisional teachings that respond to these desires. But to focus solely on rebirth and quiescence, always aloof from ordinary life, cannot fulfill the potential of the Dharma. The Human Life Buddhism I advocate today takes ordinary life as foundational. Improving and purifying it, [this Buddhism] seeks to fully understand the truth of the Dharma through the cultivation of the Human Vehicle and its fruits. Giving rise to the thought of enlightenment for the sake of all beings and cultivating the perfections of the bodhisattva, it enfolds the Heavenly and Two Vehicles into the Bodhisattva Vehicle, advancing directly to the supreme fruit of perfect illumination of reality. Being a bodhisattva precisely by being a human being and progressing on to buddhahood—this is the unique practice and fruit of Human Life Buddhism. It may be diagramed as follows:[10]

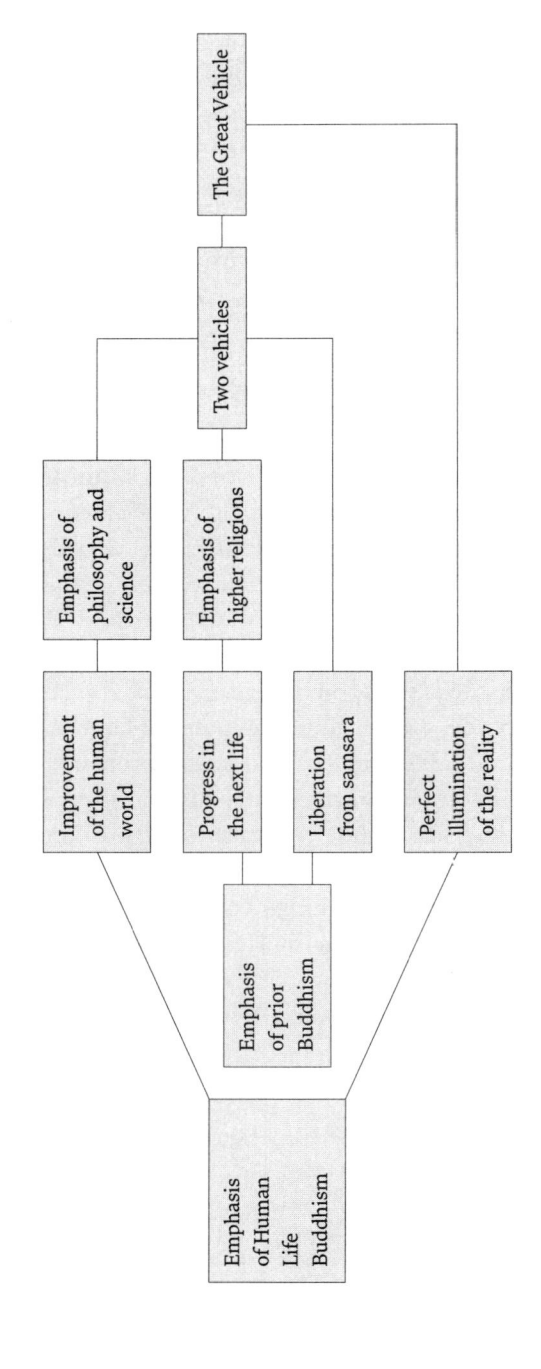

A Comparison of
Tuṣita Pure Land and the
Pure Lands of the Ten Directions

Delivered April 1936 at Xuedou Temple in Fenghua

Introduction

Now I'd like to take a moment to offer a comparative examination of the Tuṣita Pure Land and the pure lands of the ten directions.

The reason Śākyamuni Buddha spoke this *Sutra of Maitreya's Ascent* was to encourage all sentient beings now and in the future to engage in contemplation based on it and be reborn in the Inner Court of Tuṣita. This Inner Court is a pure land produced by the untainted merit of Maitreya Bodhisattva and the wondrous virtuous roots of the devas' joyous offerings. Thus, once born there, one attains nonretrogression vis-à-vis supreme and perfect bodhi. Therefore, it is by no means comparable to ordinary birth in Tuṣita Heaven.[11] We must understand pure lands are spoken of in contrast to impure lands. The circumstantial karmic recompense [of the environment] derives from the primary karmic recompense [of the body]. Where there is circumstantial recompense, there is primary recompense. Thus, a pure land encompasses the splendor of both primary and circumstantial recompense. The residences of the buddhas and bodhisattvas of the ten directions are all pure lands. The places where sages of the two vehicles and the six types of ordinary beings reside are [places where] purity and impurity are different and not uniform. Today we will focus on pure lands and make a concise comparison of the pure lands of the ten directions and the Tuṣita Pure Land.

The Pure Lands of the Ten Directions

Pure land is a broad umbrella term. It's just as if we were to say "monastery"; it would include all monasteries in China. If we hold up Xuedou Monastery, we're just speaking of one monastery. [If we speak of] Amitābha's Pure Land in the West, Bhaiṣajyaguru's Pure Land of Lapis Lazuli in the East, or Akṣobhya's Pure Land in the East and the Pure Land of Fragrance Above from the *Vimalakirti Sutra*, this is also just to hold up one particular pure land. Thus, the *Lotus Sutra* says, "When life reaches its end, the hands of a thousand Buddhas reach out to receive you and one is reborn in one of the pure lands of the ten directions in accordance with one's vow."[12] This is to say that sentient beings can be reborn according to their preferences. Chinese today generally just know of Amitābha's pure land. This is like knowing of just Xuedou, just this one monastery.

Pure lands can be roughly divided into three types: (1) Ultimate pure lands. These are the buddha lands of Dharma-nature and own-experience, which Tiantai calls pure lands of constant quiescence and radiance and splendid lands of perfect, true reward. (2) Pure buddha lands of other-experience. [These are] pure lands manifested by buddhas for tenth-ground bodhisattvas, which Tiantai calls the splendid land of perfect, true reward. These two are not attainable by ordinary beings, the heterodox, or followers of the two vehicles. (3) Pure lands for expediently receiving sentient beings. This group includes Amitābha's Land of Bliss that most are familiar with, as well as Maitreya's Tuṣita Pure Land, etc. These are especially for those who are giving rise to Mahāyāna mind and cultivating the bodhisattva path but in this life have not achieved sovereign mastery over rebirth and fear falling into evil paths in the next life. Expedient pure lands receive them, providing them something to rely on. Ordinary beings and the heterodox are attached to samsara and do not seek rebirth in a pure land. Those of the two vehicles [just] seek nirvana for themselves. Bodhisattvas at the stage of Mahāyāna sagehood each produce a lotus-store pure land, so they don't need to seek birth in a pure land. So, the pure lands manifested by the buddhas and bodhisattvas of the ten directions are set up specially to receive those who are learning to produce the Mahāyāna mind but have not attained sovereign mastery.

The Tuṣita Pure Land

Now let us take among the numberless pure lands the nearest and closest one that receives us—the Tuṣita Pure Land. The pure lands of the ten directions discussed above accept all beings from all worlds. They are like the departments of a regular university— they're established for students studying all different subjects. A monastic seminary[, on the other hand,] specializes in educating monastics. The pure land of Maitreya's Inner Court is also like this. It was established especially to receive and guide beings from this land.

Thus, we say that the Tuṣita Pure Land has three superiorities: (1) The pure lands of the ten directions accept any being who has a karmic affinity with them, but it is not easy to tell which pure land has the strongest karmic affinity with the beings of this realm. Because Maitreya Bodhisattva will achieve buddhahood in this world in the future and guide and teach the beings of this realm, we know that he has a karmic connection to the beings of this realm! He has specially manifested this Tuṣita Pure Land [for us], thus we vow to be reborn there to commune with him. (2) The Tuṣita Pure Land is in the Sahā world as we are, and moreover in the desire realm. Because this pure land of [expedient] manifestation is in the same place and realm, it has an especially close and intimate affinity with the beings of this realm, thus whereas pure lands of other quarters receive sentient beings from all ten directions, this one specializes in guiding the beings of this land's desire realm. (3) Maitreya's Pure Land is gained through human [conduct]. Rebirth there is due to people cultivating the merit of the ten virtues, which at the same time causes human morality to advance and society to evolve to become pure, peaceful, and joyous. In this way, we can stimulate Maitreya to descend earlier and thereby create a pure land on earth.

Basically, these are the similarities and differences of the pure lands of the ten directions and Tuṣita Pure Land.

(Recorded by Zhiding)

Further Reading

Asaṅga. *On Knowing Reality: The Tattvārtha Chapter of Asaṅga's Bodhisattvabhūmi*. Translated by Janice Dean Willis. Reprint, Delhi: Motilal Banarsidass, 2002.

DeVido, Elise Anne. "The Influence of Chinese Master Taixu on Buddhism in Vietnam." *Journal of Global Buddhism* 10 (2009): 413-58.

Jones, Charles B. *Taixu's "On the Establishment of the Pure Land in the Human Realm": A Translation and Study*. New York: Bloomsbury Academic, 2021.

Madsen, Richard. *Democracy's Dharma: Religious Renaissance and Political Development in Taiwan*. Berkeley: University of California Press, 2007.

Pittman, Don Alvin. *Toward a Modern Chinese Buddhism: Taixu's Reforms*. Honolulu: University of Hawai'i Press, 2001.

Ritzinger, Justin. *Anarchy in the Pure Land: Reinventing the Cult of Maitreya in Modern Chinese Buddhism*. New York: Oxford University Press, 2017.

Welch, Holmes. *The Buddhist Revival in China*. Cambridge, MA: Harvard University Press, 1968.

Master Hongyi at the age of fifty-seven in Shanghai, 1937.

4 | A Peripatetic Bodhisattva-Artist

Hongyi

RAOUL BIRNBAUM

If we can trust the tales, some of the best-known figures of Chinese Buddhist history seem to have emerged from the womb already saints. It is almost as if there had been a seamless transition from a past life of great accomplishment into this next birth, with a secure and confident memory of principles and modes of practice still intact. The history of the artist-monk Hongyi (1880-1942), much of which can be substantiated by an abundant array of primary sources, presents a very different picture. It is this tale of "riches to rags," of an elite man who at midlife turned from wealth and wide acclaim to become a Buddhist monk, who somehow managed to establish a personal transformation despite an extraordinary background of worldly privilege and renown, flaws, emotional crises, love affairs, and devastating illness that has so captivated a Chinese audience in modern times. There are collections of his writings, elegantly bound presentations of his calligraphy, and scholarly studies written about him, as well as award-winning films, stage plays and musicals, and biographical fiction (including some accounts in graphic-novel form), recordings of his musical compositions, and exhibitions of his visual art. Now, as I just came across while writing this chapter, there also are mass-produced clay portrait sculptures of him, sitting quietly in dignified meditative repose, easily available in two sizes through internet purchase.

Seeing past the caricatures and fantasies, at heart this is a man whose Buddhist renown rests most especially on notions about his life—his personal transformation and the products of that achievement—rather than institutional leadership, charismatic teachings to mass audiences, or unique practice methods.

Many educated persons in China's first half of the twentieth century considered that Buddhist principles and practices, no less the privations Buddhist monastic life, had become hopelessly old-fashioned and irrelevant. Some monks of that time sought a radical restructuring of the monastic order and a reconsideration of monastic rules. Through the conduct of his own life, though, Hongyi demonstrated within an emerging modern age the value and vital relevance of the most fundamental Buddhist teachings and practices. Hongyi's life presents us with a basic question: If we accept the validity of this description of an "ordinary" man (however privileged and talented) who became extraordinary, whose self-transformation was vividly witnessed and reported on by those around him who knew him well, then how did he manage this achievement? What are the methods by which he effected this profound transformation?

This chapter provides a sketch of Hongyi's remarkable life, his cultivation methods, and some of the most significant accomplishments of his lifetime. I have been looking at Hongyi over the past twenty-five years, using one tactic or another to begin to get some grasp of this complex man, perceiving him as if through a kaleidoscope to consider a myriad of very colorful slivers that somehow converge to form a singularly fascinating person. What I present here, written specifically for the broad readership imagined for this volume, is drawn from that ongoing, long-term research project.

This man was known by many names. In part, this was a customary practice of elite individuals, but one of his quirks is the very large number of names that he adopted when signing calligraphic work over the twenty-four years of his monastic career. In this chapter, for the sake of simplicity, when describing the period from his 1880 birth to his entrance in the monastic community in 1918, we will use the lay name by which he was most commonly known, Li Shutong; for the monastic years thereafter, he was best known as Hongyi (and his principal alternative name, Yanyin).

Initial Years: The Life of Li Shutong

Li Shutong was born in the north China port city of Tianjin in October 1880. His father already was sixty-seven. Li Xiaolou (1813-1884) was an intellectual who had passed the *jinshi* exam, the highest level of the civil service examinations. After a five-year stint in government, he left to engage in trade in salt and silver, and the family became immensely wealthy. It also became well known for generous philanthropic endeavors. All but one of his sons had died at an early age, so in his midsixties he brought a young, fourth wife (family name Wang, 1861-1905) to join this large and complex household. It is their child who is the center of this tale. Although Li Shutong's father died just a few years after the child's birth, family members looked after his education in the classics and in various traditional arts as his remarkably abundant artistic talents began to emerge.

The youth was married by arrangement at age sixteen, and this couple soon produced their own offspring. In 1898, a moment of significant political unrest in China, Li Shutong, with both mother and wife, moved from the north to the safer territory of Shanghai, where the young man received more modern educational training and also had notable romantic affairs with elite courtesans. Photographs depict him posing in the most stylish clothing of the era.

There followed some years engaged in studies alternately in Tianjin and Shanghai, until his mother died in 1905. Li Shutong by that time had broad acquaintances established among an emerging young intellectual and artistic elite, many of whom were fascinated with the notion of the "modern" and its consequences and opportunities for a China that seemed weak and backward compared to more militarily powerful nations of the time, such as Russia and Japan. Free of the obligation to care for his mother, Li Shutong became one of China's pioneering students abroad, in search of training in modern arts. He enrolled in a rigorous course of study in the Tokyo School of Fine Arts (Tokyo Bijutsu Gakkō), where he trained in European modes of oil painting under eminent Japanese artists such as Kuroda Seiki (1866-1924), who had studied in Paris. Those five years abroad were momentously significant for his personal growth and outlook. This period was marked by deep engagement with European approaches to visual expression, as well as effective songwriting. Some of these songs were wholly composed, while on occasion he created new Chinese lyrics for existing European or American melodies. With fellow Chinese students in Tokyo, he was a cofounder of the first Chinese theater group to present Western-style stage acting (with European and North American scripts in Chinese translation). Having the means to design and commission elaborate gowns, Li Shutong famously and memorably took on female roles in such melodramatic works as *Uncle Tom's Cabin* and *La dame aux camélias*. These roles were preserved in evocative photographs; a Japanese newspaper review compared him favorably to Sarah Bernhardt. While abroad, he joined the Nanshe (Southern Society), a group of revolutionary poets and artists who sought the overthrow of China's Manchu rulers. Li also created China's first magazine devoted to music, whose cover design for the first (and only) issue included an image of sheet music bearing the opening measures of France's revolutionary anthem, "La Marseillaise." Among the *Little Music Magazine*'s contents, Li drew a portrait of Beethoven and wrote a short essay that introduced him to a Chinese audience. He focused on the deaf composer's powerful will as an example for Chinese youth to consider.

After graduation in 1911, with a required final project in the form of a haunting self-portrait that he chose to paint in pointillist style (still retained in the school archives), he returned to China accompanied by a Japanese woman who had become his second wife. There was a fair amount of disarray in the world to which Li Shutong returned, including the collapse of the Manchu rule over the country (the Qing dynasty). Financial market disruptions gravely affected the family resources, and Li Shutong now had to make a living. For a six-month period, he served as editor of an arts supplement of a short-lived Shanghai newspaper associated with the Nanshe, where he designed layout, created illustrations and calligraphic headers, and commissioned pieces from leading young intellectuals.

After this return, he also began a series of positions teaching art and music in various new schools that had begun to appear as part of the educational transformation of modern China. It is said that Li Shutong introduced the first nude life drawing studio in China (a photo captures the scene), and he also encouraged young artists in the practice of plein air drawing and painting, an outdoor approach to visual representation based on direct observation that had rarely been seen in Chinese art history. Eventually he was invited to join the faculty at a progressive teacher-training institute in Hangzhou, where he remained for almost six years and gained a reputation as an unusually gifted and deeply respected instructor. Some of his Hangzhou students, roughly twenty years younger than their teacher, later became significant figures in the arts and arts education of modern China; some notable figures remained lifelong friends and key lay disciples. By this point, Li Shutong was well known as a robustly talented, highly original, and charismatic man of the arts, a member of the modern-seeking intellectual elite of an emerging China.

This acclaim and apparent success was intermixed with contradictions and concerns, for Li Shutong found that he was deeply uncomfortable, with a nagging sense of unhappiness. As he later recalled in his fifties, he first became aware of significant habitual faults around the age of thirty (he would have been a student in Japan at that time). These concerns appeared to deepen in succeeding years, and they prompted him to begin to explore various traditional approaches to self-cultivation. The most significant new influence was a comprehensive work by the late-Ming Confucian thinker Liu Zongzhou (1587–1645), who wrote extensively about modes of self-examination and the importance of moral behavior and good acts, not for the purpose of future rewards (as some others proposed, in a self-gain approach to cause and effect) but simply because that is the way one should be. Li Shutong noted in emphatic red ink on the cover of his copy of Liu's *Renpu*[1] that this was a work to be set into actual practice.

His internal discomfort was accompanied by various physical symptoms, which he recognized as elements of an underlying mental illness, a syndrome commonly labeled "nerve weakness" (*shenjing shuairuo*), in that era sometimes known in the US as neurasthenia. This disease was said to be caused by the tensions of modernity. He found a cure proposed in a Japanese magazine: a seventeen-day progressive fast carried out in a quiet place during the coldest days of the year. Li Shutong decided to give it a try during his school's winter break, and he arranged through friends to stay for three weeks in one of the local Hangzhou-area monasteries, at Hupao Springs beside scenic West Lake. He went there to gain a sense of spiritual renewal (as he put it at that time), not for any conventional Buddhistic aim, and he kept a diary of the fast, so we have a day-by-day account of this experience through his eyes. While engaged in this strange dietary regime, Li Shutong on occasion saw from the window of his guest room a young monk walking past who had about him an air of happiness—it is this impression of happiness that drew the visitor's attention. He engaged the monk in conversation and asked for some Buddhist reading matter. This marked the start of his interest in things Buddhist.

Somehow this experience set off a tidal wave in the artist's life. Soon he had adopted a vegetarian diet; set up an altar in his living quarters, where he regularly offered incense before images of Guanyin and Dizang (the two most popular bodhisattvas in the Chinese pantheon at that time, known in Sanskrit respectively as Avalokiteśvara and Kṣitigarbha); and began to read Buddhist texts, ranging from short devotional works to the philosophically sophisticated *Awakening of Faith in Mahāyāna*. Thus, he engaged in a Buddhist manner with three interleaved domains: regulated body practices, imaginative devotion, and intellectual investigation. Again and again he returned to the Hupao monastery, where he chatted with monks and participated in rituals. Also, he began studies with the well-known philosopher Ma Yifu (1883–1967), who at that time was lecturing on *Awakening of Faith*; he also met with him in his West Lake home for more private discussions. All of this profoundly affected him, and less than two years after the Hupao fast, Li Shutong had determined to become a monk. At the end of the school year, he gave away most of his possessions, returned to Hupao, and went through the hair-cutting ceremony to "leave home" (*chujia*), by which he became a novice monk. Just a few months later, he went to the major Hangzhou monastery Lingyinsi to receive the full set of monastic precepts, and thus was ordained as a full member of the monastic order. As far as we know, his two wives—one in Shanghai, the other at the family compound in Tianjin with her children—had not been consulted. Indeed, they were surprised and dismayed, but neither of them could convince their husband to change his mind.

This departure sent shock waves through elite circles, whose collective impression of Buddhist monks and monastic life was not high. The Hangzhou school headmaster addressed the students and faculty, and sharply cautioned them to respect their teacher but not imitate him. The well-known artist and theorist Chen Shizeng (1876–1923) made a fascinating painting to mark the transition in which he depicted a host of objects he had seen in Li Shutong's room, thus presenting a portrait of a complex man through his possessions.

Thus began a transformation from immensely privileged, famously talented, highly networked, and thoughtful aesthete to Buddhist monk living with minimal creature comforts. The next dozen years or so were foundational—an engagement in studies and practices by which he became both learned and transformed. This process took time and effort, of course. It appears that Hongyi stepped into a full maturity in this new identity in the early 1930s. That maturity was marked by a pivotal dream in early 1933, after which he began to teach with a new sense of confidence and authority.

Hongyi's Inner Conflicts

Before turning to discussion of Hongyi's world of practice, there is one further issue to raise about the course of his life. It is well established that a factor in the causes and conditions leading to his interest in Buddhist matters was the state of his mental health. He was stressed, on edge, and searching for answers in a world that presented him with renown but not inner satisfaction. (In a letter to a friend during this time, he said somewhat ruefully, "People say that I have a mental illness.") Accounts of some eminent Buddhist figures suggest that it is not unusual for such circumstances to propel their initial search. For Hongyi, at times there is a sense, even if overdramatic in the telling, that his acts of taking refuge are moments in which he has the feeling of saving his life. (Indeed, when we look closely at those individuals known among their peers in the Chinese Buddhist world as great practitioners, there seems to be a shared sense of the absolute necessity of their practice, that indeed they are saving their lives, and therefore they work at it with great focus and intensity.)

Emotional crossroads are not unique to Buddhist environments. For example, the medieval Italian St. Francis of Assisi went through soul-searching convolutions as a young man as he tried to find meaning and a place in life. He, too, left a background of privilege, perhaps not as grand as Li Shutong's, for a homeless life as a religious mendicant, in which he became utterly dedicated to following the example of Christ. Looking further at the life of St. Francis, it seems that even as he advanced in development, there were times when he was beset by inner struggle, even deep despair. Among the Catholic saints, he was not unique in that experience.

A careful examination of the primary sources related to Hongyi's life reveals that in his maturity as a clerical figure, he had at least two periods of very considerable strain and inner conflict. The first occurred around 1930, and it related to a growing recognition that his 1918 ordination had not been carried out according to Vinaya expectations. He concluded that he had not actually received a transmission of the monastic precepts and thus was not genuinely a *biqiu* (ordained monk). Hongyi's gradual resolution in late 1932–early 1933 of this far-reaching crisis, which struck at the core of a hard-fought identity, was eventually certified by a powerful dream (discussed below) that marked his step into maturity as a Buddhist teacher. In 1936, he grew deeply concerned about the ways in which people were beginning to idolize him and extol him in praise, and for a while he rued the choice to serve as a teacher of others. He also expressed deep regret at the shape of his homeless life, which was dominated by the need to go here and there at the invitation of others. As he pointed out, at times his life resembled that of the monk-ritualists of low esteem, who performed funerary and other rites for hire. Again, there seems to be a resolution to these concerns, but without documentary evidence of how he came to terms with his position, this particular story cannot yet be fully told. (These matters, which complicate the trajectory of a certain kind of hero's tale, are not commonly discussed in available Chinese scholarship.)

It is important to recognize that this man, seen by many within Chinese Buddhist traditions as one of the great practitioners of the modern age, remained human and at times had internal conflicts that required considerable effort to face and resolve. Perhaps others of high repute also had such conflicts, even though we do not see such elements in the historical record. These matters may not be addressed publicly because of cultural expectations of what it might mean to be an eminent Buddhist. At least in Hongyi's case, we really are looking at a human, not a superhuman. Ultimately, that may be a factor in the respect and popularity by which he is held within Chinese Buddhist communities today.

Hongyi's Practice Methods

When we look into individuals and their practice approaches, in some cases we can say very simply that Master So-and-So relied on a particular Chan meditation method, or perhaps a certain eminent layperson followed the Pure Land practice of focusing on the name of Amitābha Buddha. That terse account might be enough. Hongyi was a complex man, and his world of practice reflected his internal complexities, even as there may be an illusion of simplicity to it. His world of practice took form as an assemblage of a set of basic practices, which he stitched together to form a comprehensive and organic whole that proved effective for him. A view of the suite of these practices provides a useful vista across a fundamental range of Chinese Buddhist practices during the late imperial and Republican periods. It is the particular way that he pulled these various practices together, plus his intensity of dedication and grace of expression, that made them so unusually potent as a transformative influence. In general, it is useful to bear in mind that his mode of practice focused on incremental change. The full exposition of these methods can be seen in the teachings and reflections that he recorded in his last decade. That is where we now will turn.

One of Hongyi's monastic friends, in thinking back across his life, characterized Hongyi's Buddhist endeavors in this way: he took the *Huayan Sutra* as his conceptual realm, the Four-Part Vinaya as his practice, and birth in the Pure Land as the intended result. This terse characterization, an overview, provides a starting point for our investigation, in which we will look more closely at the constituent elements that made up Hongyi's world of practice.

Hongyi placed two factors at the core of his interior life: the act of refuge in the Three Jewels (the Buddha, Dharma, and Sangha) and the establishment of bodhisattva commitments. Refuge is the basic ritual act that places a person within the Buddhist community. It signifies a turn toward a set of defined principles, understandings, and aspirations (and thus a turn away from certain other matters). While some may see Triple Refuge simply as a one-time ritual for beginners, Hongyi considered it the foundation for all other practice elements. He devoted energy to thinking and writing about both the refuge ritual and the repeated experience of its interior process. He considered the initial rite, beyond its legal features, as a significant transmission (similar to a precept transmission) that was facilitated by an officiating cleric. Hongyi's teachings include advice to fellow clerics regarding how to ensure the effectiveness of this rite, with clear warnings regarding particular circumstances in which the transmission may be unsuccessful. As to the position of a bodhisattva, in an especially appealing calligraphic work made in 1942, his last year, Hongyi asserted simply that compassion without wisdom is the domain of ordinary folk, while a person who combines the two—compassion plus wisdom—is what is called a "bodhisattva." This was a matter that he thought about at length, and it served as a basis for his actions.

Underneath all of this, Hongyi held a deep trust in the workings of cause and effect, and he constantly urged others to think in this way. Conventionally, these are the most basic beginners' teachings. Hongyi urged constant attention to them, and often deliberately chose to speak about simple matters (as he clearly noted) rather than present any complex formulations.

In the context of his emphasis on cause and effect, Hongyi was profoundly concerned with the ethics of daily life, and he urged others to do as he had done—to engage in daily scrutiny of his activities (thoughts, words, and deeds), set against a grid of principles that he sought to embody. In this way, one becomes aware of not only individual and stray moments but also, more importantly, the patterns of one's thought and behavior. A close look at Hongyi's articulation of these practices makes clear that he owed much to his early studies of basic Confucian texts, especially the *Four Books* (the *Great Learning*, *Analects*, *Mencius*, and the *Doctrine of the Mean*) that in his day formed the foundation of traditional educational training. He continued to study these classic texts after becoming a monk, recommended them to both lay and monastic students, and when bestowing Buddhist teachings, he continued to quote from those texts to the very last year of his life. Confucian textual elements also surfaced in Hongyi's dream life to the very end. Carefully examined, there was a Confucian vocabulary of not only words but also concepts, actions, and values that formed a basic part of Hongyi's complex weaving of practice approaches. The particular line of Confucian teachings that Hongyi focused on was explicitly concerned with teachings related to self-cultivation, to individual transformation achieved through self-scrutiny and steady application of ethical principles.

In the process of self-examination recommended by Hongyi, one identifies negative and positive traits, and then seeks to focus on a few of these for constructive change. Hongyi sought to discern deep-seated problematic habits, most particularly those vexing habits that any amount of focused will could not deter. Those stubborn habits, he held, are faults established in past lives, repeated again and again. Deeply ingrained as they may be, such habitual faults can be transformed through sincere repentance and supplication for aid from the various buddhas and bodhisattvas. This is the special factor that Buddhist refuge makes possible; it is the mysterious process that distinguishes Buddhist approaches from those taught by the Confucians.

Buddhist precepts provide guidelines to appropriate living. Acceptance of these—ranging from the five basic precepts accepted by laypersons, to the complete monastic precepts accepted by monks and nuns, to bodhisattva precepts received by both lay and monastic practitioners as a culminating set—can have a significant effect on a practitioner's life. Precepts function as guiding rules, and when properly transmitted in specified ritual contexts, they also are understood to have a mystical element (the *jieti*), absorbed during the transmission rite, that connects to the force of buddhas in a way that powerfully assists an individual to respond to challenges.

This world of the buddhas and bodhisattvas was real for Hongyi. He was profoundly devotional from the very start of his conscious engagement with Buddhist worlds. Many of his practices were interwoven with this devotional element, and they make best sense when seen in those contexts. An enormous pantheon of figures stands within the Chinese Buddhist traditions, especially buddhas, bodhisattvas, and protector figures. As one reads in scriptural texts, bodhisattvas make formal vows that establish the trajectory of their life force. (Vows are aspirational promises, in contrast to precepts, which are rules that set protective restrictions and boundaries.) There are basic vows to engage in internal transformation in order to aid and liberate all beings (such vows in fact define one's status as a bodhisattva), as well as individualized vows particular to a person's special skills, talents, and aims that may be deployed in this process. These vows are central elements in the texts that introduce the buddhas and bodhisattvas. Hongyi trusted deeply in the truth of such accounts—that indeed such beings did exist, that they could be contacted, and that the power of each of these being's vows to aid others may be accessed through sincere supplication.

Accordingly, recognizing his own failings through self-examination, Hongyi established a posture of sincere repentance, and he requested aid from these beings, not only Amitābha Buddha but also most especially the bodhisattvas Dizang and Guanyin. Later in life he also turned to Yaoshi Rulai (Bhaiṣajyaguru), the buddha known as an effective healer. Hongyi called upon these potent figures for aid in his path toward liberation. He also saw them as effective examples, models for his own practices. The ritual act of making vows—done before the invoked witness of buddhas, bodhisattvas, and sages of the past—was a powerful tool in his practice arsenal that helped him to focus his energies and draw closer to the vital realms of these beings. Vows were basic to his practice life, functioning as engines or generators that produced focused energy. He encouraged his students to make vows, and on one important occasion in 1933 he made a set of group vows with eleven of his students that included a pledge of mutual aid in present and future lives.

This mode of cultivation, in which one tries to become aware of faults (at increasingly subtle levels) and makes a best effort at sincere repentance, does not tend to lead to the "enlightenment" (more properly, "awakening") claims that are part of Chan traditions (see, for example, chapters 1 and 2). Combined with Pure Land approaches (discussed below), this process of gradual purification aims to qualify the practitioner for rebirth in Amitābha's Pure Land, where genuine teachings to achieve liberation are ever available, received directly from that buddha and his bodhisattva assistants.

Hongyi saw some teachers of the historical past as especially worthy, and his study of their works and lives was more than intellectual. Their place in his life was complementary to his trust in and reliance upon the great buddhas and bodhisattvas. The most towering influence among them was the late-Ming monk Ouyi

Zhixu (1599–1655). Hongyi made intensive studies of his life and works, including composing a biography, and he internalized these investigations by modeling some texts and key actions (including some of his vows) directly on Ouyi's example. In addition to the powerful influence of such figures of the past, among living Buddhist teachers of his era, he most deeply respected the Pure Land master Yinguang (discussed in chapter 5), whom he consulted by correspondence in his early monastic years and in 1924 visited for a week on Putuo Island.

Soon after joining the monastic order, Hongyi followed Yinguang's example and made a series of linked vows regarding the course of his vocation. Among them, he pledged that he would not accept significant monastic office (as an abbot or other high-level position). He also pledged that he would not directly sponsor individuals to join the monastic order; in contrast to peers, he specifically would not create a monastic lineage, which then would be responsible for temples and property, as was the established custom at that time. Thus, he made it clear that he would not become involved in monastic politics, administration, and economic duties. Ultimately he had monastic disciples (although not through a ritual process) and there is a lineage stemming from his teachings, but this lineage has not been concerned with the perpetuation of property management or any kind of institutional status. In the context of these pledges, Hongyi differed from most senior monks of his era in that he truly was homeless, moving from monastery to monastery according to invitations and circumstances, without ever bearing administrative responsibility for the livelihood of others. While he did not have a monastic home, in the Triple Refuge he had an interior home, maintained wherever he might be.

Engagement with the *Huayan Sutra*

Hongyi read widely among Buddhist texts (as we can see attested in his records): sutras, Vinaya works, Chan treatises, traditional biographies, and numerous commentaries and essays. Among the sutras, his clear favorite was the *Huayan Sutra*, a massive collection of Mahāyāna texts that circulated in China in three translations, all of which he carefully studied. There are certain sections that he turned to again and again, and when one looks closely at the suite of chapters that Hongyi especially favored, one can see that for the most part they speak to the issue of the bodhisattva path—how to develop the mental stance and abilities of an accomplished bodhisattva, the courage and wisdom of an activated bodhisattva, the importance of vows, and so forth. There is a certain complementarity between this defined Buddhist thread and the thread of Confucian teachings that Hongyi found especially fruitful and compelling. Both are foundational and directly practical in their concerns with sagely human behavior.

In the summer of 1931 Hongyi wrote a short essay that provides a guide to reading and studying the text, suggesting an order by which the various chapters might be read. His engagement with this text, though, was far more encompassing than a regime of reading, reciting, and studying. That engagement reached into his calligraphic work, his dreams, his self-naming practices, and more. Here are a few of the ways this played out.

Hongyi's calligraphic work often presented lines from sutras, usually accompanied by an identification of the source. It is clear from a survey of the available materials that the great majority of his calligraphic work made for display (thus different from such items as letters, sutra copies, Vinaya treatises, and other manuscripts) sets forth quotes from the *Huayan jing*. More formally, in 1931 Hongyi completed a major multiyear project in which he selected and copied out three hundred couplets from the *Huayan jing* (one hundred from each of the three translations); this was published as a book intended for wide circulation. He considered this one of the major works of his later years. In a seamless way, it was a calligraphic work, an act of devotion, and an act of Buddhist dissemination. One could also see this as a considered act in which Hongyi inscribed himself into the world of the sutra, writing out these lines again and again. The year of completion, 1931, was also the seventieth anniversary of his mother's birth; Hongyi dedicated the merits from this project to her posthumous benefit and thus incorporated her in the *Huayan* world as well.

Over the years, he copied out various sutras, including selected chapters of the *Huayan jing*. In some cases, such as a 1940 copy of the verse sections of the chapter on Puxian's (Samantabhadra Bodhisattva) practices and vows, he used blood as ink, thus merging vital life fluid with the text. (Though not common, blood calligraphy is a traditional practice in Chinese Buddhist worlds, with a deep context in Chinese history.)

In early 1933 Hongyi reported that he had experienced a powerful dream, one that proved to have pivotal, life-changing force. He prepared an account immediately after awakening. This dream record reports an encounter with a dignified elder, chanting before an assembly of raptly listening persons. A placard placed before that elder was inscribed with the title of the *Huayan Sutra*, and in the dream Hongyi recognized that it was *Huayan* verses that were being chanted. Those verses spoke about the way of the bodhisattva and pointed to refuge as the foundation for making bodhisattva vows. After waking from the dream, Hongyi pledged to set these verses into practice. He inscribed his written report to the younger monk Guangqia, who had come to him the previous day to request Vinaya training, and he agreed to begin a series of lectures on key Vinaya texts.

A few years later, Hongyi wrote out numerous copies of the title of the *Huayan Sutra* and thus brought this element of the dream to material reality. Guangqia, who had become one of his principal students, donated his blood to be used as calligraphic ink for the project, and thus with these inscriptions he entered with Hongyi into this *Huayan* realm.

There is one more relevant point to consider in thinking about Hongyi's connections to the *Huayan jing*. Hongyi famously used many names during his monastic years, some 252 at least, as we can see in signatures to his abundant calligraphic work and correspondence. Some were given to him, such as Hongyi and Yanyin, the formal Buddhist names bestowed when he first took refuge and later entered the monastic order, while others were names that he had deliberately chosen. Almost all those self-chosen names were directly derived from *Huayan jing* passages. This was a further way of inscribing himself into the vast realm of this text. Engaging with the scripture in these many ways became more than simply reading and mulling over a text, however engrossing that might be. It was visceral and all-encompassing, a realm of being, a way of living.

Hongyi's Pure Land and Vinaya Practices

Li Shutong had been a well-known public person, a man active in the arts and present in some of the key intellectual circles of a rapidly modernizing China. But Hongyi (I now use the name for his changed, Buddhist persona) wanted to step away from that world, and indeed he came into Buddhist monastic life with a powerful drive for retreat. This element of Buddhist life, perhaps initially romantically conceived, held great attraction for him, and we can see from the very earliest years of his monastic life the wish to study and practice within the context of mountain solitude. Although Hongyi was never able to carry out a traditional three-year sealed retreat, he did effectively weave a regular series of shorter retreats (often a few months in duration) into his schedule of activities through the years. Despite that drive for solitude, as his Buddhist knowledge and understanding grew and he became mature in his vocation, Hongyi gradually became a public figure once again within these new contexts. He traveled about giving many talks, most of his writings were published during his lifetime (including contributions to Buddhist periodicals and elite literary magazines, which enabled extensive distribution of some key essays), and his calligraphy circulated widely.

Hongyi famously was a Pure Land practitioner. One of the concerns and anxieties of Chinese religious life centers on postmortem destinies. What happens when you die? Will you be okay? Hongyi as a Pure Land adherent was focused on rebirth in Amitābha's Pure

Land, and he urged others to work toward that end. He often gave talks to lay groups who had gathered for intensive Pure Land chanting practice. Focused recitation of Amitābha Buddha's name is a core Pure Land practice, and it sometimes is framed as preparation for the moment of death, in which the ability to concentrate on the Buddha enables you to gain rebirth in his paradise realm. Following the advice of Yinguang, Hongyi learned the meditative practice of *nianfo sanmei* (samādhi of mindfulness of the buddha), a method of deep and stable absorptive concentration on Amitābha Buddha, as taught in the *Lengyan Sutra*. Addressing a group of Pure Land practitioners in late 1932, Hongyi sought to assuage their anxieties regarding rebirth. He indicated that rather than fixating on periodic chanting practices, it would be far better to concentrate on interior transformation such that one becomes a better person. If one is successful in that endeavor, then of course as a natural result one will be reborn in the Buddha's pure land.

Following ordination procedures at Lingyin Monastery in 1918, Hongyi's friend Ma Yifu made him a gift of books: important Vinaya texts and the *Lingfeng zonglun*, a great compendium of Ouyi Zhixu's main literary works. Both gifts proved significant for the course of his lifetime. Hongyi came to accept the view that Śākyamuni Buddha, prior to his death, had instructed disciples that in his absence they should take the Vinaya (or perhaps more precisely stated, the precepts) as their master. Hongyi made this topic the center of his monastic studies, carefully determined what rules were central to monastic and lay life, and sought to revive some key monastic practices stipulated in those texts, such as the summer rains retreat and the regulation to abstain from food after noon. His extensive studies brought clarity to the structures of monastic life, and some of those works remain central to Vinaya studies and practice in contemporary monastic communities. Later on, he also composed a book on Vinaya for laypersons in which he drew from works conventionally restricted solely to monastics to bring forward important Vinaya teachings that would benefit lay practitioners.

Hongyi eventually came to champion the Four-Part Vinaya transmitted by Daoxuan (the Nanshan Vinaya), in part because of its flexibility such that it could be read in a Mahāyāna fashion, whereas the other traditions brought to China were strictly pre-Mahāyāna in formulation. Again, we can see that the basic threads of Hongyi's practice commitments emphasize procedures of daily life rather than abstract speculations or subtle philosophical thinking, and they favor teachings that support the bodhisattva path. It was ultimately the bodhisattva precepts that he valued most.

A Bodhisattva's Sphere of Activities

Although we might say that lasting impressions of Hongyi stem from images of his life, from notions about who he was and what he accomplished as a Buddhist practitioner (and that compelling tale of a journey from "riches to rags"), practically speaking he also became well known for creations and activities that brought him before the public. These could (and should) be characterized as the sphere of activities of a bodhisattva, the visible expression of his commitments. Hongyi understood the bodhisattva path as a place of action in which energy is harnessed for wholesome accomplishment that benefits others. There were three distinctive domains in which he gave expression to his practice commitments: aesthetic realms, the world of education, and the world of scholarship. In contrast to some eminent clerics who may have been monastic leaders, institution builders, and lineage transmitters, these three defined areas formed the most public elements of his life and were his contributions to benefit others.

Li Shutong had been a famously accomplished and original artist, with strong talents across an unusually broad range of disciplines: the visual arts (calligraphy, seal carving, painting, woodblock printing, and graphic design), poetry, musical composition, and stage acting. His talents had appeared early, and their expression was central to his life. In becoming a monk, he had to consider just how to proceed. Was it appropriate to engage in the senses in this way? Was he in any way violating Vinaya expectations and restrictions?

How did he want to focus and train his mind to accord with this new way of life—did immersion in aesthetic concerns divert from (or even subvert) more fundamentally crucial aims?

While there is a sense, conveyed in the "Hongyi myth" (the glorious set of fanciful tales about him), that he set all those worldly activities down when he became a monk, that is not quite true. He did step away from many of the visual arenas (such as plein air watercolor painting, paintings of nude women, woodblock prints, etc.) that earlier had been his sites of expression and activities of great enjoyment, and he no longer remained vigorously active in poetry composition. (He had already left stage acting, which had been an important pursuit while studying in Japan, and he no longer maintained the practice of seal carving, an avid engagement of younger years.) Advice from both Yinguang and his friend Ma Yifu led him to continue one element of his visual art activities: the practice of calligraphy. For many centuries calligraphy has been widely viewed as the supreme art of China's educated elite. (Traditional theory elevates this practice beyond simple and utilitarian "handwriting" to maintain that this mode of skillful application of brush and ink upon paper or silk reveals the direct imprint of the artist's mind.) Now Hongyi's calligraphic work was subordinated to a particular aim: to convey Buddhist teachings in order to benefit others. Aesthetic excellence, it was intended, could induce viewers to read and consider the lexical content of his writing (the meanings of the words). Looking back across all the explorations and changes through his lifetime, we can see that calligraphy in fact was the single discipline that threads through Hongyi's life, from childhood to his deathbed. In his maturity, through calligraphic gifts, it became an important mode by which he engaged with others, from his closest friends and disciples to respected figures and even complete strangers. It also was the art in which he especially excelled, one in which he made an unusually original contribution. Perhaps if Hongyi had continued to disperse his creative energies through the rest of his life across that same broad range of disciplines, he would not have excelled in calligraphy to the same exceptional degree. His distinctive style was perceived to convey the quality of *qingliang*, a sense of cool and calm that reflected the virtues of accomplished Buddhist practice. Eventually this calligraphic style became a visual marker or signifier for Chinese Buddhists, used in many arenas.

Li Shutong wrote many songs in his earlier years, some of which became very popular and are still sung today, such as "*Songbie*" (Farewell). Those activities came to a near halt in the monastic years. He did collaborate with the famous reformer-monk Taixu (discussed in chapter 3) to create a Buddhist anthem, "*Sanbao ge*" (Song of the Three Jewels), a refuge-taking song that remains popular in some lay populations. And in 1931, in response to requests for Buddhist songs that young people might sing, he provided lyrics for a set of five songs whose melodies were composed by his friend and former student Liu Zhiping, together with several of Liu's students. Ultimately this group of five songs was published in 1936 as *Qingliang ge* (Songs of Clear and Cool), with a book cover in elegant calligraphy provided by Ma Yifu.

Li Shutong apparently had been a very effective and indeed memorable teacher in the years after his return from Japan. That experience in some ways was formative, and those skills were carried over into the Buddhist realm, where in time he became actively engaged in monastic and lay Buddhist education. In distinctive contrast to the many persons involved in monastic education in the Republican period as teachers and curriculum innovators in newly formed academies, Hongyi could bring forward the knowledge and skills gained through extensive professional experience in his premonastic years as an educator in stable and regulated school environments. In addition to focused teaching—mainly on topics related to Vinaya—of his own monastic disciples, both individuals and in groups, he thought carefully about the comprehensive training of young monks and set out a multiyear curriculum for them. Eventually in the mid-1930s a school was created under his inspiration at Nanputuo Monastery in Xiamen to educate young monks from the neighboring region who did not qualify, either by academic skills or by their youth, for admission to the famous

Buddhist studies academy (the *Minnan foxue yuan*) also sited at the monastery. Hongyi spoke there regularly when he was in the region; some of his close friends and disciples were charged with administration and regular instruction. Another Buddhist school was created in Fujian under his inspiration, though the plans came to fruition after his death. Its purpose was to educate young women in Buddhist matters (Hongyi's initial concern was to provide an educated basis for the lives of the left-home women who formed communal lay groups in this region).

Most especially, Hongyi was an itinerant lecturer, who responded to invitations and traveled mainly in Fujian and Zhejiang to give talks to both lay groups and monastics. This practice was an important traditional element of Buddhist education in late imperial and Republican times. A sense of his engaging lecturing style can be gained from the many revised transcripts that eventually were collected and published in book form (the *Record of Lectures of Great Master Hongyi*, which includes some talks that also had been published individually in Buddhist periodicals of the day). Hongyi's peripatetic life, without an established home base, left him free of the administrative obligations that his more settled peers had to shoulder as they took responsibility for major monastic complexes. However, he found that this unsettled way of life required a steady stream of invitations to ensure survival, and at times he found it vexing.

While engagement with both calligraphy and education carried over from past experience, Hongyi's work as a textual scholar was developed after joining the monastic order. He may have read and studied in thoughtful and critical ways earlier, but after ordination he began to make thorough, organized studies of Vinaya texts, and he produced syntheses, guides, commentaries, and original teachings that have proven significant and highly influential in the Chinese Buddhist world. While some may think of him primarily as a calligrapher, in Buddhist contexts he also is especially honored for his distinctive contributions to the study and practice of Vinaya (hence the frequently encountered title of Vinaya master). As far as he was concerned, his commitment to the study and propagation of the Nanshan Vinaya, articulated in the vows of the early 1930s (as mentioned above), formed a central element of his bodhisattva work in the world. This was his contribution to the vitality of the Buddhist enterprise. At the brink of death in the summer of 1932, he composed a will in which he asked that memorial funds be used to print and circulate what he considered to that date his most important contribution, a massive volume-length explanatory diagram of the Four-Part Vinaya monastic regulations (which he had completed in 1924), rather than any expenditures on a special stupa for his cremated remains, as would be customary for an eminent monk.

Hongyi survived this illness (an infectious disease contracted in the Fujian countryside), and he lived to compose two further last statements at later health crises. Indeed, the precarity of his health was a defining element of his life, and he came to see the pressure of illness as a "great medicine" that led him to deeper levels of understanding and interior concern. In 1941 and 1942, it became increasingly apparent that his vital energy was diminishing, and he prepared for the end, eventually moving to a Buddhist care home in the Quanzhou area. His death, at age sixty-two, became itself a final teaching and, it seems, his greatest public statement. All accounts spoke to his conscious awareness and dignity in this process, in which in the last hours with the help of his attendant Miaolian he chanted the name of Amitābha and also verses from the *Huayan Sutra* on the vows of bodhisattvas. A photo taken eight hours after his death, when the doors to his chamber— sealed after the last breath— finally were opened, showed him peacefully reclined on his right side in the standard position for both sleeping and dying. This photo has circulated widely. With death seen as the final test of a lifetime of cultivation, the deathbed image often is interpreted as visual testimony to the truth of Hongyi's transformation from wealthy and privileged aesthete to profound and accomplished monk-practitioner. Some have seen the photo as witness to the genuine possibility that Buddhist practice, which many had dismissed as ancient and irrelevant, may truly have immediate practical bearing in the modern world.

The Translations

To give some sense of Hongyi's interior world, I have provided a set of four closely related documents. These deal with vows (a central element of his interior life), an instrumental dream, and an approach to addressing faults. The first text, which records a formal vow act, was composed in early 1931, and the remaining three followed in 1933. These texts are drawn from the beginning of Hongyi's final decade, which I think of as his years of spiritual maturity, and they are focused on the turning point into those authoritative years. Around 1930, Hongyi concluded that his monastic ordination in 1918 had been faulty, that he had not actually received the

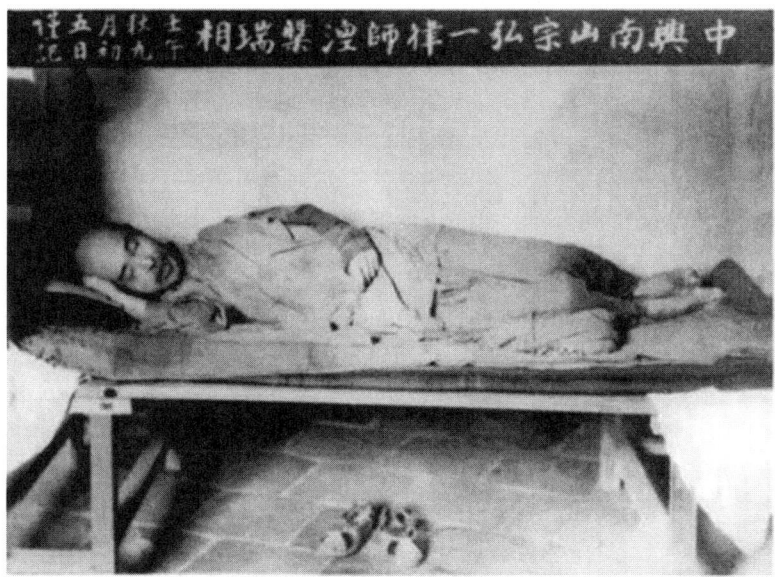

Master Hongyi shortly after his death in Quanzhou, 1942.

full complement of monastic precepts. Thus, this widely respected Vinaya master discovered that he was a *biqiu*, an ordained monk, only in name, not in reality.

He understood that beyond the personal, this was a systemic problem. As he said some years later, "To the view of an ordinary person looking out [upon us], that person would consider that the assembly of Chinese monastics is considerable, numbering at least a million. Yet actually among these million or so, if you wish to find a single genuine *biqiu*, I fear that would be a most difficult matter."[2]

He concluded that the best path was to carry out an individual rite of self-transmission of the bodhisattva precepts, a special practice sanctioned in a few key texts for circumstances where the standard method is not feasible. The standard ordination practice involves a group of senior fully ordained monastics who conduct and witness the ceremony (such persons no longer can be found, in Hongyi's view); in a self-transmission rite, the precepts are received directly from the buddhas and bodhisattvas, without need for human intermediaries. (Scriptural texts declare that only a few sets of precepts may be transmitted in this way, most importantly the basic five precepts and the bodhisattva precepts, which are a set of guidelines to support the bodhisattva aspirations equally for lay and monastic practitioners, male and female.) In connection with this ritual, between 1931 and 1933 Hongyi made three separate formal vow statements that through a clear declaration of intent established him as a bodhisattva and set specific directions of focus for this and future lives. Document I, "Text of Vows to Spread Vinaya," is the first of these vow records.

Then in early 1933, Hongyi gave a series of three invited talks at a monastery in Xiamen; a full translation of that third talk, on how to address one's faults, is included here as Document II, "An Experiment in Reforming Faults." This instructional talk provides a vivid sense of Hongyi's approach for identifying and addressing his own faults. Some hours after the third talk, Hongyi that night had a powerful dream, and he prepared a written record immediately after awakening (Document III, "Record of a Dream").

This auspicious dream bore a range of meanings for Hongyi, among them the traditional sense of confirmation through a sign such as a dream or vision that the bodhisattva precepts had been authentically transmitted. In the dream, Hongyi heard, and essentially received a transmission of, verses from the *Huayan Sutra* that emphasize the central role of refuge in the Three Jewels as a basis for generating the mind of a bodhisattva. The dream record concludes with another vow—vows were central to the way in which he organized the course of his life.

Gathering a small group of serious monastic students for intensive Vinaya studies, as he believed the dream authorized, Hongyi had them conduct together that same bodhisattva precept transmission rite to ensure that they, too, had genuinely become precept holders. In association with their bodhisattva precept transmission, the master and these monastic students made a concise set of group vows (Document IV, "Vows made by Vinaya students who have gathered to dwell in the Nanshan Vinaya Academy"). Hongyi and the eleven serious students who had come to study with him are listed at the end of the vow record; this number of students mirrors the number of figures gathered to listen to the venerable cantor's sonorous recitation of the *Huayan* verses in Hongyi's dream.

Text of Vows to Spread Vinaya

(*Hong lü yuanwen*, early 1931)

As to these [bodhisattva] precepts, I now vow to accept and uphold them, to cultivate and study them. Into the limitless future, I will never abandon them. With this merit, may all the faults that I and all beings have created since beginningless time be dissolved. For those living beings who are to receive retribution for their fixed karma, may I receive it in their stead.

Repeatedly born in dusty lands, successively turned to the unfortunate paths of rebirth [as animal, hungry ghost, or hell-dweller], passing through dusty kalpas and thus experiencing all kinds of suffering, I will steadfastly bear this with joy, to the end without regret, so that all beings may attain the buddha's way prior to me. These vows that I have expressed are genuine, not empty, and I prostrate in veneration to the Three Jewels to certify this.

I, Yanyin, have myself composed and expressed these vows of three types. Whether walking, standing, sitting, or reclining, I will ever keep them in mind, and all the merit gained from cultivating and maintaining them will be dedicated entirely to all living beings of the Dharma Realm. I vow that in this lifetime I will take on the sufferings that arise from the limitless bad acts made by living beings.

· I pledge to give up my life to protect and retain the teachings of all the buddhas of the three times!

- · I pledge to give up my life to save all living beings in the Dharma Realm!
- · I vow to take upon myself all the sufferings of all living beings in the Dharma Realm!
- · I vow to protect the Nanshan Four-Part Vinaya teachings and transmit them across the world!

ll

An Experiment in Reforming Faults

(Lecture given at Miaoshi Monastery, Xiamen,
in 1933, on the eighth day of the new year,
according to the traditional calendar)

TRANSLATOR'S INTRODUCTORY NOTES: At the end of the year in 1932 (following the traditional calendar), Hongyi gave two talks at the Miaoshi Monastery in Xiamen. The first talk, given to a group that had gathered for a period of intensive chanting, addressed basic Pure Land practices. The second talk ("At the End of Life") was a long, detailed, and practical discussion of Buddhist approaches to deathbed practices—how to prepare for one's death, how to help those who are dying, auspicious ways to die, caring for the bodies of the recently dead prior to cremation, and so forth. Keyed to its particular moment in the calendar, in this lecture Hongyi compared the moment of death to the end of the year, that point of reckoning when in Chinese worlds debts traditionally come due and must be settled.

Following those two talks, the Miaoshi Monastery abbot invited Hongyi to pass the New Year with the monastic community there and then return to give an additional talk after the main holiday festivities had concluded. It is this third talk, once again keyed to the calendrical moment (the resumption of social activities on the eighth day of the new year), that I have included here. Conceptually, it is paired with the earlier talk, "At the End of Life." Having spoken about death and endings as the old year came to a close, Hongyi now reflected on a Buddhist practitioner's constructive approach to the New Year: an internal renewal and transformation that might match the lively external environment of the traditional New Year celebrations seen all around Xiamen.

I have included this talk among the translations that accompany the essay on Hongyi for a couple of reasons. First, it is part of the complex of events occurring in 1932–33 that (we can see in retrospect) were critical to the development of Hongyi's inner life, and so it fits well with the vow texts and the dream record also presented here. These texts are all interconnected. (The dream report of Document III occurred just a few hours after Hongyi gave this talk.) Second, the talk presents a basic method of self-cultivation. It provides us with a sense of some of Hongyi's personal challenges and a glimpse of the methods he used to meet those challenges. If we ask how Hongyi was able to achieve the profound internal transformation for which he has been respected and honored, talks such as this one—resolutely basic and to the point—provide a sense of those internal dynamics and disciplines. The method Hongyi sets out bears many resemblances to self-cultivation methods of later Confucian teachings (which he had studied in earlier years), but there also are some crucial Buddhist aspects to it, as he makes clear in his concluding section.

Hongyi returned to discussion of this topic a few months later in 1933, when he addressed the small group of monks who had been engaged in serious study of Vinaya under his guidance. He again spoke about this approach to identifying faults and systematically transforming them, and he added some key points. Importantly, he noted that addressing all your faults at once is not practical, and he suggested a strategic approach by which one might identify two or three vexing issues and work on those with concentrated focus, moving on to other topics as one progresses. Hongyi stated very clearly that this kind of work, where one seeks to address personal faults and cultivate strengths, in his view is an integral part of Vinaya studies; it is not somehow a separate matter. Hongyi's teachings, as we see here in a basic form, were resolutely practical rather than speculative or theoretical.

In Hongyi's concise characterizations of each of the ten specific faults and habits that he highlights, he often enhances his discussion with brief passages drawn from a variety of texts. Most of these are taken from such Confucian classics as the *Analects* (*Lunyu*) and from a popular Qing-period collection of maxims and moral teachings, the *Geyan lianbi*. Wherever it has been possible, I have included an identification of the source at the end of the passage—for example: [*Lunyu* 19.8].

It is now the New Year according to the old agricultural calendar, and we can see that the city of Xiamen is filled with an atmosphere of renewal. New spring couplets are pasted on doorways, many people are wearing new clothing, and they are saying phrases of congratulation and wishes for happiness and good fortune in the New Year. At this time of a myriad signs of renewal, those of us who have long held trust in Buddhist teachings also should become new. What sort of newness? Just as the commonfolk paste the new spring couplets, don new clothes, and so forth, and in this way are new? No, I say. What *we* may call new is the renewal of a person by reforming faults. The four words *gaiguo zixin* (to renew oneself through reforming faults), though, are simply too broad. If one seeks to lecture on this topic, one hardly knows where to begin. Today, then, based on my experiments over the past fifty years of cultivating self-examination to rectify faults, I will raise a few concise points for you.

Before I proceed with this talk, I need to tell you that while I will quote passages that for the most part are drawn from Confucian texts, they are consonant with the Buddha's teachings. Metaphysical discussion and step-by-step cultivation methods found in Buddhist texts are most detailed, yet for those of us who are engaged in beginning studies, although there is discussion in Buddhist texts regarding matters of personal trustworthiness and how to deal with things, the explanations in Confucian texts are especially clear, detailed, and suitable for beginning studies. Therefore I will include many quotes today as an aid for those of us who study Buddhist teachings.

I have organized what follows into a general discussion followed by specific instructions. The general discussion explains the successive steps to reforming faults:

1. **Study.** One must first read many Buddhist and Confucian texts, to know in detail the difference between good and bad, and the methods of reform and change for the better. Because Buddhist and Confucian texts are as vast as a sea of fog, and one may not be able to read them all, and in addition because they may be difficult to understand, you might first read the single-volume *Geyan lianbi* [a book of maxims compiled in the Qing dynasty]. I have been reading this book since childhood. Even after taking refuge and trusting in the Buddha, I have read it often and find it especially accessible and engaging [literally: flavorful]. You can obtain a well-printed copy from the Buddhist Bookstore.

2. **Self-examination.** Having engaged in studies, you should then constantly examine yourself and determine: Have all my words and all my actions been good or bad? If they have been bad, then they should be corrected. In addition to this constant careful attention and reform of faults, every day before falling asleep you should again review in detail the actions of that day. It would be especially good if you were able to record this every day in a diary.

3. **Reform.** Following self-examination, if you become aware of a fault, then you should energetically reform it. You all should know that this matter of reforming faults is entirely honorable. It is the expression of the character of a great person. That is why Zigong [a disciple of Confucius] said, "A noble man's mistake is like an eclipse of the sun or the moon. He makes a mistake and everyone takes notice; he corrects his mistake and everyone looks up in admiration" [*Lunyu* 19.21]. There was another ancient who said, "If you are able to recognize your faults, you can be called 'bright.' If you can both recognize them and are

able to reform, you can be [called] a 'sage.'" I hope you can do this without discouragement!

As to the specific instructions, in this section I will explain respectively things that I have done over the past fifty years to reform faults and change for the better. These matters, though, are too numerous to discuss. Now, let's consider ten items that often escape the notice of ordinary people, which I would like to introduce to you. The number ten is used throughout the *Huayan Sutra*. This use of ten expresses the idea of limitlessness. Now in this remaining discussion of the matter of reforming faults, I also have raised ten items. This [use of ten] indicates that the remaining items are numerous; actually, they too are without limit. The time for this lecture is brief, and so for each of these items I am not able to present a detailed discussion; I will present only a concise explanation of the main idea. For those who would like to know more, we can discuss that on another day.

1. **Humility.** Ordinary people do not understand good and bad, they do not fear cause and effect, and they will never admit to their mistakes, no less correct them. The ancient sages, though, were not like this. Here are a few examples. Confucius said, "If I can study the *Changes* until I am fifty, I will be free of major mistakes" [*Lunyu* 7.17]. He further said, "To hear about righteousness but be unable to apply it, to be unable to reform what is not good—these are my worries" [*Lunyu* 7.3]. "Qu Boyu, who was a sage of that time, sent a messenger to Confucius. Confucius offered him a seat and questioned him, asking, 'How is your master?' The reply: 'My master seeks to minimize his faults but is not yet able to do so'" [*Lunyu* 14.25]. When sages are so modest, how can we be so complacent and proud!

2. **Vigilance in solitude.** Whatever we do, whatever thoughts arise and move our hearts, there is nothing that is not known or seen by the buddhas and bodhisattvas, extending to all the demons and gods. If you hold this in mind all the time, you will not dare do anything wrong. Master Zeng said, "One is subjected

to the [stern] gaze of ten eyes, to the [pointing] fingers of ten hands. How severe this is!" [*Daxue*]. Further, to quote from the *Odes*, "Trembling and shaking, as if on the edge of an abyss, as if treading on thin ice" [*Odes* 195; also *Lunyu* 8.3]. I constantly recall these words and do not forget them.

3. **Generosity.** The "creator of things" avoided artificiality and cleverness. When sages treat things, it is only with generosity and kindness [*Geyan lianbi*]. There are abundant ancient instructions on this topic, I will not elaborate on them now.

4. **To bear suffering.** A person of old said, "I do not know what constitutes a noble man. I only look to see a person who is willing to bear suffering in every matter. I do not know what constitutes a petty person. I only look to see a person who is willing to take advantage in every matter" [*Geyan lianbi*]. In ancient times there was a sage who had reached his time of death, and his children and grandchildren requested a final teaching. That sage said, "There is nothing else to say: you must learn how to bear suffering."

5. **Reticence.** This matter is most essential. Confucius said, "A chariot with a team of four horses cannot catch up with a loose tongue" [*Lunyu* 12.8]. How frightening! There are abundant ancient instructions on this topic, I will not elaborate on them now.

6. **Refrain from speaking about the faults of others.** An ancient said, "If you always are checking on your own faults, how are you able to make the effort to check on others?" Confucius also said, "Demand much from yourself, little from others" [*Lunyu* 15.15]. I dare not ever forget these words.

7. **Refrain from glossing over your mistakes.** Zixia said, "A lesser person always glosses over his mistakes" [*Lunyu* 19.8]. We all must know that to gloss over one's mistakes is a most shameful matter.

8. **Refrain from hiding your faults.** When we offend others in any way, we should give rise to great shame and regret, and we should generate great fear. Confess and repent past mistakes.

Do not care about your dignity, forbear in silence, or deceive yourself.

9. **When you hear slander (about yourself), do not dispute it.** An ancient said, "How does one stop slander? Answer: There is no defense" [*Geyan lianbi*]. And it is further said, "If you can absorb a small loss, then you will not suffer a big loss." I have experienced this many times over the past thirty years, and I deeply believe that these words are true.

10. **Refrain from anger.** The habit of anger is the most difficult to eliminate. A sage of old said, "Twenty years of addressing that single matter of anger, and yet I have not eliminated it" [Xue Wenqing (1389–1464), as quoted in Liu Zongzhou's *Renpu*]. But we must try our best to address it. The *Huayan Sutra* says, "One thought of an angry heart can open a million doors of obstruction." How frightening!

Due to time constraints, these remarks have been brief, but you can know from them the general idea of reforming faults. Finally, there are a few words that I would like to address to all of you. Regarding this matter of reforming faults, to speak about it seems easy, but setting it into practice is extremely difficult. When you repeatedly act to correct a fault yet repeatedly fall astray, and you find that you just are not able to master yourself, this is a situation that actually has its cause in acts established in your former lives across the beginningless past. I urge you all more than ever to constantly uphold and recite, with utmost sincerity and utmost reverence, the name of Amitābha Buddha and the names of Guanshiyin Bodhisattva and Dizang Bodhisattva. Earnestly confess and repent the acts of those former lifetimes stretching across time without beginning. From out of the mysterious darkness you will experience inconceivable acts of spiritual response. Inspired by the aid of the compassionate force of the buddhas and bodhisattvas, your karma will be dissolved and your wisdom will be made brilliant. Then very rapidly this matter of rectifying faults and self-renewal will be entirely accomplished, in this present life you will enter at ease into the precincts of the sages, and at the end of your life you will be reborn in the land of Extreme Joy. For this you can be congratulated in advance!

When common people meet in the New Year's season, they all say "Congratulations" and in this way express the wish to obtain fame and fortune. When I meet you at New Year's, I say "Congratulations" as well, so as to wish that you will be able to truly reform your faults and soon become a sage or saint, that you may quickly and most certainly be reborn in the land of Extreme Joy, rapidly achieve the buddha way (that is, achieve awakening), be able to divide your body so that you may appear across the ten directions, and entirely be able to benefit all sentient beings.

II

Record of a Dream

(Recorded in 1933, in the early morning of
the ninth day of the year, according to
the traditional calendar)

TRANSLATOR'S INTRODUCTORY NOTES: In the night after his talk on transforming faults, Hongyi had a pivotal dream. He prepared a record immediately after awakening. This was one of only three dreams that Hongyi recorded during his monastic years, and it provides a rare view of his interior world. The dream seemed to confirm the efficacy of his self-transmission of the bodhisattva precepts some months earlier, and it contained some basic teachings about a bodhisattva's interior stance, which he vowed to maintain. Earlier that day, the younger monks Guangqia (1901–1994) and Ruijin (1905–2005) had arrived at Miaoshi Monastery and presented a formal request for teachings on Vinaya. Hongyi viewed this dream as an auspicious indication that he could now begin an active, focused approach to teaching Vinaya in Fujian, in response to the request of those two monks and in accordance with his vows of 1931 and 1932, in which he had pledged to devote his life to the study and teaching of the Nanshan Vinaya. His intensive activities as an authoritative teacher now were launched. Guangqia and Ruijin ultimately became central figures among his monastic disciples.

There is far more to say about the specifics of this dream, but here I will limit discussion to one curious point. In his comments on the central figure that he encounters, Hongyi specifically uses musical terms as well as standard terminology to describe the act of reciting or chanting Buddhist verses. This is unusual. He seems to assert that this venerable figure, identified as a "cantor," was engaged in singing these verses (as he accompanied himself with a stringed instrument) rather than employing a standard mode of text chanting. Hongyi muses on that as an effective method of transmitting Dharma. This point is important in relation to Hongyi's long background as a musician and songwriter.

I should note that I have chosen to translate the word *xin* 信 in the *Huayan* verses as "trust," while others might render it as "belief" or "faith"; the meaning is found somewhere along that continuum. I have shied away from "belief" and "faith" to forestall the projection of core Christian concepts, very familiar to some, into this Buddhist environment.

On the eighth day of the first month of the *guiyou* year [1933], I went to stay at Miaoshi Monastery. That night I dreamed that I was a youth, who walked together with a Confucian master [*rushi*, "classicist teacher"]. I heard behind us a person who was sonorously chanting lines of *Huayan Sutra* verses [*gāthās*]. Listening closely, I recognized that these were writings from the chapter on [the bodhisattva] Xianshou. Hearing the syllables swelling yet distinct, I felt the profundity of this person, and I was not yet able to leave him behind. I turned back, together with the *rushi*, and saw ten or so persons seated on a mat on the ground. In their center there was a person manipulating a silk-stringed [instrument], a long-bearded elder—this was the cantor (*gezhe*). There was a paper placard before his seat on which the [full] title of the *Huayan Sutra* had been written in a single line of large characters.

I came to understand that he was preaching the Dharma through singing, and I considered him with deep reverence and respect. Accordingly I wanted to enter the seating area, so I asked among those listening if there were empty space for us. They replied that there were vacant seats at the two ends. I removed my shoes and then sought to take a seat. At that moment, the dream ended.

I recall the gāthās of the *Huayan Xianshou* chapter: there are five verses that address the practice of arousing the mind. This very night I lit a lantern and set out this record. I vow that through the endless expanse of the future, I will read and recite, accept and maintain these cultivation practices as they are spoken of there.

Yanyin [Hongyi]

I offer this to Dharma Master Purun (i.e., Guangqia). Five days later I have further recorded [the gāthās]:

> When bodhisattvas arouse the intention to seek awakening,
> It is not without cause, not without conditions.
> Giving birth to pure trust in the Buddha, Teachings, and
>   Community,
> It is by this means that they produce a broad and great mind.

> They do not seek the five cravings or royal position,
> Nor wealth, personal enjoyment, or fame.
> It is only to ever diminish the sufferings of all beings,
> And to bring benefit to the world that they arouse this mind.

> Ever seeking to enrich and bring joy to all beings,
> They majestically adorn the [buddha-]lands and make
>   offerings to the buddhas.
> Accepting and retaining the genuine teaching, they cultivate
>   its knowledges;
> To realize awakening, they arouse their minds.

> With profound trust and understanding ever pure,
> They reverently honor and respect all buddhas,
> As well as their teachings and communities.
> Making offerings with utmost sincerity, they rouse their
>   minds.

Having deep trust in the Buddha and the Buddha's teaching,
They also trust in the paths of practice traversed by the
    Buddha's disciples.
Trusting in the peerless great awakening,
By these means bodhisattvas first arouse this mind.

IV

Vows made by Vinaya students who have gathered to dwell in the Nanshan Vinaya Academy

In the twenty-second year of the Republic of China (1933), *guiyou* year, fifth month, twenty-sixth day, which corresponds to the third day of the fifth month of the agricultural calendar, the date on which we honor Master Lingfeng Ouyi's birthday, we disciples who study Vinaya respectfully state: before the buddhas, bodhisattvas, and patriarchs [as witnesses], we together have expressed the four great [bodhisattva] vows. Further, we express four special vows:

- First vow: We disciples who study Vinaya vow that in life after life we will ever be good friends and mutually support each other, without ever separating. Together we will study Vinaya, together we will spread the great Dharma, promote the sangha, and benefit all beings.
- Second vow: When we disciples study Vinaya and thereby spread the Dharma, we will be settled and tranquil in body and mind. [We will bring to this endeavor] no demonic obstructions, and be in unhindered circumstances, with sufficient economic support.
- Third vow: We vow to establish a Nanshan Vinaya Academy in the future, gather numerous persons and broadly transmit [these teachings]. We will not seek fame or reputation. We will not seek profit.

· Fourth vow: We will arouse the great awakened mind, and thereby protect and uphold the Buddha's teachings. We pledge to do our utmost to spread the Nanshan Vinaya teachings, which have been lost and for over seven hundred years were no longer transmitted; we will spread them within the world. We hope that the Dharma again will flourish, and the Buddha's sun[light] again will shine.

We further pledge that by means of expressing this vast vow [that is, the four great bodhisattva vows] and by means of the merits of the additional four vows that we have expressed, as well as all the merits generated by our future Vinaya studies, that all these merits will be directed to the benefit of all beings.

We only wish that all living beings will together give rise to this great mind, will quickly dissolve their karmic obstructions, gain rebirth in the land of highest joy, and soon achieve awakening.

We entreat all the buddhas of the ten directions, our original teacher Śākyamuni Buddha, Amitābha Buddha of the World of Extreme Joy, Guanshiyin Bodhisattva-Mahāsattva, Dizang Bodhisattva-Mahāsattva, Vinaya Master Nanshan Daoxuan, Vinaya Master Lingzhi Yuanzhao, and Great Master Lingfeng Ouyi: may you with compassionate thought take pity on us, certify and together accept [these vows]!

Attested by the Vinaya studies disciples:
Yanyin Hongyi (and eleven others, listed by name)

Further Reading

Birnbaum, Raoul. "The Deathbed Image of Master Hongyi." In *The Buddhist Dead: Practices, Discourses, Representations*, edited by Jacqueline Stone and Bryan Cuevas, 175–207. Honolulu: University of Hawai'i Press, 2007.

———. "Master Hongyi's Confucian Dreams." In *Inner Worlds: Individuals and Interiority in Chinese Religious Life*, edited by Benjamin Brose and James A. Benn. Leiden: Brill, 2025.

———. "Master Hongyi Looks Back: A 'Modern Man' Becomes a Monk in Twentieth-Century China." In *Buddhism in the Modern World: Adaptations of an Ancient Tradition*, edited by Steven Heine and Charles S. Prebish, 75-124. New York: Oxford University Press, 2003.

———. "Two Turns in the Life of Master Hongyi, a Buddhist Monk in Twentieth-Century China." In *Making Saints in Modern China*, edited by David Ownby, Vincent Goossaert, and Ji Zhe, 161-208. New York: Oxford University Press, 2017.

———. "Vinaya Master Hongyi's Vinaya Problem." In *"Take the Precepts as Your Master": Monastic Discipline and Practices in Modern Chinese Buddhism*, edited by Ester Bianchi and Daniela Campo, 23-94. Leiden: Brill, 2023.

Finaldi, Gabriele, and Joost Joustra, with André Vauchez. *Saint Francis of Assisi*. London: National Gallery, 2023.

McGuire, Beverly Foulks. *Living Karma: The Religious Practices of Ouyi Zhixu*. New York: Columbia University Press, 2014.

Tarocco, Francesca. *The Cultural Practices of Modern Chinese Buddhism: Attuning the Dharma*. London: Routledge, 2008.

ter Haar, Barend J. "Buddhist Monks and Oral Performance." In *Chinese Buddhism and the Scholarship of Erik Zürcher*, edited by Jonathan A. Silk and Stefano Zacchetti, 188-232. Leiden: Brill, 2023.

Yu, Jimmy. "Blood Writing as Extraordinary Artifact and Agent for Socioreligious Change." *Humanities & Social Sciences Communications* 7, no. 3 (2020), https://doi.org/10.1057/s41599-020-0497-1.

Portrait of Master Yinguang, date and location unknown.

5 | Pure Land Patriarch

Yinguang

CHARLES B. JONES

Mention the name of the Venerable Yinguang (1862–1940) in Chinese Buddhist circles and you will find that people think about him in several different ways depending on the context. In the setting of Chinese Pure Land Buddhism, he is the last in a series of thirteen "patriarchs" (*zu*) who defined and transmitted orthodox Pure Land teaching and practice. Within the sociological study of Buddhism during the late Qing/early Republican period, he exemplifies how Buddhism began to let go of its traditional reliance on rural elites and shifted its appeal to a modern, educated, urban audience using the latest advances in mass media. At the same time, a more Buddhist-centered study of this history places him among the "four eminent monks" (*si da gaoseng*) of the Republican period; in this context he is associated with a revival of the Pure Land dharma gate and represents a "traditionalist" approach.[1] Finally, his biography reveals one of the most singular figures in Chinese Buddhism. He saw himself as a reclusive monk who only wanted to be left alone to pursue his own practice and never sought fame, high rank, or influence. Nevertheless, once his fame spread, he used it quite cannily to propagate Buddhism. We will see him from all these angles below.

Chinese Pure Land Buddhism

Yinguang is primarily known as the thirteenth patriarch of the Pure Land tradition. Pure Land began to develop in China in the fourth and fifth centuries C.E., consolidated its most characteristic teachings and practices in the mid-seventh century, and gained self-consciousness as a distinct "dharma gate" (famen) by the Song dynasty (960–1279). At that time, the tradition began to draw up lists of monks whose lives and teachings helped to establish Pure Land orthodoxy. These lists of patriarchs did not represent a lineage of masters and disciples but a roster of fathers of the tradition put forward by influential authors or community acclaim.[2]

We find the charter narrative of the Pure Land tradition in sutras that tell the story of the Buddha Amitāyus or Amitābha. As he embarked on his path, he made a series of forty-eight vows before the assembly of the Buddha Lokeśvararāja to set his trajectory, focusing mainly on the features of the buddha land he would establish. All buddhas had such lands as external manifestations of their mental purity, but his would be the best of them all. He vowed that ordinary, unenlightened beings would be able to come to this land by means of very simple practices such as calling his name or doing good deeds and dedicating the merit to rebirth there. Certain passages affirmed that even the most wicked and unaccomplished people could gain access, though the text of the eighteenth vow excluded those who committed the five worst offenses or slandered the Dharma (an issue in which Yinguang had a personal stake, as we will see). Once there, they would enjoy perfect conditions for the pursuit of enlightenment: no distractions, no scarcity, great comfort, and a buddha and attendant bodhisattvas at hand to provide instruction. If these conditions were not met, he declared, he would not accept perfect enlightenment. Since the sutras affirm that he succeeded in his quest, it stands to reason that all his vows came true, opening a path out of rebirth and suffering even for people who would never be able to undertake arduous study and practice in the present world.

In China, various thinkers further refined this basic doctrinal framework. Most crucially for understanding Yinguang's teaching, they distinguished "self-power" (*zili*), meaning the devotee's own efforts, from "other-power" (*tali*), indicating what the Buddha Amitābha did for them through the fulfillment of his vows. Some readers may have already heard these terms in connection with Japanese Pure Land teaching, which holds that self-power accomplishes nothing in this world, and one must rely exclusively on the Buddha's power. Chinese masters never went this far. While they agreed that one cannot reach enlightenment on one's own, they held that one should still do as much as one can and rely on Amitābha's vows to make up for what one lacks. If we keep this in mind, we will not be surprised to see that Yinguang recommended that his followers put forth as much effort as they could.

Because Chinese Pure Land retained a place for self-power in the religious quest, it did not become a single-practice school as in Japan. One could engage in a variety of practices and dedicate their merit toward rebirth in the Pure Land. However, the tradition still focused on a constellation of practices grouped under the term *nianfo* as the essential component that guaranteed success. Because the term *nianfo* covers several types of practice, we will not translate it. The first word, *nian*, can mean either to have something in mind or to speak aloud, while *fo* means "buddha." Thus, the practice of *nianfo* comprises mental visualization of Amitābha, concentration on his name as a mental sound-image, or oral repetition of the name using the formula *Namo Amituofo* (Homage to Amitābha Buddha). Yinguang commended all three variations to his followers and regarded nianfo as a serious form of self-cultivation.

Yinguang's Early Life and Monasticism

Yinguang's biography brings us face to face with a man who never once doubted the course his life would follow.[3] He was born on the twelfth day of the twelfth month in the eleventh year of the Xianfeng reign period of the Qing dynasty (January 11, 1862).[4] His birth name was Zhao Shaoyi, and his place of birth was Chichen East Village in what is now Heyang county, Shaanxi Province. For the first six months of his life, he could not open his eyes and cried constantly, foreshadowing a recurring eye disease that played a role in his turn to Pure Land.

Not much is known about his family since the turmoil of later years caused the loss of local records, and Yinguang himself did not speak much of them. They were farmers, and Yinguang had two older brothers. The oldest, named Zhao Conglong, was a Confucian student, while the second oldest, Zhao Panlong, tended the farm. Yinguang studied the Confucian classics with Conglong and displayed such an aptitude for learning that his family hoped he would pass the civil service examinations, join the imperial bureaucracy, and bring them security and prestige. Reflecting on his studies later in life, Yinguang revealed mixed feelings. On the positive side, he credited Confucian studies with giving him a spirit of self-sufficiency, and throughout his monastic career he attended to his own affairs—cleaning his own quarters, washing his own robes, and so on. Negatively, the official Confucian commentaries and the examination culture of his day were very anti-Buddhist, and during his studies he adopted this bias and wrote essays disparaging the Dharma. As he said in an autobiographical statement around 1927,

> I read and studied from the time I reached boyhood, and thus I imbibed the anti-Buddhist poison of Han [Yu], Ou[yang Xiu], Cheng [Yi and Cheng Hao], and Zhu [Xi]. Fortunately, I did not have the talent of Han, Ou, the Chengs, and Zhu, and this put a bit of a dike between us, [otherwise] I would have led both myself and others astray and fallen into the Avīci hell in my next life. From the age of fourteen or fifteen onward, I experienced illnesses for several years. From that time, I began surveying thought more broadly, from the ancient to the modern, delving into the scriptures and other books. I began to see that all the views of those who expounded these [anti-Buddhist] theories—Han, Ou, the Chengs, and Zhu—merely stood outside the gates.

They most definitely did not measure up to the profundities within the hall! The year after my capping ceremony, I left to become a monk and practice Pure Land exclusively.[5]

The "capping ceremony" (*guanli*) typically took place when a young man reached the age of twenty *sui* and marked his entrance into adulthood.[6] The figures Yinguang names were all Confucian scholars of the Tang and Song dynasties who wrote against Buddhism, and the last one, Zhu Xi (1133–1200), authored the official commentaries on the classic texts that all students memorized.

The "illnesses" to which Yinguang refers were continuations of his eye problems, which caused him to question his exclusive study of Confucianism. He began reading more widely and found Buddhist texts helpful in understanding his life and problems. He felt remorse for having read and espoused the anti-Buddhist views of the Confucian texts and connected his actions to the chronic illnesses of his youth. He signed his early publications "the eternally ashamed monk" (*chang cankui seng*) on this account. After a time, he formed the determination to seek ordination as a Buddhist monk.

Knowing that his family would oppose him, he waited for an opportunity to slip away. Once, when Conglong went to the city of Chang'an (today's Xi'an, about 131 miles or 210 kilometers from their home), Yinguang accompanied him. When Conglong returned home without him, Yinguang saw his chance. He departed for Mount Wutai, a set of five peaks sacred to Buddhism and dotted with many temples large and small. Once there, he found a monk named Daochun (?–1891) at the Lianhua Grotto Temple (*Lianhua dong si*) who was willing to take him in. Life with Daochun was very austere. In a letter written in 1932 to his lay follower Shao Huiyuan, Yinguang said that the master could only provide him one robe and one pair of shoes, he had no money, the quarters were bitterly cold, and they cooked their own meals.[7] For three months, Daochun drilled Yinguang on monastic discipline and introduced him to Chan and Pure Land practice. Finding Chan difficult, Yinguang decided to focus on Pure Land.

Three months later, his brother Conglong located him. Yinguang relates what happened next:

Not quite three months later, my eldest brother tracked me down and said our mother was gravely ill, so I followed him home. Halfway there, my eldest brother produced a set of lay clothes and sternly told me, "If you don't get out of those monk's robes, I will have to kill you right here!" What else could I do? I followed him. When we got home, I found my mother in good health. My eldest brother said to me, "Who told you you could go off and leave home on your own? From now on you will forget all about it, or I'll have to punish you severely!" My family members thought I would sneak away, so they kept a close watch. Then we got some happy news from relatives and my elder brother took me along to help celebrate. At the banquet they served meat, and I ate a lot, which greatly pleased my brother because he thought it meant I would not try to get ordained again and their watchfulness had paid off. One day, my eldest brother was off visiting relatives, my second eldest brother was in the fields drying grains in the sun. . . . I stole back the monk's robe and about two hundred cash and fled to the Lianhua Grotto Temple where Master Daochun was. Afraid that my brother would come for me again, I did not stay there long, and took off again the next day. Master Daochun knew a monk who practiced austerities. He gave me a silver coin, something people from Shaanxi rarely see. The money shop could not exchange it, so I went to a jewelry store where I converted it to eight hundred cash.[8]

Yinguang made his way south until he came to the Lianhua (Lotus Blossom) Temple in Hubei Province. The abbot noticed his diligence and literacy, so he put Yinguang in charge of "sunning the scriptures," or periodically taking texts from the library and sunning them outside to prevent the growth of mold. This gave him the opportunity to read further in the Buddhist canon, and in due course he encountered the Song dynasty layman Wang Rixiu's

(?-1173) *Longshu's Pure Land Writings* (*Longshu jingtu wen*), which not only deepened his knowledge of Pure Land but also strengthened his resolve to be of service to the monastic community. As he reports, it inspired him to take on the additional work of hauling firewood and boiling drinking water for the other monks.

When the monastery's quartermaster took ill in 1882, the abbot put Yinguang in charge of the storeroom. Here he showed himself extremely conscientious in handling monastic property. Although he was not yet fully ordained, he conducted himself in accordance with the monks' precepts. The rules against misappropriation of the common property of resident clergy struck him with force, and a couplet hanging on the storeroom wall reminded him of the heroic honesty of two legendary figures of the Chan school.[9] He recounted later that in handling sugar, he always used a piece of paper as a scoop so that none of it would stick to his hands and tempt him to lick his fingers.

In 1882, Yinhai Dinggong (d.u.) of the Shuangxi Temple in Shaanxi was conducting monastic ordinations and invited the guest prefect of the Lianhua Temple to serve as the celebrant. This monk knew that Yinguang had not yet received the full precepts, so he took him along for ordination. Because he was literate, the temple asked Yinguang to record everything. Writing late into the night by lamplight caused his eye problems to recur, but he kept at it, concentrating on nianfo day and night. By the time the ordination period ended and his writing assignment was complete, he had made a full recovery. This solidified his exclusive devotion to Pure Land practice and convinced him that sincere nianfo could cure illness. He was now fully ordained under the dharma name Shengliang; he took Yinguang as his "courtesy name" (*zi*).[10]

Over the next several years, he moved around to various temples. In 1886, he went to the Zifu Temple on Mount Hongluo near Beijing, which had been the home of the twelfth patriarch of Chinese Pure Land, Jixing Chewu (1741-1810).[11] After a trip to Mount Wutai in 1887, he returned to the Zifu Temple, where he held various posts such as manager of the itinerant monk's hall, verger, and monastery manager. He also served as keeper of the scriptures, enabling him to read through the entire canon. In 1890, he went to the Long-quan Temple in Beijing, working in the refectory for six months. In October, he began solitary practice in various places, cultivating himself away from the crowds and setting down the roots of future attainment. In 1891, he went to the Yuanguang Temple in Beijing, where he stayed for the next two years. In 1893, when Yinguang was thirty-three, Venerable Huawen, the abbot of the Fayu Temple on Mount Putuo in Zhejiang, came to ask for a copy of the canon, and the monks recommended that he engage Yinguang to help manage the transfer. He liked Yinguang's diligence and piety, so he asked him to help transport the scriptures back south and subsequently invited him to live in the sutra pavilion. Thus, Yinguang moved to the sacred Buddhist island of Mount Putuo, where he would remain for the next three decades.

Yinguang's Later Career and Emergence as a Public Monk

Early in his residence at the Fayu Temple, the contradiction that defined his later monastic life began to come into view. By temper-ament, he sought solitude and quiet, preferring to keep to himself for reading and practice. At the same time, his singular and sin-cere devotion to Pure Land practice, his ever-growing erudition, and his ability to give inspiring dharma talks attracted attention and brought him into the public eye. During Yinguang's first four years there, the monks of the temple made increasingly frequent requests of him to present sutra lectures and sermons. Beginning in 1897, he undertook two consecutive three-year periods of "sealed confinement" (*biguan*). This was an established monastic practice wherein a monk or nun requested to be sealed into a confined space for intensive meditation and study uninterrupted by other responsi-bilities. However, it is important to note that it did not entail cutting off all contact with others. The room in which the practitioner lived always had a little window for receiving food, water, supplies, and visitors. When he came out, he moved into private quarters behind the temple, but after a time the monks earnestly requested that he return to the community so they could benefit from his attainments.

Thus far, demands on Yinguang's time and talent had come only from the other clergy of the Fayu Temple, but by the early twentieth century this would change. In 1898, he met the lay devotee Gao Henian (1872–1962), and it was he who began pushing Yinguang into the currents of the contemporary Buddhist revival. Gao had come to the Fayu Temple to write about Huawen (the monk who brought Yinguang to Mount Putuo), and he met and talked to Yinguang at the window of his hermitage. After Gao returned home, he sent letters, which Yinguang answered with long and elegantly written responses. Yinguang inspired Gao to take up Pure Land practice, and Gao wanted to share his newfound master's teaching with others. In 1912 Gao gathered up several manuscripts and had them printed without attribution in the Shanghai journal *Foxue congbao* (Buddhist Studies Journal). Both clerics and laypeople were impressed with these writings, and the lay Huayan specialist Xu Weiru (1878–1937) made inquiries about the author's identity. After discovering it was Yinguang, he collected three of the master's letters from his friends and published them under the title *Yinguang fashi xin'gao* (Letters from Dharma Master Yinguang) in 1917. From this time forward Yinguang became well known under his real name.

By 1918, Xu Weiru had gathered twenty-one essays and letters and published them in Beijing under the title *Yinguang fashi wenchao* (Essays and Notes of Dharma Master Yinguang). In a letter to Shao Huiyuan, Yinguang complained,

> From Guangxu 19 (1893) I had been at Mount Putuo just being an idle rice-eating monk....I never wrote the two words [of my name] "yin guang" on any paper to ask someone to do something, so for more than twenty years I was peaceful and happy. Later, when Mr. Gao Henian handed a few miscellaneous essays over to a Buddhist journal for publication, I still did not use the name "Yinguang." This lasted up to Minguo 3 to 5 [i.e., 1914–

1916). Afterward, Xu Weiru gathered these together and privately printed the *Wenchao* in the capital. Since then, I get bundles of letters every day and stay busy answering them for people and listening to the most absurd things that people say. They seek to take refuge [with me], but all I am doing is accompanying them in faith.[12]

Since this activity encroached on time he wanted to use for religious cultivation, Yinguang described Gao as "meddlesome" (*duoshi*). The *Yinguang fashi wenchao* went through many editions, expansions, and revisions over the years, and remains in circulation today. It was not until 1919 that Xu Weiru convinced him to begin accepting lay disciples and granting them dharma names. Men and women arrived every day because of the popularity of the *Wenchao*.

It was also during his time at the Fayu Temple that Yinguang began sponsoring sutra printing. The first time he stepped off Mount Putuo was in 1918 when he arranged for the publication of *Anshi quanshu* (The Complete works of [Layman] Anshi), a compendium of morality texts by the Qing dynasty Pure Land devotee Zhou Mengyan (1656-1739). He was accompanied by Gao Henian, and they went via Shanghai where, through Gao, he met many important figures in the Buddhist world. He returned to Shanghai again with Gao in 1919 and delivered lectures on Pure Land to still more well-known Buddhist figures and publishers. After the lectures, the Jian brothers, a pair of tobacco tycoons, gave him one thousand yuan to print sutras, which was enough to cover the costs of his previous printing ventures as well. Inspired by Yinguang, they founded the Shanghai Buddhist Pure Karma Society (*Shanghai fojiao jingye she*) and even set up its headquarters in their mansion. Yinguang also founded the Propagation Society (*Honghua she*) to sponsor the publication and reprinting of many Pure Land classics and Buddhist sutras.

Mechanized publishing was a new medium in China at that time, and Yinguang was quick to see its potential utility in propagating his message of Pure Land traditionalism and Confucian virtue. He was also entrepreneurial in his search for funding, working with such notable figures as the doctor, publisher, and Buddhist lexicographer Ding Fubao (1874-1952). As the scholar Jan Kiely has noted,

> Ding Fubao recalled how Yinguang's shrewd cultivation of influential supporters, his indefatigable persistence and his personal charisma contributed to his publishing success. Not long after he first wrote to Ding about a publishing project, Yinguang appeared at Ding's Yixue Books office in Shanghai to make the case, in person, for the printing of five thousand copies of the *Compendium of Anshi*. Observing the monk's worn clothing and straw sandals, Ding concluded that Yinguang could barely afford the initial printing cost for one thousand copies at the cheapest rate of one silver dollar per volume. A few days later, Yinguang appeared again and ordered another five thousand copies. Again, Ding instructed his printers to print only another one thousand volumes. This pattern continued until Ding realized that, within a month, his press had produced more than thirty thousand copies of the volume. Later, Ding visited Yinguang and found him meeting with a high-ranking Navy Department official from Fujian. He observed that the official was so impressed with Yinguang that he wrote a check on the spot for one thousand *yuan* to support the monk's printing projects. Ding never again questioned Yinguang's ability to pay for his printing costs.[13]

Yinguang also taught the importance of compassionate bodhisattva practices, and one outgrowth of this was the establishment of prison ministries under his guidance. In 1922, Yinguang began to accept invitations to preach in prisons. Seeing how effective he was, his followers established the Society to Inspire Reform in Prisons (*Jianyu ganhua hui*) with Yinguang as honorary director. Yinguang assigned his follower Zhide (d.u.) to carry out the ministry, and both guards and prisoners were visibly moved by his lectures. The society grew and soon extended its activities to other prisons.

Many monastic and lay followers asked him to leave the relatively inaccessible Fayu Temple and relocate to another, more convenient site. He received numerous petitions to move to Hong Kong, but in

1930 his clerical follower Zhende advised him that Zhejiang Province had a large and active Buddhist community and promised him that the Baoguo Temple in Suzhou would grant him another three-year period of sealed confinement upon arrival. Yinguang was convinced and moved to Suzhou after more than thirty years at Mount Putuo. Despite going back into seclusion, Yinguang's propagation activities did not abate; in fact, Hongyi (a Vinaya reformer and another of the eminent monks of the period; see chapter 4) said it was his most prolific decade. He continued to lead a very frugal and simple life and carried out the usual monastic duties.

With the financial support of several lay followers, Yinguang continued to print Buddhist sutras and other texts for free distribution. He had reprinted the *Ten Essential [Texts] for Pure Land* (*Jingtu shiyao*), a set of Pure Land writings compiled by the Ming dynasty master Ouyi Zhixu (1599–1655); the *Five Pure Land Sutras* (*Jingtu wujing*); and several temple gazetteers. These all had a great influence on later Pure Land practitioners. In 1931, at Yinguang's suggestion, the Propagation Society moved its headquarters to the Baoguo Temple to be near Yinguang. The following year, his assistant Mingdao died, and he took over all its operations himself. He was already seventy-five, but he continued to lead the society until the year before he died.

By 1936, the eastern provinces were in turmoil following the Mukden Incident (September 18, 1931), in which Japanese forces initiated their invasion of Manchuria. Yinguang responded by directing his fundraising efforts toward war relief. He accepted an invitation to speak in Shanghai at the Dharma Meeting to Protect the Nation and Allay Disaster (*Huguo xizai fahui*) under four conditions: (1) that they not give him a welcome or a sendoff; (2) that he not ride in a car; (3) that they not put on a feast for him; and (4) that there not be too many attendees. He brought only one attendant and walked from the train station himself. After the eight-day meeting, he took all the money given to him by the thousand or so people that took refuge with him at the event and donated it to disaster relief. In the years following, he presided over many similar events.

The War of Resistance against the Japanese began in 1937, bringing danger closer to Yinguang's doorstep. Many followers implored him to leave the Baoguo Temple and move higher up Lingyan Mountain, but he refused, stating that if he died, he would go to the Pure Land. Finally, however, his followers undertook the formidable task of renovating the Lingyan Shan Temple. This temple had been affiliated with Yinguang since 1926,[14] and those directing the renovation promised he could run it in accordance with his ideals. In October of that year, he moved up the mountain and took up residence there. In order to realize his vision of a strict monastic life focused on Pure Land practice, he laid down the following rules:

1. Regardless of the abbot's own tradition, he had to take strict monastic discipline and Pure Land practice as the foundation. Abbots also could not ordain disciples, in order to prevent the evil of lineage domination.
2. Abbots would assume office in rotation and not according to seniority in order to allay the suspicion that a monk of mediocre virtue occupied a higher rank than a monk of eminent virtue.
3. There would be no transmission of precepts or lecturing on sutras in order to avoid the appearance of ostentation. Though there would be daily lectures, preachers were not to ascend the dais and outsiders would only be allowed to listen.
4. The sole activity would be nianfo. Outside of hosting a "Buddha Seven" (*Foqi*, i.e., a seven-day nianfo retreat), no other dharma service could take place.
5. No one would be allowed to tonsure personal disciples.

These five provisions not only retained Yinguang's emphasis on Pure Land as the temple's sole practice but also represented an effort to democratize the sangha by eliminating seniority and entrenched lineages, which had been avenues for monopolizing power within temples in the past. These rules remain in force at the temple today.

By 1939, when he was seventy-nine years old, Yinguang withdrew from administrative duties and began to concentrate on nianfo. In letters, he began planning for his own death and giving instructions for his funeral arrangements. Since he felt assured of rebirth in the Pure Land, he did not want anything pretentious or distracting, so he limited the plan only to the simplest of rites and minimal material expenditures. On the twenty-seventh day of the tenth month (November 26, 1940), he reported the first premonitions of his impending death. For the next several days he showed signs of decline, though he occasionally rebounded somewhat and resumed his normal routine. He gathered his monks and followers and gave them instructions and assignments for the future of the temple.

On the morning of the fourth day of the eleventh month (December 2, 1940), he sat up in bed and said, "Nianfo and see the Buddha; I will assuredly be born in the west!" Having said this, he uttered one loud nianfo. He turned to an attendant, washed his hands, and said, "In dependence on the Buddha Amitābha's guidance, I will go. Everyone nianfo, make vows, and be reborn in the west[ern Pure Land]." Then he sat up on his pillow. An attendant said, "You are not quite upright." Yinguang sat up straighter and continued to nianfo. His monastic attendant Miaozhen arrived, and Yinguang gave his final instructions to maintain the temple as a haven of Pure Land practice. After that he said nothing more. His lips moved with the nianfo, and he passed away that same day.

Yinguang's Teaching and Practice

In China, proponents of Pure Land have conceptualized the relationship between the believer, the Buddha Amitābha, and the Pure Land in two ways. The first is called "western Pure Land" (*xifang jingtu*) and teaches that the Pure Land and its buddha literally abide far to the west of our present world. The goal of practice is to align one's mind with that buddha in a state of "sympathetic resonance" (*ganying*) through constant and sincere practice. At the end of one's life, the buddha will come and escort one to rebirth in his buddha land. The second is called "mind-only Pure Land" (*weixin jingtu*), and it holds that both the buddha and his land are ultimately manifestations of one's own mind. To hold the Buddha Amitābha in mind is simply to detect one's own buddha-nature. Yinguang held firmly to the first model. In his writings he counseled strongly against "psychologizing" the buddha and repeatedly urged his followers to believe firmly that Amitābha and his Pure Land exist and that, upon death, they would go there instead of following the path upon which their karma would otherwise lead. This will be apparent in the translation below.

Yinguang taught that one needed the following beliefs and attitudes when engaging in Pure Land practice. First, one had to believe that this Sahā world is suffering, while Sukhāvatī (i.e., the Pure Land) is bliss. Second, one needed faith that Amitābha is a manifestation of one's mind, while at the same time one was manifesting in Amitābha's mind. This teaching came from his reading of the *Recorded Sayings* of the twelfth Pure Land patriarch, Jixing Chewu. The mutual regard that caused the practitioner and Amitābha to appear as images in each other's minds accounted for the working of *ganying*, or "sympathetic resonance" that connected them. As Yinguang put it, sentient beings are like water; Amitābha is like the moon. When their faith is firm, then sentient beings will resonate (*gan*) with Amitābha, who will respond (*ying*) to them. Note that this differs significantly from the "mind-only Pure Land" view described above, as it maintains that Amitābha is real and separate from the believer and is not just a symbol of innate buddha-nature as held by practitioners who sought to combine Chan (Zen) with Pure Land.

Third, one need not worry about the exclusion of those who committed the five grave deeds or slandered the right Dharma in the eighteenth vow of the *Larger Sutra*. This only applies during one's lifetime. At the moment of death, Amitābha would come for anyone who practiced with faith. As we saw, Yinguang thought he had slandered the Dharma by repeating the Confucian anti-Buddhist rhetoric he had imbibed in his youth. This third belief gave him hope that he could still achieve rebirth.

Fourth, one needed firm belief in the law of cause and effect, or karma. Amitābha was not a savior figure whose vows nullified one's past karma; rather, one's practice established a connection with Amitābha's vow power that redirected one's karma into a more direct path to buddhahood. To be sure, Yinguang taught that human effort alone was insufficient. However, as the translation shows, he took Pure Land to be a serious practice in the present life and not an excuse to put off practice until after rebirth. Thus, he consistently counseled his followers to practice conventional Confucian virtues in their daily lives and to attempt as much Buddhist practice as they could.

For him, nianfo encompassed all other methods of cultivation: devotion, meditation, study, ritual, ethics, and so on. For some practitioners it might lead to the attainment of samādhi, or deep meditative concentration, but for most it would not. Pure Land was the best of all "dharma gates" precisely because it could accommodate all believers, whether of superior, middling, or inferior capacities, and had the support of all Buddhist scriptures.

Yinguang's program of practice for most of his followers looked like this: The method of gathering the mind (*she xin*) begins with deep sincerity. When sincerity is achieved, then perform nianfo aloud, concentrating on the ear to hear one's recitation exclusively and clearly. As the length of time one can maintain focus on each word and phrase increases, the body and mind will achieve greater unity. When sleeping or undressed for the bath, when using the restroom, or when in an unclean place, one may only recite silently. When reciting the Buddha's name, there is no need to go into a state of concentration. Just bring the mind, tongue, and ear together around the name. If one can focus all six sense faculties in the act of nianfo, then all karmic obstructions will be eliminated. Whether aloud or silently, nianfo arises in the mind, exits the mouth, and enters the ear. When it arises clearly from the mind and voice and enters clearly into the ear, then one has successfully begun to focus the mind.[15]

Yinguang is famous for devising a method of refocusing the mind if it started wandering. As he wrote to a follower, when reciting the

Buddha's name, either aloud or mentally, do it in groups of ten. However, do not count the repetitions vocally or using a rosary. Instead, simply be aware in a nonverbal way when one has reached ten recitations. This practice sharpens one's focus on the recitation without the added activity of counting creating a distraction.[16]

While this seems aimed at an educated audience with the time and opportunity to meditate, we must remember that Yinguang adjusted the practice to match individual circumstances and abilities. For a great many of his followers, he said that simple oral repetition was sufficient. As noted above, Chinese Pure Land masters never adopted the belief that self-effort counted for nothing, and so they always taught their followers to do whatever level of practice they could. As I have shown elsewhere,[17] the more one did in this lifetime, the shorter the period of time one spent in the Pure Land and the sooner one could become a buddha and begin saving other beings. Thus, even a person whose life had been wasted in evil or idle pursuits could attain rebirth through simple deathbed recitation of the Buddha's name, but they would spend a longer time in the Pure Land, while someone who had practiced virtue and self-cultivation would be there for a shorter time. We must not think Yinguang inconsistent if he recommends arduous practice for some while allowing that a lower level will still be effective for others.

Yinguang's Engagement with Modernity

Beliefs and practices such as these naturally lead one to think of someone like Yinguang as a "traditionalist." While his message reflected premodern conceptions of Pure Land practice, he was willing to embrace emerging technologies to get that message out. Like Christian evangelists in the West who successively adopted printing, radio, movies, television, and the internet to propagate "that old-time religion," Yinguang saw the potential in modern print culture for spreading his message. Put another way, he accepted modernity without adopting modernism.

On the intellectual level, this also meant engaging with modern Buddhist studies in a way premodern promoters of Pure Land never needed to. For example, one traditional method of defending Pure Land against the accusation that it was a peasant practice unfit for serious practitioners was to assert that even the great bodhisattva Samantabhadra had vowed to achieve rebirth in the Pure Land as witnessed by the *Huayan Sutra*. Yinguang could not bring this argument forward without qualification. In his *Treatise Resolving Doubts about Pure Land* (*Jingtu jueyi lun*), a critic argues that since modern textual studies have shown this section of the sutra was inserted later, it cannot serve as a defense of Pure Land. Consequently, Yinguang could not simply invoke the "king of sutras" for support, but he was compelled to mount an argument for the critical passage's authenticity.[18] The only way to be a strict "traditionalist" was to ignore modernity altogether and carry on in willful isolation. Yinguang chose to engage the modern world, which required that he modify his traditionalism to meet it on its terms.

Thus, while his placement among the "four eminent monks" sets him up as the representative of traditionalism, in fact his stance is ambiguous, and this ambiguity led to him standing for conflicting ideals that straddled the interests and needs of the urban elites and the masses of Buddhist devotees. For example, his Pure Land teaching had only a limited rationalizing effect, as when he told a wealthy Hong Kong businessman to prioritize congregational Pure Land practice over devotion to the bodhisattva Tara and participation in a spirit-writing cult, but without questioning the reality of these practices or their objects. In fact, he never doubted the existence of Buddhist or Daoist ghosts and spirits at all.[19] Many aspects of his life and teaching did not sit well with a modern social sensibility or scientific outlook. While he raised funds for charitable relief work, he never questioned any societal arrangement or political practice on a systematic level. Unlike Taixu (see chapter 3), he never tried to square Buddhist cosmology with modern astronomy. Taixu speculated that the depiction of the world in traditional Buddhism as a central mountain with four radiating continents may refer to planets in the solar system;[20] Yinguang was unconcerned with such questions. He also cited miracles in his promotion of Pure Land, as when he claimed, as noted above, that the practice of nianfo had cured his eye disease. At a time when the law made a formal distinction between "good" religion (*zongjiao*) and "bad" superstition (*mixin*), protecting the first and suppressing the second, such beliefs worked against the efforts of Buddhist leaders to legitimize Buddhism before the law.

Still, Yinguang's reputation remains high to this day. He was added to the roster of Pure Land patriarchs almost immediately after his death. Just as he used the most modern technologies of his day to get his message out, in the ensuing decades his followers used film, DVDs, and now the internet to promote his vision of a self-sufficient Pure Land dharma gate unmixed with Chan elements.

The Translation

As we saw above, once his writings began circulating and his fame spread, many people from all over China wrote letters to Yinguang seeking his insights. In this response to Chen Xizhou, Yinguang first lays out the suffering inherent in our present world and the great difficulty of escaping it through practicing Buddhism on one's own. Next, he describes the bliss of rebirth in the Pure Land and exhorts Chen to have complete faith that Amitābha will bring him there for rebirth after death, thus avoiding the further suffering that would otherwise await him. Finally, he cautions against reading the Pure Land in a psychological or metaphorical way, advising instead that Chen believe in its literal existence as described in Buddhist scriptures.

YINGUANG

On True Faith and Ardent Vows

Letter to Chen Xizhou

When we speak of "faith," we mean that one must have faith that the Sahā world is really and truly suffering, while the [Land of] Utmost Bliss is really and truly blissful. The suffering of the Sahā world is immeasurable and boundless. In general, it is encompassed within the eight kinds of suffering. These are birth, old age, sickness, death, separation from what we desire, association with what we hate, inability to get what we desire, and the raging flames of the five aggregates. Beings at every level, from those who are noble for a time to those as humble as beggars, experience these eight kinds of suffering. The first seven types are the results of karma from previous lives. With some reflection one can know the truth of this on one's own, so it does not require a detailed explanation and I will not waste brush and ink detailing them. The eighth, "the raging flames of the five aggregates," arises from the movement of thoughts in the present mind, and the actions [deriving from these thoughts] become the causes for the suffering one will receive in the future. Cause and effect lead one on continuously and without end; from kalpa to kalpa there is no way to break free.

The five aggregates are form, sensation, perception, intention, and consciousness. Form is the physical body, which receives the retributions of karma. Sensation, perception, intention, and consciousness are objects impinging on the mind, which gives rise to illusions and errors. Based on the illusory and erroneous dharmas of body and mind, along with the dusts of the six realms of sense objects, delusions arise and karma is created. It is like a blazing hot fire that one cannot quell, and so we call it "raging flames." In addition, aggregate (*yin* 陰) also means "to cover," and so its pronunciation is the same as [the word for] "shadow" (*yin* 蔭).

Because these five aggregates cover over one's true nature, it cannot manifest. They are like thick clouds covering the sun. Though the sun rises, its light is brilliant, and it is not itself diminished, clouds keep us from enjoying its brightness. In the same way, as long as worldlings have not yet brought an end to their afflicted karma, then the obstructions of these five aggregates will keep the sky of [true] nature and the sun of wisdom from appearing.

The eighth kind of suffering is the root cause of all suffering. Among those who cultivate the Way, if the strength of their meditative samādhi is deep, then they will not grasp at anything in this world of the six dusts and will not give rise to more aversion or attachment. If they redouble their efforts and enter into realization of no-birth, then their delusive karma will be thoroughly purified, and they will cut off samsara at the root.

However, this practice is not at all easy. In the generation of the end [of the dharma], achieving it is truly difficult. Therefore, one has to cultivate pure karma exclusively and seek rebirth in [the Land of] Utmost Bliss. Supported by the power of the Buddha [Amitābha's] compassion, one achieves rebirth in the west[ern Pure Land]. Having attained rebirth, one is then born by transformation in a lotus bud and avoids the suffering of birth [from the womb]. One has the features of a pure youth, one's life span equals that of space itself, and one's body is free from all misfortune. One does not even hear the names "old age," "sickness," "death," and so on; how much less would [one experience] them in actuality? One attends personally upon the Buddha in the company of the sages. The water, the birds, and the groves of trees all produce the sound of the Dharma. Following one's fundamental nature, one goes from hearing to realization. Having directly fathomed the unattainable, what cause is there for dissatisfaction? Think of clothing and clothing comes; think of food and one obtains food. The towers, pavilions, halls, and quarters are all made of the seven jewels solely by transformation without any human effort. In this way, the seven sufferings of the Sahā world become the seven pleasures.

[In the Pure Land], one will have supernatural powers and great majestic strength. In a single instant one can travel to all the buddha lands of the ten directions without moving from one spot in order to worship the buddhas. One will seek out those who are superior and transform those who are inferior. One's mind will possess great wisdom and eloquence. From within a single dharma, one will universally discern the true characters of all dharmas and be able to teach the Dharma according to other beings' capacities without any errors. Even when speaking in conventional language, one will accord with the wondrous principle of the true character. Without the raging flames of the five aggregates, one feels the bliss of enjoying the stillness of body and mind. Thus, the sutra says, "No form of suffering is found there, one receives only the various pleasures. Therefore, it is called 'Utmost Bliss.'"[21] The suffering of the Sahā world is unspeakable; the bliss of Utmost Bliss is beyond compare.

Only deep faith in the Buddha's words absolutely free from doubt and perplexity can be called genuine faith. Be careful not to go making your own ignorant guesses based on the views of other religious paths that state that all the various inconceivable splendors of the Pure Land are just a matter of allegory or metaphors for psychological states and lack reality. With these kinds of heterodox opinions and false views, one loses the benefits of rebirth in the Pure Land. One cannot fail to know the great harm that comes of this![22]

Further Reading

Chen Chienhuang. "The Process of Establishing and Justifying the Thirteen Patriarchs of the Lotus School." Translated by Charles B. Jones. *Pacific World: Journal of the Institute of Buddhist Studies*, 3rd ser., 19 (2017): 129–48.

Jones, Charles B. *Chinese Pure Land Buddhism: Understanding a Tradition of Practice*. Pure Land Buddhist Studies. Honolulu: University of Hawai'i Press, 2019.

———. "Mentally Constructing What Already Exists: The Pure Land Thought of Chan Master Jixing Chewu (1741-1810)." *Journal of the International Association of Buddhist Studies* 23, no. 1 (2000): 43-70.

———. *Pure Land: History, Tradition, and Practice.* Boulder, CO: Shambhala, 2021.

———. *Taixu's "On the Establishment of the Pure Land in the Human Realm": A Translation and Study.* New York: Bloomsbury Academic, 2021.

Kiely, Jan. "The Charismatic Monk and the Chanting Masses: Master Yinguang and His Pure Land Revival Movement." In *Making Saints in Modern China*, edited by David Ownby, Vincent Goossaert, and Ji Zhe, 20-77. New York: Oxford, 2017.

Yinguang. *Pure-Land Zen, Zen Pure-Land: Letters from Patriarch Yin Kuang.* Translated by Thich Thien Tam. New York: Sutra Translation Committee of the United States and Canada, 1993.

———. "Treatise Resolving Doubts about the Pure Land (*Jingtu jueyi lun*) by Master Yinguang (1861-1940)." Translated by Charles B. Jones. *Pacific World: Journal of the Institute of Buddhist Studies*, 3rd series, no. 14 (2012): 27-61.

Master Benkong sometime after her ordination in 1950.

6 | From Laywoman to Tiantai Master

Benkong

BEATA GRANT

Born in 1900, it was not until nearly half a century later that the woman who would come to be known as Master Benkong (Original Emptiness; 1900-1969) would be ordained and subsequently named an official lineage holder in the tradition of Tiantai Buddhism. Before that, she was known primarily as a poet, educator, scholar, and Buddhist laywoman whose many published works appeared either under her family name of Zhang Ruzhao or Zhang Shenghui, the dharma name given to her by the famous reformer-monk Taixu (1890-1947; discussed in chapter 3).

Benkong was born in Cixi, a town located just east of Ningbo in the southeastern province of Zhejiang, to a merchant family with a long tradition of scholarship. When she was only two years old, her father died suddenly, leaving his wife, Mrs. Yang, to singlehandedly run the family business as well as care for Benkong, her elder sister Ruyue who was six, and her younger brother Lu'an who was just a toddler. Although Benkong was an intellectually precocious child, Mrs. Yang's hopes were pinned on her only son. Instead of encouraging Benkong to continue her studies at one of the girls' schools that were beginning to be established during this period, her mother arranged for her fifteen-year-old daughter to marry the scion of a local Cixi family. Determined to continue her education, Benkong persuaded her husband to move to Shanghai, where she studied English at the YWCA while he frequented the city's many nightclubs and bars. Shortly before turning twenty, she became pregnant and returned to Cixi to have the baby. She then returned to Shanghai alone and, without any financial or moral support from her family, continued to pursue her educational aspirations. It was not easy: She was about to graduate from the Shouzhen Middle School, a British-run Christian school, when she was informed that she could not receive her diploma unless she became a Christian. She had to drop out from another school because she could no longer afford the tuition. In 1925, she was expelled from yet another college for having been arrested and thrown briefly in jail for distributing leaflets during the May Thirtieth Incident.[1] Finally she succeeded in earning a degree in English from the National University.

It was in 1925 as well that Benkong published her first collection of poetry, *The Verdant Heavens Collection of Poems and Lyrics* (*Lütian yishici ji*), which was very well received and helped establish her reputation as a significant literary talent. Although later both she and her Buddhist teachers often referred to poetry writing as an obstacle to spiritual practice, during this period it most certainly helped her through some of her most difficult times, and even, she writes, kept her from committing suicide. While she wrote on a wide range of topics, the following short verse, entitled "Feelings," is a good example of the poems in her first collection:

> The past years of pain and sorrow
>   have been full of suffering.
> My life has been an unhappy one
>   that has left me feeling adrift.
> But—just look at that hoary pine
>   way down in the deep ravine:
> Having weathered wind and frost
>   it has become ever greener![2]

Although Benkong had originally planned to study medicine, she became increasingly involved in the fledgling women's movement in China and even managed to obtain a scholarship to go to the United States to study the social position of women there. However, her mother intervened and, in Benkong's own words, "came up with a hundred strategies designed to keep me from going." Her plans thwarted, she fell into a deep depression and, after months of barely eating or sleeping, became quite ill and was bedridden for nearly a year. During this dark period, she relied heavily on the support and friendship of the Presbyterian missionary Aimee Boddy Millican (1384-1974), whom she had met when she had first come to Shanghai.[3]

Benkong's idealism led her in 1925 to take up a position with the Zhejiang Office of Justice of the Guomindang Nationalist Government, which had been established that year. This would be her one and only encounter with the world of politics, and she soon left her job, having become quickly disillusioned. In 1927, the revolutionary, philologist, philosopher, and, latterly, Buddhist layman Zhang Tai-yan (1869-1936) recommended Benkong for a much more suitable position overseeing the organization of the first Nanjing Municipal Library, a position she would hold for four years. During this period, she also began to read even more widely in both Chinese and Western works of literature, philosophy, and natural science. She was excited at first by the thought of Western thinkers such as Arthur Schopenhauer and Friedrich Nietzsche. However, none of these fully satisfied her, and gradually she began to look more deeply into Indian philosophy and, closer to home, the neo-Confucian thinkers of the Song and Ming dynasties. Both her mother and grandmother had been lay Buddhists, but it was only now that she began to learn more about the work of contemporary Buddhist reformers such as Chan Master Jichan (a.k.a. "Eight Fingers," discussed in chapter 8).[4]

Meeting Master Yinguang

It was in the summer of 1928, while on holiday at Mount Putuo, an island just off the coast of Shanghai, that Benkong met the great

Pure Land master Yinguang (1861–1940; see chapter 5), the first of her four primary religious mentors. On her visit to the great master, who was then living at Putuo's Dharma Rain Temple (Fayu si), she presented him with a copy of her recently published collection of poetry. To her surprise, while Master Yinguang acknowledged her literary gifts, he sternly reproved her for what he considered to be a very un-Buddhist indulgence in self-pity and resentment. (This tension between her love of poetry and literary pursuits in general, along with her yearning for an authentic lived spiritual life, would continue for many years and was not easily resolved.) After her meeting with Yinguang, Benkong's personal interest in Buddhism began to deepen, and several years later she took formal refuge with him. At that time, she wrote a letter to Aimee Boddy Millican in which she carefully laid out what she felt to be the major differences between Buddhism and Christianity, gently telling her friend that she had made her choice and that from this point on would not welcome any attempts to persuade her to change her mind.

Benkong's growing commitment to Buddhism as a way of life can be seen in her acquisition, in 1930, of a small piece of property in the foothills just outside of her hometown of Cixi. She named it the "Gaya Farm and Forest" (Gaya nonglin), after Bodhgaya, the site of the Buddha's enlightenment. For much of the rest of her life, it would serve as Benkong's home base, where she grew her own food, studied, wrote, meditated, and received guests.

Although many of her politically active friends accused her of turning her back on the world, Benkong by no means lived a life of quiet seclusion. In fact, she became increasingly involved in the Buddhist reform movement. At the request of Taixu's senior student Daxing (1900–1952), then the editor of the popular Buddhist periodical *Sound of the Sea Tide* (*Haichao yin*) founded by Taixu, she wrote a piece entitled "I Believe in Buddhism," which was reprinted in at least two other Buddhist periodicals, and several years later, even translated into Japanese. This would be followed by dozens of articles and essays published both in the *Sound of the Sea Tide* and other Buddhist periodicals. The topics of these written pieces reflected Benkong's wide-ranging scholarly interests. Just a few examples include "A Comparative Study of Christianity and Buddhism," "Buddhist Thought in the Poetry of Bai Juyi," and "Tolstoy and Farming Chan," in which she compares Leo Tolstoy's later reform efforts on his estate, Yasnaya Polyana, to those of Tang dynasty Chan monks determined to be self-sufficient. Benkong also wrote important articles on the status of women in Buddhism both past and present, and biographies of contemporary monks, nuns, and laywomen. She also continued to write poetry, although now her poems were more directly inspired by her newfound Buddhist faith. In 1934, she published a collection entitled *The Seagull Collection* (*Haiou ji*). In 1935, she published poems and essays on specifically Buddhist topics in a collection entitled *Prajñā Flowers* (*Bore hua*), a preface for which was written by Master Taixu. By this time, Benkong had become one of China's most well-known and highly respected Buddhist laywomen.

Meeting Master Jueming

In 1936, Benkong was invited to head a new seminary for Buddhist nuns associated with the Fachang Temple in Ningbo. It had been established by Taixu and Jiang Ruilian (1890-1937), the younger sister of the Nationalist government leader, Jiang Jieshi (Chiang Kai-shek, 1887-1975). Although the seminary disbanded after less than a year, it was there that Benkong met the Chan Master Jueming (ca. 1896-1939). Benkong's religious exchanges during this brief period with this extraordinary nun were so intense and life-changing that she would later refer to her as the second of her most important religious mentors.

A spirited anti-Qing political activist and educator in her early youth—her great hero was the feminist revolutionary martyr Qiu Jin (1875-1907)—Jueming had become disillusioned with politics and in 1920 took ordination at the Haihuai Temple in Yixing, Jiangsu Province, with Linji Chan Master Miaocan Qingxu (d.u.), whose dharma transmission she later received. After Miaocan Qingxu's death, Benkong studied with other eminent teachers, including two of the most famous early Buddhist reformers and educators, Chan Master Yingci (1873-1965) and Tiantai Master Dixian (1858-1932). In time, Jueming herself became known for her deep mastery of the *Śūraṃgama Sutra* and other important Buddhist texts, on which she lectured widely. She was also known for her strict ascetic practice and for being as eccentric, fierce, and spiritually uncompromising as some of the old Tang dynasty Chan masters were said to have been. Like Master Yinguang, Jueming also felt that Benkong's considerable literary and intellectual talents had ultimately become impediments to her spiritual advancement, and she urged her to become a nun. Benkong was not, however, yet ready to take this next step. Indeed, she had always disapproved of women becoming nuns as a way of escaping unhappy personal circumstances rather than because they felt a genuine call to the religious life.

Meeting Master Jingkuan

After the seminary was disbanded, Benkong returned home to Cixi where she would spend the war years. It was there that she began an intensive period of scriptural study and meditation practice with the man she would regard as the third of her four major teachers: Chan Master Jingkuan (also known as Jingguan, 1872-1943). Tonsured at fifteen, Jingkuan had been ordained at eighteen at the Guoqing Temple on Mount Tiantai, the home temple of the Tiantai school of Chinese Buddhism, and subsequently received dharma transmission from the eminent Tiantai master Dixian. He was a deeply learned scholar as well as a highly realized practitioner, and he soon acquired a reputation for his eloquent dharma talks. As was not uncommon during this period, Jingkuan also studied with several well-known Chan teachers, including the Linji Chan master Qingquan Yinkai, the abbot of the prestigious Jiangtian (Jinshan) Chan Monastery, one of China's most important Chan Buddhist training centers. Impressed by Jingkuan's abilities, Qingquan Yinkai also bestowed dharma transmission on him and not long afterward recommended that he succeed him as abbot of the Jingtian Chan Monastery, a position Jingkuan held for five years before retiring due to poor health.

Benkong had actually met Jingkuan briefly during a visit to Jingtian Chan Monastery in 1930, at which time he had remarked that she was "half a monastic," and predicted that they would meet again seven years later. By this time, Jingkuan was residing at Cixi's Chongfu Temple, not far from where Benkong lived. Over the next several years, she received intensive training from Jingkuan, who, apparently intent on training her to be a dharma teacher, provided her with detailed oral commentaries on the major Buddhist scriptures, after which she was instructed to convey her understanding to the nun who had come with her from the seminary as well as to the residents of local nunneries. Benkong greatly appreciated both Jingkuan's commitment to rigorous practice and his wide-ranging and comprehensive mastery of all the major schools and traditions, including Chan, Tiantai, and Pure Land. A major essay she wrote during this period, entitled "Chan and Tiantai," reflects her deep interest in the syncretic approach embodied by Jingkuan.

Meeting Master Genhui

It was around this time that Benkong first became interested in the Lotus Samādhi, one of the fundamental practices of Tiantai Buddhism, which was most fully elaborated upon by the great Tiantai master Zhiyi (538–597) and is still practiced today. Hearing that Tiantai Master Genhui (1881–1951), a good friend of Master Jingkuan's, was conducting a Lotus Samādhi retreat in Ningbo, she decided to attend and try it out for herself. Master Genhui, who was born to a farming family and was drawn to the religious life as teenager, was one of the many dharma successors of Tiantai Master Dixian, and for a time he served as Dixian's personal attendant. In 1932, while on a closed retreat at the Puji Temple in Cixi, Genhui had a life-changing experience while practicing the Lotus Samādhi. After this, he became an especially strong proponent of this practice and subsequently conducted many twenty-one-day retreats, which were attended by both monastics and laypeople.

When Benkong met with him before the retreat began, he expressed his general disappointment, if not outright disdain, for women and girls who, while they expressed interest in studying Buddhism and might even sit for a short intensive retreat, often left the temple having completely failed to grasp the true Dharma. Rising to the challenge, Benkong expressed her fierce determination to persist in her practice until she had grasped the authentic Buddhadharma, regardless of any difficulties she might face. Moreover, she vowed that once she had attained some measure of realization, she would dedicate herself to teaching other women. In fact, Benkong, who had devoted much of her life to the cause of women's education, appears by this point to have herself become disillusioned at what she perceived as many women's continued narrowness of vision and their unwillingness to join forces to work for the betterment of society. In this she reflects the despair felt by many of her reformist contemporaries in the face of political corruption and the devastation wreaked on China by war. For Benkong, it seemed increasingly the case that the only liberation worth its salt was spiritual rather than political.

Benkong's first twenty-one-day retreat with Master Genhui proved to be very significant, and, as she would later explain, afforded her with spiritual insights and experiences that she had not been able to attain with her previous practices, including more traditional forms of Chan meditation. Master Genhui was known for his uncompromising, even harsh, training methods, and retreat participants were afforded no comforts whatsoever. Benkong, however, appears to have found Genhui's strict discipline of great benefit; she mentions, for example, his use of a judicious whack of the stick traditionally used in Linji Chan Buddhist meditation halls to keep students from dozing off. Benkong would go on to study more intensively with Genhui and to participate in many more such retreats. As an indication of her deepening commitment to Buddhist practice as well as scholarship, around this time Benkong also formally took the bodhisattva vows at the Chongfu Temple, with Master Jingkuan and Master Genhui both presiding.[5] After the death of Master Jingkuan in 1943, Master Genhui became her principal teacher.

In 1945, Master Genhui was named the abbot of the Guanzong Lecture Monastery in Ningbo, which had been founded in 1919 by Dixian. It was an important center of monastic training known for its relatively more conservative and traditional methods and curriculum, although it had fallen into disrepair during the war years. Master Genhui invited Benkong not only to become an instructor at the Guanzong Lecture Monastery but also to assume responsibility for recording and transcribing many of his sutra lectures and dharma talks. Then, in 1949, the year the People's Republic of China was established, Master Genhui invited her to take up residence in the nearby Wonderful Voice Vihara (Miaoyin jingshe), where he had lived before becoming abbot. There, Benkong—still a laywoman—continued to engage in her own practice, as well as give dharma talks. Finally, on February 8 of the following year, Benkong requested ordination. Master Genhui, now ailing and near death, officially named her as one of his four dharma successors (and the only woman) and a forty-fifth generation Tiantai master.

Benkong's full transformation from scholar-poet to Buddhist master is exemplified by the fact that when she too fell seriously ill, in 1951, she asked her disciple to burn the poems and essays she had written over the previous two decades. Fortunately the disciple turned them over to a lay devotee instead, and 1953 saw the publication of The Mist and Waters Collection (Yanshui ji), a final collection comprised of twenty-seven prose pieces and 146 poems.

Unfortunately, very little is known of the last decades of Benkong's life, especially since she no longer took it upon herself to write about her personal experiences as she had previously. We know that after recovering from her illness, she continued to lecture widely in the Shanghai and Ningbo areas. She also appears to have finally realized her dream of traveling abroad, and between 1954 and 1956 she made several visits to India and Japan. The next we hear of Benkong is 1968, when during the turbulent first years of the Cultural Revolution, she was ordered to Shanghai to undergo a year of "reeducation" and self-criticism, no doubt particularly severe because of her earlier close association with Chiang Kai-Shek's family and the National government. In 1969, the Wonderful Voice Vihara was turned into a factory, although Benkong adamantly refused to disrobe. Her health had always been precarious, and the privations and punishments endured during this time finally broke her. In September of that year, Benkong passed away at another small temple in Cixi. In 1994, the Wonderful Voice Vihara was restored and is today once again a working Buddhist convent. A commemorative hall in which hangs a large photograph of Master Benkong has kept her memory alive.

The Translation

In 1936, Benkong published a long essay comprising a scholarly introduction to the basic doctrinal teachings of Tiantai together with personal accounts of her first experiences as a (lay) participant in a Lotus Samādhi retreat conducted by Master Genhui.[6] Tiantai is an indigenous school of Chinese Buddhism known for its emphasis on both scriptural study (especially the *Lotus Sutra*, which is held as the culmination of the Buddha's teaching) and meditative practices as a means of achieving awakening. In terms of the latter, it is known for the so-called Four Samādhis. While the term *samādhi* is commonly thought to refer to a state of meditative absorption or bliss, in this case, it also refers to the various disciplines and practices used to realize these awakened states—in other words, the means as well as the ends. These meditative practices were most fully elaborated upon by Zhiyi in various texts such as the monumental *Clear Serenity, Quiet Insight* (*Mohe zhiguan*) and more specific practice manuals such as the *Procedure for Lotus Samādhi Penitence* (*Fahua sanmei chanyi*), a detailed guide to one of the most well known of the Four Samādhis and one that is still practiced today. It is also the one with which Master Genhui, and later Benkong, would come to be most closely associated.

The Lotus Samādhi is actually divided into two types of twenty-one-day practices, which Zhiyi regarded as ultimately complementary: the Lotus Samādhi without Characteristics and the Lotus Samādhi with Characteristics. The first of these focuses primarily on maintaining a constant and single-minded contemplative awareness of the ultimate emptiness of all things regardless of what one is doing. The second of these, often referred to as the Lotus Samādhi Penitence, comprises a structured sequence of ritual activities including a formal veneration of the buddhas and bodhisattvas, reading and recitation of the *Lotus Sutra*, seated meditation, and perhaps most importantly, the heartfelt confession and repentance of sins committed over one's lifetimes past and present that have been caused by an unenlightened use of the six sense faculties: the eyes, ears, nose, tongue, body, and mind. Benkong participated in both types of Lotus Samādhi practices, and in her essay and elsewhere, she writes about her experience with them. The translation below is her narrative account of her initial experience with the Lotus Samādhi with Characteristics.

BENKONG

The Actual Practice of the Lotus Samādhi with Characteristics

For seven or eight years, I had been engaged in research on Song-Ming neo-Confucian thought and Western philosophy as well as Buddhism. Whenever I had a little free time from my work, I would do some casual reading in the Buddhist scriptures, but my investigations were amateur and my understanding cursory. Although I was just a Buddhist follower who had taken the three refuges but had not yet gone so far as to take the five precepts,[7] in my heart I felt an earnest desire to seek out the Dharma. So, in 1934, I resigned from several of my teaching positions and went to Wuhan to study and practice.[8] In 1935, again because I wanted to practice the Dharma, I also resigned from several of my official posts. When it comes to Mahāyāna repentance rituals, normally nonordained persons are not allowed to participate. But since it is written in *Clear Serenity, Quiet Insight* that "lay people are also permitted [to cultivate this practice] but they should make ready three simply sewn robes in preparation for [taking part in] Buddhist rituals,"[9] I went ahead and prepared a set of cotton robes. I was, however, still not allowed to enter the inner sanctuary [as a layperson] and could only carry out the repentance rituals, sutra recitations, and seated meditations in the outer sanctuary.

A few days before the start of the repentance practice period,
I composed this pentasyllabic old-style poem[10] to present to Meditation Master Genhui, the Lotus Altar Master:

I've learned by experience about society's changes,
And about people by having had dealings with them.
Understanding as I do the illusions of this floating life,
Why would I get caught up seeking profit and fame?
Out of the limelight, I've been happy in my retreat;[11]
Living incognito and keeping close watch over myself.
I've assiduously explored and examined the Three Baskets,[12]
And meticulously assessed and appraised the ten schools.[13]
Words have become a hindrance and I've made little headway:
I've an intellectual understanding[14] but shamefully no
    practice.
I've been wasting my time on fruitless and empty pursuits,
When will I ever be able to realize the Buddha's Way?
I have had the fortune to meet a clearsighted man,
And with great joy commit all my heart and soul.
When the icy winds dispel the frost and snow
The buds on the winter plum trees appear;
It is between rows of boulders standing tall
That the water in the creek is limpidly clear.[15]
I entreat the master to plant the standard of the Dharma,
And with sword in hand,[16] promulgate the true teaching.
When the six thieves[17] willingly acknowledge their chief,
The eight winds[18] will grow silent and not make a sound.
If the crooked timber stays close to the master craftsman
His rules of practice will naturally cause it to straighten.
Unruly soldiers must be controlled by an intrepid leader
If they are to enjoy a long march of ten thousand miles!
I vow to do away with my habit of exaggerating,
And learn from the simple ways of countryfolk.
I vow to cut my attachment to literary pursuits
And to stop complaining that life has been unfair.

For moral discipline, I will rely on the Ten Recitations,[19]
And aspire to carrying out the four bodhisattva vows.[20]
I will do my utmost to cultivate the six perfections,
And when it is called for, I will study the five sciences.[21]
Instead, I will make utmost use of this lifetime,[22]
To look deeply into the principles of the unborn.
I only hope for your compassionate acceptance,
Of this humble expression of sincerity.

At two o'clock on the morning of October 15, 1935, we entered the sanctuary and made obeisance to the Three Jewels as well as a penitential offering.[23] Then, kneeling, we meditated on the lines about the ten mentalities that go against and [the ten mentalities that go] with the flow of samsara:[24] "Today, facing the buddhas of the ten directions and the bodhisattva Samantabhadra, we [declare our] deep belief in causality, arouse a deep sense of shame, publicly confess and repent, sever all thoughts that continue [from previous misdeeds], arouse the mind of bodhi, and encourage the three karmas (of word, thought, and deed); review the serious transgressions of the past, and rejoice in even the slightest bit of virtue on the part of both commoners and sages. We remember the great virtue and wisdom possessed by the buddhas of the ten directions, which can save and rescue us as well as all sentient beings, taking us from the two seas of death to the banks of the three virtues.[25] From beginningless time, due to [our] not understanding that all the dharmas are intrinsically empty, we have committed all kinds of evil. Now that we understand emptiness, we seek awakened wisdom and for the sake of all sentient beings, widely engage in all kinds of good and completely sever all evil."[26]

[As I meditated on these words], I couldn't help but be secretly filled with joy: it was as if all the buddhas and bodhisattvas were intent on engaging in practice for all sentient beings and not just for themselves, which accorded completely with my innermost aspirations. Having had a deep experience of the world—the hot and cold of human relationships and people's dirty and devious ways—I realized early on the intrinsic emptiness of all things. As my basic needs were met, I did not need to rush about seeking more, and could instead indulge my love of poetry and books, or of carefree wandering among forests and streams.[27] Why would I want to put so much effort into seeking the Buddhadharma [especially when I was] despised by others for doing so?[28]

However, I found my thoughts returning again and again to those of my compatriots indulging themselves in sensual desires, harassing and fighting each other, hating and killing each other. As they lost their way, they became more and more degenerate. If I did not make every effort, however modest, to dispel their mental clouds of confusion and awaken their correct understanding, I would truly be falling short on my duties as an ordinary woman![29] When my thoughts reached this point, I began to silently pray: "If during these twenty-one days I am able to attain a modicum of spiritual insight, then I must take every opportunity that arises to do the best I can for the benefit of both myself and others so as to repay the compassion of the Three Jewels."

On the afternoon of the third day, as we were reciting the text of the six sense faculties confessional, [30] we came to this passage: "Through innumerable existences, the function of your sense faculty of sight has caused you to yearn for and become attached to various kinds of forms. Because of your attachment to various forms, you have been passionate about the smallest of matters. Because of your passions for the smallest of matters, you [have been reborn in] the body of a woman.[31] Wherever you take birth, in life after life, you are attracted and attached to all kinds of forms. Forms spoil your eyes, and you become a slave to emotion and passions: forms thus make you wander throughout the three realms [of samsara]."[32] I suddenly found myself filled with mixed emotions, and my tears fell like rain, dampening my clothes. When it came time to sit in meditation, all the sufferings I had endured over the first half of my life appeared in detail before me. I tried everything I could to dispel them, but to no avail.

I've always been conscious of things I've done in the past, but ordinarily I would make use of the rational mind to purge it almost completely away. Now, propelled forward by the radiance of the

Buddha's mind, the shadows cast by the six sense fields of the past rose again in my consciousness where they had been hidden away. Therefore, during the evening period of repentance, I fervently beseeched the Three Jewels to assist me in clearing away these serious hindrances (to awakening). It has been several months since I performed this deep repentance and, fortunately, I've not experienced this sort of deluded mind-state again.

On the fourth day, we recited the passage from the introductory chapter of the *Lotus Sutra*: "And I see Buddha sons whose minds have no attachments, who use this wonderful wisdom to seek the unsurpassed way,"[33] and from the chapter entitled "Expedient Means": "The Buddha, through the power of expedient means, has shown them the teachings of the three vehicles, prying living beings loose from this or that attachment and allowing them to attain release."[34] I could not help but reflect on the words of Lu You: "The ability to remain unswayed by external things is [true] learning; that which uncultivated people love [cannot really be called good] poetry."[35] As for me, I am by nature very straightforward; as soon as there is the possibility of unpleasant words [being exchanged], I drop it and just leave. I am also a person of deep feelings: when I hear the birds, my heart is startled and facing the flowers, I shed tears.[36] I am always being moved by external things; I am always being stirred by my surroundings. Although I've tried very hard to change this around, in the end I've not yet been able to completely eradicate [these failings]; in fact, sometimes I cannot avoid becoming excited by memories of the pleasures of the chase, and like Mr. Feng, find myself longing to return to my former métier.[37] The *Platform Sutra* says. "If you are able to transform things, then you are equal to the Tathagata."[38] We know, then, that the Buddhadharma is indeed more excellent than the way of Confucius. Because for Buddhism, it is not just that the mind can be unattached and unswayed by externals; it is also able to reverse the myriad streams and return them to their intrinsic nature.

On the evening of the sixth day, when it was time to recite the sutras, because all the seats were occupied by others, I went to sit in the corner of the room. I was seated rather far from the lamps and, unable to make out the characters of the *Lotus Sutra* text, I placed it up on a bamboo stand so I could read it. However, finding it still difficult to read clearly, I was looking all around for a more suitable spot when Meditation Master Genhui noticed me and scolded me, saying, "If you are so stupid, how can you recite the sutras! If you drop down the bamboo stand, the meaning of the sutra will automatically become clear." Although I could not help but feel mortified, I had an inkling of what he meant.[39]

On the seventh day, as we were reciting the six sense faculties repentance, we came to the lines, "As for the sins committed by the tongue [such as] careless speech and frivolous talk…uttering unhelpful words and fomenting disorder, preaching a Dharma that is not the Dharma…pushing one's views when one is in the wrong, is like stoking the fire."[40] I felt deeply ashamed that ever since childhood I have delighted in reciting poetry and have written many lyrics about the charm of the scenery. I've enjoyed engaging in pleasantries and often crack jokes and make fun of things for no reason at all. I have also tended to think highly of myself and have often indulged in sophistry. When I served as the administrator of such and such a school, being partial, I would strongly laud its instruction. I sincerely hope that from now on I can control my speech and be more circumspect in my writings. If something is not fair-minded, I will not say it. If something is not important, then I will not take up the pen. As a reminder against making these kinds of mistakes, I will inscribe on my chair these lines by eminent Master Yongming: "Only when one is slow to speak can one distinguish the fork in the road; only when one acts like a fool can one shut the gate of [fighting over] right and wrong"[41]

On the first day of the second week, as we were sitting in meditation, I heard the swallows outside the window noisily scrambling over their nests, and a girl student flashed me a smile.[42] I smiled back but then suddenly found myself being scolded by Master Gen who had seen me: "You say that your remorse should be very deep, but if you do not thoroughly take yourself to task and diligently work to purify yourself, then there will be no gate through which you can enter the Way!" Although I could not keep my face from turning red and my ears burning, in my mind I felt cool and refreshed!

On the third day of the second week, we recited the [lines from] the "Expedient Means" chapter of the *Lotus Sutra*: "It would be better if I did not preach the Law, but quickly entered into nirvana."[43] We know, therefore, that even someone as great and powerful as our teacher Śākyamuni Buddha still felt some hesitation before beginning to teach. When it comes to ordinary earthbound mortals like us, to want to spread the Buddhadharma at a time when different religions vie for dominance in a degenerate age is truly as difficult as ascending into the sky! Just thinking of it strikes fear into my heart.

On the fifth day of the second week, Mr. Millican[44] sent me a letter by express mail which said, "The Sir X____ of England has invited you to go with us to India to visit Y___[45] and participate in the work of world peace. The date is fast approaching so I hope you can quickly pack and come to Shanghai so that we can travel there together." Although I couldn't keep my heart from pounding with excitement, I went to discuss the matter with Master Genhui. Upon receiving a profound teaching about the harm caused by fame and fortune, I felt ashamed of my inability to control my nature and that I was often stirred up by external circumstances. I then lost no time in resolutely but politely turning down the invitation.

On the first day of the third week we were reciting from the "Distinctions in Benefits" chapter of the *Lotus Sutra*: "For countless kalpas dwelling in a deserted and quiet place; and if he practices sitting and walking exercises, banishing drowsiness, constantly regulating his mind, and as a result of such actions is able to produce states of meditation..."[46] For the first time I began to understand that if one wants to give rise to meditative concentration, one needs to focus the mind. If the first thought is not controlled, then deluded notions will enter through that first thought; if the second thought is not controlled, then deluded notions will enter through that second thought. But if one can control every thought, then one can quiet each thought. One must try to follow [the advice of] Dharma Master

Shenxiu: "At all times you must strive to polish it, and must not let dust alight."[47] Comparing my experience with the lines of this gāthā, I find it is reliable and borne out by the evidence.

At dawn of the fifth day of the third week, while reciting the six sense faculties repentance, we came to the passage that reads, "Śākyamuni Buddha is called Vairocana Buddha, the universally pervading one. One should understand that all things are Buddhadharma, but because of the discriminations of deluded conceptualizations, one suffers all manner of anxieties. Thus although I am in the midst of enlightenment, I see only impurity. Although I am in the midst of liberation, only entanglements arise."[48] Suddenly I felt that in the present moment my body and mind and the objective world had all disappeared, the [sense of] a separate self and [notions of] right and wrong had nowhere to stand. A pure ocean of awakening as vast as space; a sliver of spiritual luminosity, shining without boundary. It was not something that words could describe, not something that brush and ink could paint. Normally I felt the activities of worship and repentance went on too long and that they were tiring, but this time they seemed to be over in a snap of the finger. It was truly a case of "doing the Buddha's work in a great dream, sitting in meditation in the bodhimandala of the moon's reflection in the river."[49]

To sum up the results of my practice of the Lotus Samādhi with Characteristics, I was unable to purify the six sense faculties or to open forth the wise vision of a Buddha.[50] But my heart of faith was suddenly awakened, and I experienced dharma joy.[51] The four elements feel light and smooth, and I am filled with strength and vigor.[52] Moreover, I am now aware of the sins of the six sense faculties committed in the past and the causes that gave rise to them. I have generated a profound shame as well as profound fear [of what these sins can lead to.] I truly hope that from now on I will be able to control my anger and restrain my desires and do the work of "subduing myself and returning to the rites."[53] I no longer have any desire to engage in idle and foolish talk or in thoughtless activities that add to my ignorance. I will work hard to be a "fool" who is content with the way things are and let other people insult me if they so desire, calling me slow-witted and dull. I will seek to do nothing more than "eradicate past karma in accord with conditions and desist from creating any new calamities."[54] [As the verse goes],

> The myriad things can all be found in this Way,
> Its one taste[55] points to a preordained affinity.[56]

Further Reading

Grant, Beata. "Thirty Years of Dream-Wandering: The Conversion Narratives of Zhang Ruzhao 張汝釗 (1900–1969)," *Nan Nü: Men, Women and Gender in China* 19, no. 1 (2017): 28–63.

Luk, Charles, trans. *The Surangama Sutra (Leng Yan Ching)*. London: Rider, 1966.

Stevenson, Daniel. "Four Kinds of Samadhi in Early T'ien-t'ai," in *Traditions of Meditation in Chinese Buddhism*, edited by Peter Gregory, 45–96. Honolulu: University of Hawai'i Press, 1986.

———. "The T'ien-tai Four Forms of Samadhi and Late North-South Dynasties, Sui, and Early T'ang Buddhist Devotionalism." PhD diss., Columbia University, 1987.

Swanson, Paul L., trans. *Clear Serenity, Quiet Insight: T'ien-Tai Chih-I's Mo-ho Chih-Kuan*. Nanzan Library of Asian Religion and Culture. Honolulu: University of Hawai'i Press, 2017.

Watson, Burton, trans. *The Lotus Sutra*. New York: Columbia University Press, 1993.

Portrait of Master Changxing, date and location unknown.

7 | Student and Huayan Master

Changxing

ERIK HAMMERSTROM

This chapter introduces one part of an introductory Buddhist text published in 1928 in the revolutionary Chinese Buddhist journal *The Sound of the Sea Tide*. Its author, the monk Changxing (1896–1939), was a gifted student and teacher of Buddhism. He was well acquainted with many of the figures discussed in this book, and although he is not as well known as Taixu (chapter 3) or Xuyun (chapter 1), he had a significant impact on monastic education in China. Like most Chinese Buddhists, Changxing studied and taught broadly in the Mahāyāna tradition, but this chapter will focus on his legacy as a teacher of the school of East Asian Buddhist philosophy known in Chinese as Huayan. Huayan thought, which elaborates on the interconnectedness of all things, is not well known in the West but its teachings suffuse the entirety of East Asian Buddhism.

Changxing's Career in Buddhist Education

Changxing was born in 1896 in Rugao, which lies along the north bank of the lower Yangzi River roughly two hours north of Shanghai by car. Changxing's family took him to receive basic Buddhist ordination at a local temple when he was eleven, but he did not shave his head and he continued to dress as a layperson. He was a precocious child, and his family made sure he was steeped in classical Chinese learning from an early age. In 1905, the imperial Chinese government undertook major reforms in education, and new schools began to teach modernized curricula that included Western subjects. Many provincial governments established teacher's colleges to prepare people to serve in the new public schools that were being created across the empire. Because of his talents, Changxing's Buddhist master sent him to attend the teacher's college that had been established in Jiangsu Province. The training he received there helped him build a firm foundation for the vocation in monastic education that he pursued for the rest of his life.

The Empire of China fell in 1911, and in 1912 the democratic Republic of China took its place. Changxing graduated from the teacher's college in 1912 in the midst of these historic events and, at the age of sixteen, he traveled downriver to Shanghai to enroll in a brand-new monastic training program called Huayan University. Structured around an extensive series of lectures on the *Huayan Sutra*, this program was the brainchild of the monk Yuexia (1858–1917). He is widely revered today as the founder of modern Chinese Huayan studies, and all the major teachers of this tradition today trace their lineages back to him. Because he did not leave any writings behind, his legacy is defined entirely by the students he taught and the successes they had in passing their education on to others. Changxing was one of these students.

Huayan University received its initial funding from Liza Roos Hardoon (1864–1941), a biracial French-Chinese woman. An ardent supporter of Buddhism, she hosted the Huayan University in buildings on the grounds of the palatial estate she owned with her husband, a wealthy Jewish businessman from Baghdad named Silas Hardoon (1851–1931). Yuexia ran his program according to the strict rule of the traditional Chinese Buddhist monastic code. Because of this, he insisted that Changxing, who was still dressing and living like a layperson, first return to his hometown to get his head shaved by his master and then go to one of the major public monasteries to receive full monastic ordination. Changxing followed Yuexia's guidance and was ordained at Mt. Baohua, the most respected ordination monastery in the region.

Every day at Huayan University, its five dozen students attended the lectures given by Yuexia on the *Huayan Sutra*, as well as supplemental lectures delivered by his longtime assistant Yingci (1873-1965), and even other students, who were selected by the traditional system of drawing lots. They also engaged in two hours of meditation each day. Yuexia's insistence on a rigorous following of the monastic rule eventually led to an emotional and permanent falling out between him and Liza Hardoon, and he was forced to move the school to the nearby city of Hangzhou in 1914. Yuexia and the students who came with him, including Changxing, were able to complete the planned course of study at Haichao Temple in 1916.

Although he had now completed a full intensive study of the *Huayan Sutra*, the longest sutra in the Chinese canon, Changxing was not finished with his studies. Upon graduation, at the age of twenty, he sat a Chan retreat at Tianning Monastery under Yekai (1852-1922), Yuexia's own Dharma master. Changxing then spent two years studying Tiantai philosophy with Dixian at his Guanzong Research Society. Having established a firm foundation for himself in Chinese Buddhist doctrine and practice, Changxing was ready to make the transition from student to teacher.

The monastic educational scene in China was in a great deal of flux in the early 1920s. The establishment of the Republic did not recreate Chinese society or its traditions overnight, and many new initiatives came and went amid the social churn of the 1910s and 1920s. For Changxing, this meant that he spent the rest of his life trying to create a stable institution in which he could teach the next generation of Chinese monastics. He first accepted a teaching invitation from Yingci, who was Yuexia's senior student and one of the teachers at Huayan University. Yuexia had passed away in 1917, and Yingci wanted to carry on his teacher's legacy by relaunching Huayan University in the city of Changshu, near Shanghai. The new Huayan University started in 1920, but it was forced to shut down the following year after its funding ran out. In the aftermath of the school's failure, Changxing went upriver to the neighboring Anhui Province to teach at a monastic school there. After two years Changxing relocated this school, and most of his eighty students, to the Southern Putuo Temple, located many miles to the south in the coastal city of Xiamen in Fujian Province. This new school proved to be just what Changxing was hoping for, and with the support of the temple's abbot and Taixu, the school became the Minnan Buddhist Institute, which was one of the longest-lived and largest monastic schools of the era. Changxing served as the school's vice principal and taught classes. The piece that is translated here is taken from a short book he published during his time teaching at the institute, which he most likely created for his students as a general introduction to Buddhism.

Changxing collaborated with Taixu on several other educational ventures before traveling back to Jiangsu in 1931 to assume the abbotship of Guangxiao Temple. He had received dharma transmission in the Linji Chan lineage from the temple's former abbot, Pei'an (n.d.), in the summer of 1924. (Unlike Japanese Buddhism, Chinese Buddhism is not sectarian, and it is not unusual for monastics to receive dharma transmission in a Chan lineage, even if they focus their practice or study on another school of Buddhism, such as Huayan.) At Guangxiao Temple, Changxing began to lay the groundwork for another Huayan training program at the temple, but he became ill and had to hand both the abbotship and the running of the school over to his student Nanting. Changxing moved to Shanghai to convalesce and eventually recovered from his illness enough to accept a position as secretary for the Chinese Buddhist Association. In this important role of national leadership, he tried to play a mediating role between the supporters of the great reformer Taixu and the more conservative supporters of Yuanying (1878–1953). These two formidable monks had quite different visions for the future of Chinese Buddhism, and this produced ongoing tensions within the organization. The Japanese invasion and retreat of Chinese forces from Shanghai in 1937 put an end to the organization, however, and amid the social pressures of life in wartime Shanghai, Changxing's illness returned, and he passed away in 1939.

Like his teacher Yuexia, Changxing's greatest legacy lay in the lives of the hundreds of students he taught over his career. He believed deeply that the strength of Chinese Buddhism depended on the education of its monastics, and several of his students went on to have impacts in Chinese Buddhist history. Perhaps most notable among these was Nanting, who is an important link in the modern Huayan lineage. Nanting fled to Taiwan after the Communists won China's civil war, and he eventually founded the Huayan Lotus Society there. It is one of the most robust Huayan-centered groups in the world today and has trained hundreds of nuns in the intricacies of Huayan thought.

Huayan Philosophy

The school of thought discussed in this translation is known by several different names. In China it is often referred to as the Xianshou school, which is what Changxing calls it here. Xianshou is another name for the monk Fazang (643–712), who is usually celebrated as the most important architect of the school's philosophy. Throughout East Asia, and even in China, however, the school is more commonly referred to as the Huayan school, taking its name from the sutras that it claims as the primary source of its teachings.

There are three versions of the *Huayan Sutra* used throughout East Asia, which were translated into Chinese in the fifth through eighth centuries C.E. This text is known in English as the *Flower Garland Sutra*. In Sanskrit this text could be called the *Avataṃsaka* or *Gaṇḍavyūha Sutra*, but this cannot be confirmed because there is no Sanskrit version of the text. Although Changxing, and the larger Buddhist tradition, claim that there was a single, original *Huayan Sutra* taught by the Buddha, contemporary scholars have concluded on the basis of text-critical methods that the *Huayan Sutras* were likely created by combining multiple texts that were already circulating independently. This combining may have happened somewhere in central Asia. Regardless of its provenance, the eighty-volume version of the *Huayan Sutra* is the longest single text in East Asian Buddhism. It discusses an extensive range of Buddhist doctrine, from ideas about the true nature of dependent origination to the many practices and stages of the bodhisattva path. Because of its breadth and profundity, the *Huayan Sutra* came to be identified by Buddhists in East Asia as a record of the first teachings given by the Buddha and is considered to encompass and express the entirety of the Buddha's enlightenment. That enlightenment is described as synonymous with the Dharma Realm, the totality of existence in all its inexpressibly glorious and "flower-adorned" (the literal meaning of *huayan*) profusion. The sutra describes the Dharma Realm as equal to the mind of all buddhas, and none other than the very identity of Vairocana, the great sun Buddha.

In order to make sense of this expansive, somewhat positive, and ultimately unfathomable vision of reality, a new school of thought developed in China during the Sui and Tang dynasties (sixth through ninth centuries C.E.). Building on the ideas of earlier thinkers, a handful of monastic writers expanded on the basic premise of unity and causal connection presented in the *Huayan Sutra* to form a coherent body of philosophy and practice that sought to explain its dharmic truth. By the eleventh century, the Chinese tradition recognized five Huayan thinkers as the key contributors, or patriarchs, of the school. In order, these were Dushun (557–640), Zhiyan (602–668), Fazang, Chengguan (737–838), and Zongmi (780–841). Fazang is generally considered the greatest thinker, but Chengguan's extensive commentaries on the *Huayan Sutra* probably had the greatest impact over the course of history. In the translation below, Changxing makes use of both of these masters' ideas.

Huayan writings aim to describe the indescribable. Unlike Chan masters, whom they greatly influenced, Huayan writers did not shy away from diving into discursive language to try to get their point across. For this reason, it is useful to give an overview here of some of the main concepts that Changxing uses in the text below. The first thing we see in the text, after an introduction of the Huayan school's main thinkers, is a systematic discussion of all the various doctrines within the Buddhadharma. Such discussions are not unique to Huayan, but Changxing uses a classification scheme that was commonly used in Huayan texts.

In China, Buddhist texts were introduced over many centuries and came from all its different traditions. In order to make sense of all of these texts, scholarly monks and laypeople developed systems for classifying texts and the doctrines they contain. These schemes relied on both history (the order in which the Buddha presumably taught the various sutras) and philosophy (the profundity of the truths expressed in those sutras). English speakers do the same thing today when they divide Buddhism and Buddhist texts into the three vehicles of Theravāda, Mahāyāna, and Vajrayāna, as each of these is also defined historically and by the texts that they venerate. Changxing himself uses two overlapping ideas to think about the entire Buddhist tradition. The first is historical—the "three times." Today most secular scholars agree that the Theravāda texts are the oldest Buddhist texts, followed by Mahāyāna sutras, followed lastly by Vajrayāna texts. According to the Chinese three-times scheme that Changxing uses, the Buddha taught the *Huayan Sutra* first, then the texts of the Theravāda, and then various Mahāyāna texts, before finally teaching the *Lotus Sutra*.

In the historical scheme of the three times, we see a connection to the other scheme Changxing uses, which is doctrinal. This is called "the five classes of teachings." According to Huayan thinkers, the Buddha began his teaching career by preaching the *Huayan Sutra*, but because the Huayan tradition classifies its doctrines as the "complete" or "perfect" teaching, this text is listed as the fifth of the five teachings. The Buddha soon realized that the teachings of the *Huayan Sutra* were too advanced, so he went back to the beginning and started with basic doctrines, which are the Theravāda (or Hinayāna) teachings. These were followed by teachings of increasing complexity, which are all part of the Mahāyāna but are divided into "preliminary" and "final." The fourth class of teaching includes Chan practice, which is called "the sudden teaching" because it leads to sudden awakening. The fifth class of teaching also includes the *Lotus Sutra*. Both the *Huayan Sutra* and the *Lotus Sūtra* are said to teach the truth that in reality there is only one Buddhist path, and that all Buddhists, even Theravāda Buddhists, are actually on their way to becoming bodhisattvas. This is why these two sutras are said to teach the Single-Vehicle Mahāyāna. Up to this point, the Huayan approach to classifying the various texts and teachings of Buddhism is mostly shared with the Tiantai school, but what is distinct about the approach of the Huayan school is that it sets the *Huayan Sutra* aside as unique in making the truest statements about the nature of reality. This is why Huayan writers like Changxing refer to the *Huayan Sutra* as the "unique" or "distinct" teaching of the Single-Vehicle Mahāyāna. This is a major point of difference between the Huayan school and its traditional rival, the Tiantai school, which places the *Lotus Sūtra* at the pinnacle of Buddhist texts.

So what exactly is this unique doctrine of the *Huayan Sutra*? According to the thinkers of the Huayan school, the unique contribution of the *Huayan Sutra* is its teaching of the holism of all things as they arise in a mutual cocreation, which they refer to as "nature origination." Huayan philosophy is an attempt to describe reality using positive language that is different from the negation of Mahāyāna emptiness philosophy. The underlying goal of both approaches is the same, though: to help us lessen our attachment to the labels we apply to the things that happen in our lives. Emptiness philosophy tries to help us see that our labels for things (like "me" or "my car") are not really things at all, because those things do not have an underlying permanent substance that corresponds to those labels. Huayan philosophy adopts a different approach by emphasizing the cocreative side of all things in the universe. Also, instead of talking only about material things, Huayan philosophers talk about the phenomena in the universe, which are referred to in Chinese as *shi*. Shi include not only objects but feelings, situations, and events. All things and events in the universe are simultaneously creating and being created by all other things and events. Nothing is independent by itself, but because each thing or event is the result of everything else, there is also some sense in which it has a reality to it. But the reality of one thing or event is not the entirety of reality. This is the principle of mutual cocreation, which is the fundamental principle of reality, which is called *li* in Chinese. "Nature origination" is the process by which shi and li mutually exist within each other and give rise to the whole of reality.

This all sounds beautiful, but because it is not easy to learn to see reality in this way, the Huayan thinkers created a number of conceptual frameworks we can use to practice thinking through the interdependent nature of reality. The first of these was laid out in a text called the *Contemplation of the Dharma Realm*, which Changxing mentions in the first paragraph of this translation. Attributed by the tradition to Zhiyan, the second Huayan patriarch, it outlines a progressive series of contemplations designed to lead the practitioner into a complete and correct understanding of reality. The *Contemplation of the Dharma Realm* is the fundamental text of the Huayan school, and continues to be widely studied, usually alongside commentaries by Fazang and Chengguan.[1]

Fazang and Chengguan expanded on this earlier work and added new tools for helping people to see the nature of reality. One approach was to analyze things using mereology, the study of parts and wholes. One method they offered for how to think about this was the concept of the six characteristics (a concept that Changxing alludes to). When we think of any one thing or event, it is part of the whole of reality, and that thing or event can be said to have six different relationships with the whole, simultaneously. The six relationships that one thing can have to the whole of reality are: unity with the whole, separateness from the whole, identity with the whole, difference from the whole, formation of the whole, and disintegration of the whole. As humans we tend to focus on just one aspect of a thing's or event's participation in the totality of reality, and this inflexibility in our views causes us a lot of suffering. Buddhas can see all perspectives at the same time, but ordinary beings cannot. So Huayan texts tend to involve a lot of shifting back and forth in one's viewpoint.

Besides the six characteristics, another well-known Huayan teaching on how to expand one's understanding by taking different perspectives on things is the ten profound (or mysterious) gates. The ten profound gates are different viewpoints from which we can look at the causal relationship between things. Even in English they tend to have fairly abstract names, but the basic idea behind the ten gates is that one should practice thinking about the things and events in one's life from a variety of perspectives, until one realizes that all of these perspectives are equally true. To take but one example, think of the English idiom "cannot see the forest for the trees." What this means is that if one only looks at individual trees, one does not understand that they are actually part of a larger entity, an identity called a forest. Taking the myopic view, one might cut down each individual tree, one at a time, thinking each is just a tree, until eventually the entire forest is gone. The fifth of the ten profound gates, the somewhat densely worded "gate of both concealment and revelation completely attained," tells us that when we focus only on a tree, its identity as a tree is "revealed" and its identity as an element of a forest is "concealed." Conversely, if we zoom out and think only of the forest, then "forest" is revealed and "tree" is concealed. Huayan tries to teach us to see the truth of both realities—tree and forest—at the same time. This is relatively easy to do when we are talking about forests and trees, but it can become quite difficult when we are talking about accidents, enemies, death, or sadness.

The goal of Huayan philosophy, like all Buddhist teachings, is the alleviation of suffering. Its teachers believe that by learning to see the deep interconnection between all things, to learn to see the harmonious mutuality that exists behind our narrow views of separate things, we will be able to put down our attachments and the dis-ease they cause us. Changxing believed in this teaching. Living in a time of civil and international strife, he deeply believed that if we could learn to see all members of the human race as part of our own family, we would build a more compassionate world.

The Translation

Changxing left a number of written works behind, including commentaries on the *Awakening of Faith in the Mahāyāna*, the *Sutra of Perfect Enlightenment*, and a text on Buddhist logic. He also wrote a complete introduction to Huayan. The following translation is drawn from *An Outline of Buddhism*. In this text, Changxing attempts to explain Buddhism using many of the new terms and ideas that were circulating in China. He uses novel Chinese terms like *cosmology*, *science*, *psychology*, and *philosophy* to locate Buddhist thought within the world of modern knowledge. He introduces basic Buddhist teachings, as well as the histories of the various schools of philosophy and practice in China, all of which he frames within general questions of human purpose and meaning. The section translated here comes from the chapter on the different schools of Chinese Buddhism. Although it is the only section where he explicitly focuses on the Huayan school, the overall organizing ideology of the *Outline* is deeply Huayanistic in nature. He uses the particularly Huayan idea of "nature origination" to explain the relationship of Buddhism to modern cosmology, and he ranks and organizes the Buddhist teachings using a traditional Huayan framework.

CHANGXING

The Xianshou School

The Sanskrit version of the *Huayan Sutra* is one hundred thousand verses long, but the first Chinese translation included only thirty-six thousand of these verses.[2] Using the first Chinese translation of the sutra, Master Dushun of the Tang dynasty wrote the *Contemplation of the Dharma Realm*. In this work he used the idea of universal pervasion and inclusion to show the truth of the nonobstruction of all phenomena. The Venerable Zhiyan built on Dushun's writings by creating the ten profound gates, which he combined with the teaching on the six characteristics. Based on their work, Fazang assessed all the teachings given by the Buddha in his lifetime and divided these into three time periods and five classes of teachings. Fazang identified the Huayan concept of the origination of the Dharma Realm as the unique teaching of the Single-Vehicle Mahāyāna, which he said was the highest and most revered teaching in Buddhism. Around this time, the Khotanese monk Śikṣānanda produced a new Chinese translation of the *Huayan Sutra* in forty-five thousand verses, and Chengguan wrote an important series of commentaries on this version of the sutra. His commentaries are both comprehensive and thorough, and they carefully tease out the essential and important ideas in the text from the less essential ones. It is fair to say that there is nothing like his commentaries.

We can diagram Chengguan's classification of the Buddha's teachings like this:

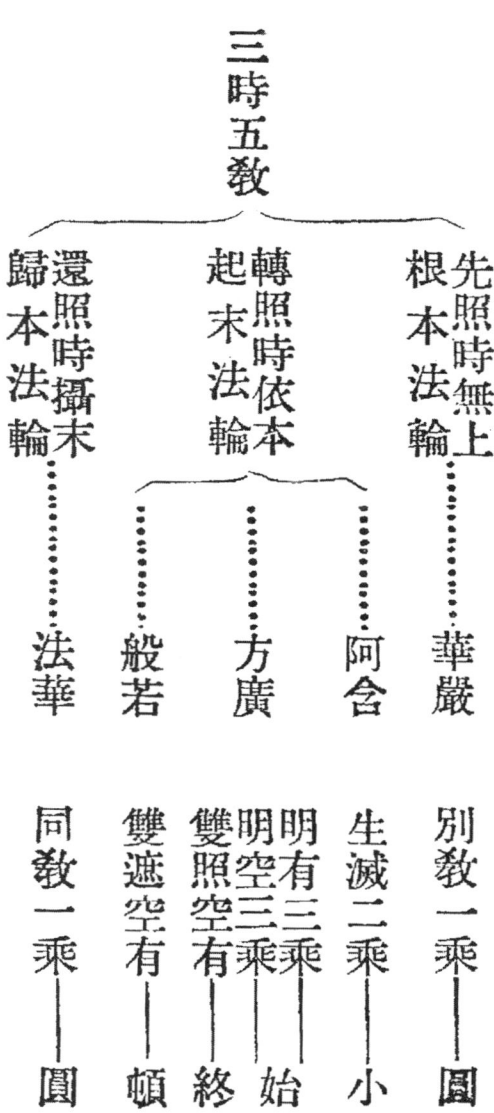

Diagram showing Chengguan's classification of the teachings
(translated on next page).

The Three Time Periods and the Five Teachings

1. The first elucidation: the unsurpassed fundamental dharma teachings
   a. The *Huayan Sutra*
      i. The unique teaching of the Single-Vehicle Mahāyāna
         • The complete teaching
2. The period of transmitting the teachings: using the fundamental teachings to create supplemental explanations
   a. The *Āgamas*
      i. Teaching of birth and death, found in the two vehicles of the *śrāvakas* and *pratyekabuddhas*
         • Hinayāna
   b. The *Vaipulya* sutras
      i. Explanations of phenomenal existence, found in the Bodhisattva Vehicle, the third vehicle
      ii. Explanation of emptiness, found in the Bodhisattva Vehicle, the third vehicle
         • (both i and ii =) Preliminary Mahāyāna
      iii. Illumination of both emptiness and form
         • (both ii and iii =) Final Mahāyāna
      iv. Obscuration of both emptiness and form
         • The sudden teaching
   c. The *Prajñāpāramitā* sutras
      i. ii–iv.
3. The period of returning: using the supplemental explanations to lead people back to the fundamental teaching
   a. The *Lotus Sutra*
      i. Common teachings of the Single-Vehicle Mahāyāna
         • The complete teaching

The nature of things can be described using one of four explanations, which correspond to the first four classes of teachings identified by Fazang. He categorized all the various doctrines taught in Buddhism into five categories, which are: Hinayāna, preliminary and final Mahāyāna, the sudden teaching, and the complete teaching. Let us turn to the four ways of explaining the nature of things.

First, if we were to focus on discussing the conditioned arising of things, then we are positing a kind of provisional existence to them. This is a Hinayāna doctrine. Second, if we were to focus on things' lack of an inherent essence, we will say that everything is completely empty. This is the preliminary teaching of the Mahāyāna. Third, if we were to consider that insofar as the qualities of things correspond to their essential nature, which is empty, then forms are empty; at the same time, insofar as the essential nature of things is the basis for their qualities, then emptiness has form. This is referred to as the final teaching of the Mahāyāna because it explains both emptiness and form. Fourth, if we were to focus on the essential nature of things in order to exclude their qualities, then those qualities disappear and there are no existing things left. But if, on the other hand, we focus on the qualities of things in order to exclude their essential nature, then the essence of things is hidden, and the fact that things are empty disappears from view. This is the sudden teaching that discards both emptiness and form.

There is, in fact, a deeper truth that lies at the heart of these four explanations, which is that if we take in everything together, emptiness and form are completely intermingled and there is no difference between them. This is the viewpoint of the complete teaching that points to the boundless origination of things, which is why it is the greatest of the five teachings. Every thing in the universe mutually interfuses and interpenetrates one another. This is the true nature of reality.

Among the three time periods of the Buddha's teaching, his initial elucidation of the *Huayan Sutra* is referred to as the fundamental dharma teaching. He used the uniquely complete teaching of the Single-Vehicle Mahāyāna to explain the true nature of things, which is that the overarching essence of reality (*li*) and the boundless phenomena that compose it (*shi*) all multiply interweave, mutually infusing each other without obstruction.

After he gave his first teachings, the Buddha began transmitting more general teachings. He taught the *Āgamas*, which contain only the Hinayāna teachings on birth and death. Later in this second period, the Buddha taught the *Vaipulya* sutras, in which he narrowly explained four perspectives on emptiness and existence. He taught about conditioned arising and the empty and essenceless nature of things. This is why Fazang said these sutras contain both the preliminary and final Mahāyāna teachings. After that, the Buddha taught the *Prajñāpāramitā* sutras. Although these say that all dharmas are empty, their true inner meaning is to describe a reality that is beyond words, which can only be understood through one's own direct and unmediated experience of it. This is why these sutras are classified as the sudden teaching. The doctrines that the Buddha set forth during this middle period of his teaching all start from the concept of conditioned arising but only explain one part of it, which is why they are said to use fundamental concepts to create supplemental explanations.

During the third and final period of the Buddha's teaching, on the occasion when the Buddha preached the *Lotus Sutra*, he taught that all beings can become buddhas and that all beings are, in actuality, practicing only Mahāyāna Buddhism. In other words, in this period the Buddhas used supplemental explanations to return to the fundamental teaching. The *Lotus Sutra* relies on teachings that are common with the other three vehicles, and it does not yet clearly explain the doctrine of boundless dependent origination, which is why it is only called the common complete teaching and not the unique complete teaching.

What sets the unique complete teaching apart from the others is its view that in the endless field of dependent origination, all things are mutually intertwined and infused with one another so that the appearance of even one mote of dust is an event that is felt throughout the entire universe. This is just as Zhuangzi said: "Heaven and earth are of one attribute, the ten thousand things are one horse."[3] The ancient worthies often used the ten profound gates and the six characteristics to explain this teaching.

The ten profound gates are:

1. The gate of simultaneous complete correspondence (the ocean gathers a hundred rivers)
2. The gate of the free nonobstruction of breadth and narrowness (a one-foot-wide mirror showing a thousand miles)
3. The gate of the one and the many containing each other without becoming identical (lamplight in an empty room)
4. The gate of the mutual identification of all things (one hundred objects, all made of gold)
5. The gate of both concealment and revelation completely attained (a crescent moon in the autumn sky)
6. The gate of the tiniest particles each containing one another (a bottle full of mustard seeds)
7. The gate of Indra's net (two mirrors reflecting each other)
8. The gate of using phenomena to demonstrate the Dharma (a cloud appears in the vast sky)
9. The gate of the various phenomena of the ten times being different but mutually formed (crossing the world in a night's dream)
10. The gate of subject and object completely illuminating all qualities (the stars salute the North Pole)

Because sameness and difference are mutually pervasive and do not hinder one another, each of these ten profound gates subtly contains all the other nine, and together they form a limitless perspective on reality.

Turning now to look at the six characteristics, the way in which a single thing is part of a plurality of things is called the characteristic of unity, but the fact that the plurality of things is not the same as the single thing is called the characteristic of separateness. The way in which "this" and "that" are both part of the same whole is called the characteristic of identity, but the fact that they do not overflow or impinge on each other's identities is called the characteristic of difference. The tendency things have to combine into new forms is called the characteristic of formation, but the fact that individual things continue to maintain their separate existences even after they combine to form other things is called the characteristic of disintegration.

I will explain these six characteristics using the first of the ten profound gates: the gate of simultaneous complete correspondence. We could start by saying that a single person's peaceful existence is none other than the peaceful existences of all the people in the world. Likewise, it is necessarily the case that if everyone in the world lived in peace, then this one person would be able to enjoy a peaceful existence. Each one—the single person on the one hand, and all the people in the world on the other—serves simultaneously as the cause and condition of the other, and they correspond completely to each other. Why do I say this? Let's say I want to talk about the peaceful existence of this one person in terms of their family relationships. This person has six kinds of relatives: father, mother, older and younger siblings, spouse, and children. And each of these relatives has their own relatives, also of the six different types, and so it goes, on and on. Parents have parents, who themselves also have parents, and on and on with no beginning. Children have children, who have their own children, and on and on without end. Siblings have spouses, who have their own siblings with spouses, in a network of connections that spreads out in all directions without end. This is why I can say, without exaggerating, that all human beings are my relatives.

I could also talk about all the various relationships that make my life possible. I depend for my survival on the work of the farmer for the food I eat. The clothes I wear and the tools I use are produced by craftspeople, and they come to me through the trade of merchants. I depend for a place to live on the work of carpenters and construction workers. The boats, trains, carts, and horses that I rely on for travel depend on the people who run the machines and the grooms who care for the horses. And the farmers, craftspeople, merchants, and grooms all have their own needs as well, and on and on it goes, in a series of infinite intimate connections. Because of this, all of the human industry on Earth is not possible without the existence of a single person.

If we look at this from another angle, from the perspective of the cultivation of knowledge, today knowledge is divided into various specialized branches of learning that each carefully pursues its own specific goals. But these ways of knowing all make up a unified whole that cannot be divided, and each branch of learning mutually informs the discoveries of the others. For example, if a student of historical geography does not understand the theories of chemistry or physics, they will not be able to make sense of the evidence presented in the rock strata that have accumulated over time. If they do not understand social, economic, educational, or political systems, they will possess a knowledge of diachronic history but not of synchronic history. If they are ignorant of the vicissitudes of human psychology, they will not understand systems of literature or philosophy. Because of all of this, they will see only the merest outline of historical geography and will not understand its vital foundations. Therefore, if one truly wants to understand historical geography, they absolutely must have knowledge of other relevant fields of study. All disciplines of knowledge are like this. In other words, if I have enough mastery in a field of knowledge that I can produce new discoveries within it, then we could certainly say that I have benefited from the insights of all the various specialist scholars of the past. This is not an exaggeration. If we look at this from the relationship between all the knowledge produced by the scholars of all the different fields of knowledge, we can say that I have assembled all their knowledge, from the past and the present, within myself. This is why the Buddha said that at the moment when one dharma is understood, all dharmas are understood; and at the moment when all dharmas are understood, one dharma is understood. The one embraces all things, and all things enter the one.

If we think about all of this in terms of a single person's relatives, their survival, and their knowledge, we can say that one person must connect themselves completely to all of humanity, only then can they create a family. They must seek after all the material goods on Earth, only then can they nourish their body. And they must collect all the knowledge on Earth, from the past and the present, only then will they be able to attain peace of mind. So, at the moment when a single person appears, that person contains all the people, all the material goods, and all the knowledge of the entire world.

This is why we say that for a single person to have a peaceful life, everyone in the world must have peaceful lives.

This is what the gate of simultaneous complete correspondence means. One person can represent the entire world. This is the first of the six characteristics, the characteristic of unity, which describes how the one can be completely identified with the many. Furthermore, even though any one person could represent the entire world, when you look at each specific person, material thing, or branch of knowledge, they are distinct from all others. This is the characteristic of separateness, which describes how the many are not the same as the one. In other words, the elements that make up all human beings, material things, and branches of knowledge are the same as the elements that make up the entire world. Each element is in complete harmony with the others, not standing in the way of any of them. Together they form a whole, and yet each rests in its own identity and does not mix with the others. It is only because they do not mix that they can preserve their own particular identities. This is why we say that in identity there is difference. Likewise, it is only because each thing has its own particular identity that it can function as an elemental constituent of the world. This is what we mean when we say that in difference there is identity. The world is formed through dependent origination precisely because each thing rests in its own identity and performs its own function completely. This is what we mean when we say that in disintegration there is formation. Dependent origination can only occur through the complete exhaustion of each thing's power, and so we see that as each of the myriad things rests in its own identity, it does not appear to create anything at all. This is what we mean when we say that in formation there is disintegration.

This is how the six characteristics interfuse each other, intermingling infinitely. If we look at things from the perspective of the three characteristics of unity, identity, and formation, then we see the entire Dharma Realm as a single whole, interconnected and involved, an indivisible unity. When viewed from the perspective of the three characteristics of separateness, difference, and disintegration, however, we see the Dharma Realm as a composite of countless different elements, which are unknowable to each other, separate and unable to be combined. Each element is only able to fulfill its function completely because it does not merge with other things; and the whole is able to function only because of its indivisibility. All things are equally important to the total working of the whole, and each thing is indispensable because each has its own particular function. The equality and indispensability of things is what creates the capacity for them to completely integrate with one another to form the whole.

What I have offered is an explanation of the gate of simultaneous complete correspondence, which contains the entire teaching of the six characteristics. The other nine gates are also like this. These Huayan teachings of the six characteristics and ten profound gates can be applied to absolutely anything. I am deeply impressed by this. Is this not the reason why Huayan is the supreme teaching, which surpasses the doctrines of the other two time periods?

Further Reading

Cleary, Thomas. *Entry into the Inconceivable: An Introduction to Hua-yen Buddhism*. Honolulu: University of Hawai'i Press, 1983.

Cook, Francis Dojun. *Hua-yen Buddhism: The Jewel Net of Indra*. College Park: Pennsylvania State University Press, 1977.

Hammerstrom, Erik. *The Huayan University Network: The Teaching and Practice of Avataṃsaka Buddhism in Twentieth-Century China*. New York: Columbia University Press, 2020.

Osto, Douglas. *Power, Wealth, and Women in Mahayana Buddhism: The Gandavyuha-sutra*. New York: Routledge, 2008.

Park, Jin Y. *Buddhism and Postmodernity: Zen, Huayan, and the Possibility of Postmodern Buddhist Ethics*. Lanham, MD: Lexington Books, 2010.

Welch, Holmes. *The Buddhist Revival in China*. Cambridge, MA: Harvard University Press, 1968.

———. *The Practice of Chinese Buddhism, 1900-1950*. Cambridge, MA: Harvard University Press, 1967.

Williams, Paul. *Mahayana Buddhism: The Doctrinal Foundations*. New York: Routledge, 2008.

Master Jichan (center) showing the severed fingers on his left hand. Tiantong
Monastery, circa 1906–1909.

8 | The Plum-Blossom Monk

Jichan

JASON PROTASS

The Chinese monk Jichan (1852-1912) played many roles during his lifetime—for instance, becoming the administrator of important Chan temples and the teacher to future Buddhist leaders. One of his most famous students, Taixu (discussed in chapter 3), later recalled that Jichan had an exquisite ability to test the insight of students.[1] He pressed disciples with gong'an—most often "What is your original face before parents were even born?"—and was able to guide students to profound awakening. Taixu remembered Jichan as a skillful teacher with boundless energy, who never missed a single summer or winter retreat. Students flocked to learn from him.

His accomplishments in practice and his training of disciples notwithstanding, Jichan is best known for the thousands of poems he wrote and published in his lifetime. Many of his poems point to specific Chan teachings, and some of his poems served as vehicles for instruction.[2] Jichan's poetry allowed him to address worldly concerns as well, such as the suffering of people during wartime. In addition, poetry was a medium for this monk to connect with secular elites. Drafting, circulating, and reciting poetry was a normal activity for the educated classes in imperial China.

For Jichan himself, however, poetry sometimes was an expedient means to convey Buddhist teachings, a karmic fetter, or the locus for a spiritual struggle. He at times questioned the idea that poetry itself could be a Buddhist practice. In his poems he repeatedly says that his fondness for poetry is an obstacle to total liberation. Nonetheless, poetry was a fundamental part of Jichan's life, and his works remain a source of inspiration to Buddhists.

Jichan became known as a poet-monk, a reputation he still has today, thanks to his prolific poetic publications. However, the term *poet-monk* is often used to suggest something more romantic. Jichan was foremost an ardent practitioner. He was not even interested in poetry until he was twenty years old—very late for a Chinese poet. His poetry is grounded in the seriousness of his commitment to the Buddhist path. The most obvious manifestation of his seriousness is also the reason for his nickname, "the Eight-Fingered Ascetic." In 1877 he sacrificed the pinkie and ring finger from his left hand in a fiery ritual in front of relics of the Buddha. Jichan was a fervent practitioner of Buddhism and simultaneously a person susceptible to poetic reverie.

Jichan's Early Life

Jichan wrote several autobiographies, which are my main source for reconstructing the following details.[3] Jichan had a difficult youth. He was born in Hunan to a family surnamed Huang in the first year of the Xianfeng reign (1851-1861) of the Qing dynasty. This same year also witnessed the birth of the Taiping Heavenly Kingdom, the beginning of the deadliest civil war in human history. By the Gregorian calendar, Jichan's birthday was January 23, 1852, shortly before the new lunar year. When small, he liked to accompany his mother to Buddhist rituals and events, but she was sickly and died when he was five years old (seven *sui*).[4] He later mentioned her passing in one of his earliest poems, "On Shaving My Head, a Poem for My Little Brother" (translated below as I.2). A few years later, Jichan had barely started learning the Confucian *Analects* when his father's sudden death threw him into the poverty of an orphan. At first Jichan lived with a poor farmer, tilling the fields, and then he performed menial tasks for local families in exchange for housing.

He did not have parents to provide him food to eat. His labor provided sustenance for himself and his younger brother. Given these dire conditions, he had to discontinue his formal education. No one then could have predicted that this poor boy would become one of the best-known Buddhist poets of his era.

In his autobiographies, Jichan writes that one rainy day he was plowing a farmer's fields with a draft ox when he caught sight of white peach trees in bloom along the hedge. A gust of wind shook the flowers loose and they started to fall. He burst into tears. Shortly after that day he sought to become a Buddhist monk. He joined the novitiate, and a few months later he received the full monastic precepts, all in 1868 when he was between sixteen and seventeen years old. He was given the dharma name Jing'an (Reverential Peace) and the courtesy name of Jichan (Entrusted to Chan). It was almost a decade later that he gave himself the nickname "Eight-Fingered Ascetic" (*Bazhi toutuo*).

In 1877, Jichan arrived at the historic Ayuwang Monastery. He had already studied with several well-known teachers and had experienced an awakening confirmed by Chan master Hengzhi Wulai (1811–1875), a master known for his own meditative achievements, but Jichan had not yet completely realized his goal. Taixu would later write that Jichan was never complacent in his practice, and he was assiduous in his pursuit of wisdom and meditative concentration. Ayuwang Monastery has been in use since the third century C.E. and is famous for possessing the parietal bone of Śākyamuni Buddha, a relic said to have survived the crematory fires that consumed his body after his *parinirvāṇa*. Relics like this exude a kind of charisma. They provide a visceral connection to the Awakened One and frequently inspire acts of piety. Here, Jichan decided to make an offering of his own fingers. Jichan may have been zealous and extreme among his contemporaries, but he was not unique in the history of Chinese Buddhism. Many others had done this before him.

The practice of bodily sacrifice is partly based on a chapter of the *Lotus Sūtra*—perhaps the single most important Buddhist scripture in East Asia. The practice also finds inspiration in Jataka tales, ancient texts recounting previous lives of the Buddha, narrating the virtuous and self-sacrificial qualities he cultivated over countless lifetimes before being born as Prince Siddhārtha. Siddhārtha in his final lifetime left his stately home to pursue intense ascetic practices. All these selfless acts had to be done before he could become the Awakened One.

We can only speculate about the physical, social, and spiritual preparations Jichan undertook for the ordeal. He may have informed someone in the leadership of his plans. He likely soaked a cloth in perfumed oils and wrapped tightly the two smallest fingers on his left hand. In front of the skull bone of Śākyamuni, Jichan surely intoned prayers, inwardly clarified his intentions, and demonstrated his irreversible will to achieve liberation. He ignited the oil-soaked cloth.

For the remainder of his life, Jichan was renowned for the seriousness of his practice. He spoke plainly and forcefully. Everywhere he went, his dedication to the Buddhist path was always visibly at hand. Jichan lived during the early history of photography, and there are several known photographs of him. In some photographs, he lifts his left hand up toward the camera. In a photograph by Ernst Boerschmann, reproduced at the beginning of this chapter, Jichan holds a long rosary with prayer beads across his body. It is running through each of his hands. A viewer can see the depth of Jichan's commitment to Buddhist practice moving through his eight fingers.

Jichan as Poet

Although Jichan gained a positive reputation through various accomplishments—for instance, serving as the principal force behind the modern reconstruction of Tiantong Monastery— already in his lifetime he was best known as a poet. He published semi-regularly in his lifetime, writing nearly two thousand poems. According to Jichan, his ability to compose traditional Chinese poetry, a genre known for its profound difficulty, arrived suddenly one day when he was about nineteen years old.

Having missed out on an education as a child, Jichan was not initially inclined to literary or aesthetic pursuits. To the contrary, he was dubious of the ornate flourishes of literary monks. His conversion to poetry took place when he was a student at Renrui Monastery on Qishan, west of Hengyang City, Hunan. There he studied with his first great master Hengzhi Wulai. Hengzhi was also from Hunan and likewise grew up in a poor family. Jichan recalled that one other student in particular, named Jingyi Sican, enjoyed writing poetry and had a big influence on him in this regard. Jingyi was also from Hunan but had the benefit of an education as a child. Later, both Jingyi and Jichan were recognized as dharma heirs of Hengzhi Wulai, making them dharma brothers.

In 1869, when Jichan was seventeen years old, he arrived at Renrui Monastery. Jingyi was already an advanced senior student and was serving in the roles of *shuozuo* (head student; J. *shuso*) and *weinuo* ("rector," or the second in charge; J. *ino*). During breaks in the formal monastic schedule, Jichan would practice extra meditation and ascetic cultivation. Jingyi by contrast used any rest time to compose poems for his own enjoyment. At that time, Jichan believed that if a person was truly dedicated to realizing liberation, they could not spend even a moment of our brief human lives on frivolous entertainment, such as poetry. He thus spoke bluntly to Jingyi, chastising him for spending so much time and effort on profane literary pursuits. According to Jichan's first autobiography, Jingyi responded, "You spend your black-haired youth practicing so intensively, though the future in which you will realize buddhahood is immeasurably far away. As for the wisdom and samādhi of writing, I worry I won't be able to realize it in this lifetime." In other words, the possibility of becoming a buddha by sitting in meditation requires countless lifetimes, whereas the possibility of achieving a spiritual insight from textual study can be realized in this life. In a later autobiography, Jichan remembered Jingyi instead saying, "Your dusty head and dirty face are only suited to studying the Chan of withered trees. How could you understand what is in the heart of a person destined with karma for both literature and

Buddhism?" In other words, to shun language and insist on silent sitting (like a cold dead tree) is a deluded attitude that has not yet realized the truth of nonduality. In both versions of his story, the episode clearly encapsulated for Jichan a recurring motif in his life and a theme in his poetry: the tension between the ascetic path of Buddhist monastic training and the aesthetic life of a person endowed with a poetic sensitivity to the world. At the time of this conversation, Jichan had not yet composed a single poem.

According to Jichan's autobiographies, his poetic career began unexpectedly several years later, in 1871, when he took a short leave from Qishan Monastery to visit a maternal uncle in Yueyang (northern Hunan). There, Jichan joined friends in climbing the famous Yueyang Tower that overlooks the eastern shore of Lake Dongting. Rebuilt many times, the impressive structure was first constructed for military use in the third century. It was made famous by poets of the Tang and Song dynasties (such as Du Fu, Li Bai, and Fan Zhongyan). Inspired by the view (and the echoes of those earlier poems), Jichan's friends began playing a parlor game to compose their own poems. Jichan, not yet a poet, excused himself and sat quietly and meditated. After some time, he lowered his gaze and beheld the colors and shapes of the enormous body of water. All at once an entire poetic phrase appeared in his mind: "The waves of Dongting carry this solitary monk." Despite that he had never studied poetry before, the cadence of the words formed a perfect line of verse.

Jichan soon shared his experience with a learned friend named Guo Jusun (d.u.). Guo confirmed that this was an original line of poetry and was stunned that Jichan could produce such a lovely line. This moment of poetic creativity seemed inexplicable. Guo decided this was a spiritual mystery. He told Jichan that his karma from previous lives clearly connects him to poetry. It was Guo who encouraged Jichan to cultivate his gifts. Guo taught Jichan about poetry from the anthology *Three Hundred Tang Poems*. One by one, Jichan learned each poem by heart, memorizing it after a single reading, and he quickly absorbed all three hundred poems.

Two of Jichan's earliest surviving poems were revised and completed in 1873. One poem from 1873 is called "On Shaving My Head, a Poem for My Little Brother." This poem (I.2) is autobiographic and narrates his path to becoming a monk. It is the very first poem in several publications by Jichan. The other is to his dharma brother Jingyi (I.1). The poem is about missing a close friend, and the poem wishes to close the distance that separates them. Although the poem begins very early in the morning, it is already too late; upon waking the poet-monk already feels a sense of longing. When he says that a wild goose has departed, the wild goose is a metaphor for a messenger—it is as if the mail has already gone for the day and there is no way to send a message to his friend. The poem turns its attention to the beauty of a hermetic delight. Because the poem is addressed to Jingyi, that implies, first, that Jingyi is someone who can also appreciate such small everyday joys; second, Jingyi is a person who would appreciate Jichan's keen desire to share that moment with the right friend, even if that friend is far away. The poem registers the kind of friendship that exists between poet-monks.

Jichan became obsessed with poetry. He wrote that he felt a tremendous burden if he sensed one word was not quite right, sometimes forgetting to eat or sleep while he wracked his brain. He likely felt that his word choice was too facile, or that it did not quite capture the right nuance, texture, or timbre of a scene. It is said that he once finished a poem years after he started it, when he finally found the right word. Such stories are entirely plausible, however, we should note that Jichan's life story dramatizes a romantic ideal familiar to readers of Chinese poetry. The ideal of *kuyin*, "bitter intoning" or "painstaking composition," was popular among a set of late Tang poets. It is associated with Jia Dao (779–843) in particular, who had been a Buddhist monk before returning to lay life. One can compare a kuyin poet to a "starving artist," one toiling to craft a perfect literary artifact to the point of physical and mental suffering.[5] Kuyin was also associated with the feeling of being completely absorbed in poetic craft. Most of these themes appear in Jichan's poetry.

Though he would complete between 15 and 132 poems in any given year for the rest of his life, Jichan always considered himself poorly read. He continued to study the great Tang and Song poets, especially those whose sensibilities lent themselves to a poet-monk. As a result, his poetry is full of echoes to classics of Chinese poetry. His poems are relatively easy to read and yet are also satisfying to a well-educated reader. At the same time, however, his sudden infatuation with poetry also brought an uneasiness. Jichan could not neglect his proper duties as a monk. It seemed worrisome to be so infatuated with something aesthetic and pleasurable. He may have worried: Were his intentions in studying and composing poetry really aligned with his dedication to the Buddhist path? This was not a tension he could readily resolve—and it remained a live question that runs through many of his poems.

Even as his study of poetry began, Jichan continued his rigorous Chan training under Hengzhi Wulai. One day, he was investigating the gong'an of "What is your original face before mother and father were born?" when both inwardly and outwardly the world fell away. He was in this deep meditation for most of the day. Then he heard the sounds of a nearby brook and had an awakening. Hengzhi Wulai recognized Jichan as a dharma heir. And so, Jichan began a lifetime of balancing his Buddhist monastic occupation and his calling as a poet.

It is reasonable to suspect that the received story of Jichan's life has been subject to some embellishments. Our understanding of his experience is shaped by the ways in which Jichan chose to represent himself through self-narrative. Others reiterated and amplified the most compelling parts of his story. It is likely impossible that we will ever know what "really" happened on the day that Jichan suddenly had his first poetic insight, for example. At the same time, it is unlikely a coincidence that Jichan is said to have experienced the poetic equivalent of a sudden awakening—the ultimate ideal in a Chan master's life. His story may also remind us of the Sixth Ancestor Huineng in the *Platform Sutra*, who was an illiterate student and had no intention becoming a poet, but thanks to his spiritual genius, he ended up composing a famous verse. To at least some extent, preexisting cultural frameworks appear to have determined the narratives that Jichan and others used to make sense of his life.

It seems Jichan and those around him (such as Mr. Guo) did understand his life story in these religious terms. We should not suspect them of fabricating these events out of whole cloth, nor of exaggerating their significance. To the contrary, the hagiographic embellishments of Jichan's life are like a map that point us toward what he and his contemporaries regarded as the most salient details of a life well lived. His autobiographies help us understand what animated his poems.

Jichan's poems register the same tensions seen in his autobiographies. For example, some of his poetry refers to his untiring urge to make more poems as a spiritual hindrance. He playfully imagines a "poetry demon" is haunting him. That poetic image is first found in Tang and Song poetry. It was a creative way for monks and others to talk about their complex relationship to poetic craft. On the one hand, Jichan (like many others) recognized that it is ostensibly possible for a monk to write poetry that brings others toward the truth of the Dharma or inspired practice and contemplation. Such a solution, however, is easier said than done. Jichan was not one to write exclusively dogmatic poems. On the other hand, if poetry really had become an attachment or a fetter on his path, then Jichan ought to forsake poetry. He parted with two fingers—was letting go of poetry more difficult than that? For Jichan, the answer was yes—poetry was something that welled up within him, that was larger than himself, and that he could not stop. As a result, he often registered this tension between asceticism and aesthetics in his poetry. This is a classic theme of Chinese Buddhist poetry, too, a topic that monks turned to again and again over centuries. In this way as well, Jichan engaged the long tradition of poet-monks admirably, and he was praised by his contemporaries as one of the foremost poet-monks of his day.

The Flowering Plum Tree

Above all else, Jichan loved the flowering plum tree. He was some-times called "the plum-blossom monk" because of his poetic obses-sion with the flowering plum.[6] His first collection, published in woodblock print in 1881 with nearly three hundred poems, was entitled *Songs to Savor the Flowering Plum*. Selections are trans-lated here. He later published a small booklet titled *Smaller Col-lection of White Plums* in 1904, with only eight poems. A complete translation is below. He published other times in his life as well.[7] His plum-blossom poems are laden with allusions to earlier poets. At the same time, he added a new layer of Buddhist meaning to the long Chinese tradition of celebrating the plum-blossom tree.

The natural behavior of the Asian flowering plum tree, *Prunus mume*, has potent symbols that are associated with the virtues of a gentleman hermit—and by extension those of a Buddhist monk. The flowers of the plum burst forth before the end of wintry weather. Plum blossoms commonly display white, pink, or red petals. Its flowers are the first of the year and a harbinger of spring. Poets note that snow often falls again after the plum has bloomed, generating a unique seasonal experience of early spring's light-colored blossoms against late winter's snow. The trees display a delicate beauty amid inhospitable conditions. For the Buddhist monk, this flowering tree also symbolizes how hardship is not separate from the manifesta-tion of one's full potential—an idea that can be compared with the lotus blossom that grows in muddy water.

However, other qualities of the tree do not make it an obvious candidate to serve as the symbol for a poet. By common standards, its flowers are not bright and showy, neither are they especially fragrant. Even an old plum-blossom tree will not have grown espe-cially tall. Its limbs and boughs tend to be thin or gnarled. When other flowers reach their full bloom, people gather for feasts and entertainment. The plum, in comparison, appears to be a relatively unassuming tree. If, on the one hand, the plum did not garner a feast, on the other hand it is these same subtler qualities—austerity and restraint—that drew the imagination of China's scholarly class (including erudite monks) who saw their own lives mirrored in this underappreciated flower.

The literary history of the flowering plum in China begins somewhat later than that of other flora. He Xun, a poet of the Liang dynasty (502-557), was among the first to admire the virtues of plum blossoms, tending flowering plums during a period of political turmoil. Jichan refers to He Xun in a poem translated here (II.5). In Tang dynasty poems as well, such as those by Li Bai, plum blossoms are associated with exile and displacement. Many poems also compare the delicate blossoms of the plum with the beauty of a woman—a trope that Jichan avoided reiterating himself.

Jichan's poems most often reference the patriarch of plum-blossom poetry, Lin Bu (967-1028), who lived during the early Song dynasty. The Song dynasty is associated with the birth of a literati culture, as the new government cultivated a class of scholar-officials. Many members of the intelligentsia who sought freedom from the drudgery of bureaucratic life found inspiration in Lin Bu's poems. The famous Song-era ink paintings of flowering plums are virtually synonymous with these literati ideals. As for Lin Bu, he spent much of his life in rustic retirement on an island called Solitary Hill (Gushan) in West Lake, part of Hangzhou city. He was a recluse who refused employment, never married, and lived a simple life. Lin Bu is often called a "hermit," but he did not live alone in a remote mountain. He maintained regular social intercourse with nearby monks and fellow poets. The most famous of Lin Bu's poems is probably "Small Flowering Plum in a Hillock Garden," which praises the flowering plum as better than those flowers that cannot survive in winter. In that poem, one couplet has been most celebrated since the Song dynasty: "Sparse shadows cast oblique lines over clear shallow water; / Hidden fragrance wafts in dim moonlight."[8] The couplet depicts something completely ordinary (a tree's shadow) that is too subtle for a common viewer. The branches themselves must be thin if they can cast such delicate shadows. By naming the shape of moonlight shadows, and a faint breeze wafting the blossoms' delicate perfume, the poet asks his reader if they are also the kind of person who can appreciate quiet beauty. Jichan referred to this couplet often in his poetry. The sharing of such a moment of appreciation was itself important to him as a poet and as a Chan teacher. In the poems below, you can see his references to Lin Bu and the inspiration Jichan drew from this poem.

Classics of Chan Buddhist literature draw an analogy between the flowering plum and awakening. The flowering plum bursts forth from the desolate landscape of winter. Jichan explored this theme in "Facing a Plum Tree and Having an Insight." The third couplet of that poem refers to a famous Song-dynasty Chan story. The *Liandeng huiyao* (*Essential Records of the Linked Flames*) records the story as follows:

> Long ago, there was an old woman who supported a hermit for twenty years. She regularly sent a girl of sixteen or seventeen by herself to offer food and wait upon him. One day she told the girl to grab him firmly, and ask, "That moment just now, how about it?" The hermit responded, "I am a withered tree atop frozen rock; three months of winter with no warmth." The girl reported this to the old woman. The woman said, "For twenty years I've been giving alms to a common bloke." She threw out the hermit and burned down the hermitage.[9]

This story points to the nature of Chan awakening. It is not merely the rejection or negation of desires, a kind of stoicism. The monastic path to awakening does require self-restraint. However, the constant application of restraint itself is not freedom. Awakening is a kind of breakthrough. In his poem, Jichan uses a poetic metaphor to describe that kind of breakthrough. The "three months of winter with no warmth" are like the deluded world of samsara. The plum blossom is an awakening that emerges suddenly from those unlikely conditions. Jichan compared the blossoming plum to Chan awakening in other poems as well.

Jichan's poems also describe white flowering plum blossoms against white snow. In such an image, the flowering plum blends seamlessly with its landscape—though Jichan can still discern it. This subtle way of seeing, written into many of his poems, is one way that Jichan infuses these plum-blossom poems with Buddhist philosophy. In his poetry, the pureness of the white blossom may symbolize the thusness of being, or buddha-nature. This thusness is universal, not exclusive to oneself, and so it is also imminent in things outside oneself. Seen from this profound perspective, the boundaries between the self and the other begin to blur—the essence of the flowering plum is no different from that of the snow. However, seen from the perspective of our ordinary experience, each separately existing thing retains its individuality—flowers and snow are distinct phenomena. In his poetry, Jichan suggests that the truth is simultaneously both (and thus neither one) of these—like a white flowering plum blossom and the snowy landscape.

Jichan's language is plain and clear and yet full of energy, which makes it fitting that he took the flowering plum as his personal emblem. Many poems show parallels between the poet and plum. In "Searching for Plum Trees after Snowfall," there is an echo between himself, leaning on a goosefoot staff, and the plum tree with its shadows reaching through the fog. It is as though the goosefoot staff is holding him up in a way that parallels how he imagines the long angular shadows of the tree are buttressing the mist. Many of this plum-blossom monk's teachings were expressed through such poetry.

Poetry and Friendship

Though Jichan's flowering-plum poems often depict the poet as a solitary explorer, he also composed numerous poems directly addressing friends and associates. Poetry was still an ordinary part of social life for educated men in early modern China. These social poems form a substantial part of traditional Chinese poetry and are not unique to Jichan. Indeed, it would have been odd if Jichan had not written poems like these.

Several of Jichan's poems are to two artistic members of a prominent Hunan family. He was friendly with Chen Sanli (1853-1937), a well-known poet who was about his same age. Chen Sanli's father was Chen Baozhen (1831-1900), a reformist-minded official who was governor of Hunan. Jichan also corresponded with Chen Sanli's eldest son, Chen Shizeng (1876-1923), a well-known artist who was a precocious painter in his youth, later celebrated for his promotion of traditional literati styles of painting. By coincidence, Shizeng's younger brother was Chen Yinke (1890-1969), one of modern China's most famous historians.

Jichan's social relationships can be useful context for interpreting these poems. A reader can glean a lot of information by paying careful attention to the poems' long, descriptive titles. For example, a suite of three poems is entitled "Mr. Infatuated with Plum Blossoms Asked Chen Shizeng to Sketch the Likeness of White Plum Blossoms, I Added Three Poems in Acclaim" (II.2). From this title we know that Jichan's three poems were inspired by a painting done by Chen Shizeng. Plum-blossom paintings by Chen are in museums today and can be seen online. The painting, moreover, was created in response to a request by someone whose nickname was Mr. Infatuated with Plum Blossoms. That person is Li Ruiqing (1867-1920), a well-known calligrapher who would become a leader of modern fine arts education in China. The title of the poem chronicles an elite literary and artistic world, and lets the reader know the immediate audience for Jichan's poems. In another poem addressed to Chen Shizeng, "My Feelings as I Set Off from Young Master Chen" (III.3), Jichan seems to be responding to the young artist's sentimentality as they part from each other. Jichan here presents himself as an older and wiser friend who can see through such worldly feelings even though he still feels them. Jichan also wrote poems addressed to monks, recording a social web of fellow Buddhists. Those poems sometimes register his comradeship. For example, the poem addressed to Venerable Pure Karma (II.3) works the word *karma* from the monk's name into the body of the poem, rendering the poem into a unique literary gift for his friend.

Jichan wrote additional poems on paintings, such as "On a Painting of Fishing the Snowy River" (III.1). That painting was surely based on the very famous poem by Liu Zongyuan (773–819) known as "Snowy River," which includes the couplet, "The old man in solitary skiff with straw cloak, / is alone fishing the snowy river." This was a common theme for traditional landscape paintings. The original theme concerns an elite bureaucrat's desire to escape the world of administration and politics. Jichan's poem is skillful for how it transforms that classic theme into a meditation on Buddhist philosophy. Fishes who chase the shadows of plum blossoms can never have their hunger sated. A reader may compare the poetic image with how most people, deeply deluded about the nature of samsara, will chase ephemeral solutions to our insatiable desires.

Jichan's Death and Legacy

The final act for Jichan involved a dramatic episode that transformed how he would be remembered. In 1911, the Xinhai Revolution toppled the Qing dynasty government. After nearly three centuries of Manchu leadership over late imperial society, and after millennia of other forms of imperial governance, a vision for a new Republic of China began to take shape. On the first day of 1912, Sun Yat-sen was inaugurated as the first president of the provisional government. On March 11, a body of representatives convened in Nanjing to ratify the Provisional Constitution of the Republic of China. However, power had already begun to shift from Nanjing to Beijing. The political events that unfolded in the subsequent months, years, and decades are too complex to outline here. Suffice it to say that the twilight of imperial China, a momentous event in world history, was the backdrop to the end of Jichan's life. And his actions at this time were essential to how he would be memorialized by later Chinese Buddhists.

The fall of the imperial government meant the loss of the legal protections that had been afforded to Buddhist and Daoist monks and nuns for centuries. Although the new constitution guaranteed "freedom of religion," that often did not translate into real protection on the ground for traditional Buddhist monks and their temples. At the same time, the new regime encouraged social groups to organize in a new manner. The government did not want to interface with individual monks or temples and instead would respond to larger civil organizations. Buddhists quickly began to organize into associations.

Numerous Buddhist associations were created, though most can be understood as big dreams with few actual members or activities. Buddhists focused on creating associations to seek legal protection for monastery assets. This focus emerged in response to one of the goals of revolutionary intellectual elites, which was to create a modernized mass education system. The fiscal realities of turn-of-the-century China were dire, and the fall of the old empire did not improve the economy. To generate the resources needed for these new schools, local officials simply took buildings, land, and property away from Buddhist temples and placed them under local government control. Such expropriation by the state was a serious threat to Buddhist monastic communities.

Some Buddhist associations were created to enact modernist agendas. One of Jichan's most reform-minded disciples, Taixu, set up an aggressively reformist "Society for the Advancement of Buddhism." As mentioned in chapter 3, Taixu and his associates used the newly available legal instruments to seize control of the famous Jinshan Monastery, with the intention of transforming its property and holdings into a modern educational facility. Soon the monks of Jinshan fought back, and the conflict came to blows. A court jailed some of the monks and ceased the operations of Taixu's revolutionary association.

Jichan co-organized what would become the first national Buddhist organization in modern China. As the abbot of Tiantong Monastery and a prominent monastery administrator, he established a provincial association. Then he worked with delegates representing seventeen province-wide Buddhist organizations. Monks representing all corners of the new nation gathered at Liuyun Temple in Shanghai. On April 1, 1912, the delegates voted to establish the General Buddhist Association of China. They passed several resolutions (including a resolution requesting the government protect monastic property). The General Buddhist Association of China elected Jichan as the national association's first president. The association petitioned the government to ratify its charter and give it official recognition.

Though the president of the fledgling organization, Jichan temporarily returned to Mount Tiantong. At one point earlier that year, he had gone to Nanjing to visit Sun Yat-sen to discuss the importance of government protection for Buddhist temples. However, Sun soon resigned as provisional president in an agreement that ceded the office to Yuan Shikai, who held power in Beijing and was able to arrange the abdication of the child emperor Puyi (1906–1967; r. 1908–1912). In April of 1912, the center of government moved from Nanjing to Beijing. Over the next several months, the General Association's petitions and correspondence with the government would not receive a response. The national Buddhist organization would not be recognized by the government. Come the ninth month of the year, Jichan was in Shanghai again to mark the Double Yang Festival (*Chongyang jie*). There, he decided he would travel to Beijing to press the government to recognize the association and to support the needs of the country's Buddhist institutions.

Jichan traveled to Beijing with his disciple Daojie. They lodged at Fayuan Temple, one of the city's oldest and most symbolically significant Buddhist temples. After nine days, Jichan had an audience with a government minister named Du Guan. Jichan asked Du to ensure the government honor the protections to temples promised by the Provisional Constitution. Accounts of what happened next vary, but Jichan and Du had some kind of row. Some accounts record that Du at first responded to Jichan's requests with silence. Others state that it was Du who grew furious at the old monk and insulted him. Du at one point slapped Jichan on the face, according to one account. Supposedly Jichan was very angry but bit his tongue because it is not right for a monk to speak from anger. Whatever happened, Jichan returned to Fayuan Temple empty-handed. The requests of the General Buddhist Association had been rebuffed.

That night, Jichan died at Fayuan Temple, immediately after the row with Du. Speculation ran rife about the cause of Jichan's death. His disciple Daojie found his body in the morning and reported that Jichan had not been ill. He was only sixty years old. Jichan's unusual death began to be discussed in the press. It seemed obvious to many that the government had somehow caused the death of this eminent monk. It was widely believed that Jichan acted honorably in his encounter with Du, who left him humiliated and angry. That Jichan had died at Fayuan Temple, the most symbolic Buddhist institution in Beijing, only added to the sense that the new government was not acting as a good steward of the nation's Buddhist traditions. In response, the Yuan Shikai government recognized the General Association's charter, a move that granted the organization official status, and promulgated an order against appropriating temple assets.

Many Buddhists felt that Jichan had given his life in exchange for modern Buddhist legal rights. It seems fair to say that he was remembered as a martyr for the survival of Chinese Buddhism in the modern world. Jichan's portrait and poetry were regularly reprinted in Buddhist magazines, even twenty years after his death. Although Jichan's General Association would soon be banned by Yuan's government in 1915 (and the confiscation of temple assets resumed), its influence continued to resonate over the decades. Even today, nationally minded Buddhist organizations such as the Chinese Buddhism Association based in Taipei, Taiwan, trace their own history back to this first national Buddhist association and regard Jichan as the organization's first president.

The memory of how Jichan died influenced one strain of how later Chinese readers interpreted his poetry. Although Jichan was known as a poet of the plum tree during his lifetime, since the mid-twentieth century he has been celebrated in China for his "patriotism." Taixu wrote a biography for Jichan in which he titled one section "Love of Country" (*aiguo*). Indeed, Jichan made poetic observations about life during a time of war and the disintegration of the Qing nation. It is perhaps more accurate to say that Jichan wrote poems that addressed the suffering of ordinary people during the privations of the First Sino-Japanese War. One might say that he was expressing compassion in his "patriotic" poems. Still, it is unexpected for a Buddhist monk to write poems about secular affairs, such as politics and war. A monk could attract criticism for stepping beyond religious matters. These poems constitute a relatively small proportion of Jichan's total oeuvre and were not widely celebrated during his lifetime. Nonetheless, they have become a prominent part of his legacy in the most recent decades.

One of the most often referenced examples is a line that is often taken out of context from poems that Jichan wrote after seeing a young man named Hu return from battle with a wooden leg: "Our national humiliation not repaid, how shameful the army is held back!" A year after war broke out in 1894, a regiment of the Hunanese army was at the port city of Niuzhuang (modern Yingkou, Liaoning) facing off against the Japanese and suffered terrible losses. Very shortly after their defeat, the Qing commander Li Hongzhang in 1895 signed the Treaty of Shimonoseki, which ceded extensive territories to Japan. The loss of life felt all the more senseless afterward. The poem adopts Hu's voice as a persona, and it is written in the voice of the young soldier in order to explore the suffering of ordinary men in war. The persona of the poem registers a sense of national shame because the one-sided military losses have not yet been avenged. Out of context, that line suggests that Jichan wanted the Chinese army to attack the Japanese. However, in the next line of the poem, the speaker of the poem turns around to see that all his comrades have died. Altogether the poem acknowledges the desire for revenge but shows that it will only lead to further suffering. It would not be accurate to say that the first line directly reflects Jichan's own attitude toward war (especially when read out of context). Jichan was troubled by the senselessness of such disfigurement, permanent injuries endured by ordinary men. Although I am skeptical of using the word *patriotic* to label these poems, because of their importance to one strand of modern Chinese interpretation, I have translated a representative sample for the reader (see III.4 and III.5).

The Translations

The range of Jichan's concerns can be seen in the following selection of poems. I have drawn these poems from three of his publications. The first five are from *Songs to Savor the Flowering Plum*, the aforementioned collection of roughly three hundred poems published in 1881, when he was just twenty-nine years old. Second, I have provided a complete translation of all eight poems from the booklet *Smaller Collection of White Plums*, published in 1904 in Ningbo. Copies of this booklet were available for sale, and the carved woodblocks were kept at Tiantong Monastery and made available to anyone who wanted to print copies to distribute. Third, I selected ten poems from Jichan's *Complete Works*, also known as *Eight-Fingered Ascetic's Poetry and Other Writings*, published posthumously in 1919. Some of those poems had also been published earlier in Jichan's lifetime. After each translation I indicate the year that poem was written based on the research of the Chinese scholar Mei Ji. When I was selecting poems, I aimed to balance several aspects of Jichan's legacy. I included the verses most often cited in later Chinese literature and anthologies as well as lesser-known poems that I felt would convey the pith of Jichan's teachings.

JICHAN
I

Songs to Savor the Flowering Plum, Selected Poems (1881)

(I.1)

Thinking of Jingyi, My Chan Friend

I think of you, but cannot see you.
Morning after morning comes this fog of disappointment.
In the slanting rays of dawn the wild goose has already departed,
Gone to deliver a distant message for someone else.
At once an oriole flies
Out the valley, sings from a majestic tree.
I dawdle & pace, east & west.
Who will speak with me about hermetic delights?

(1373)

(I.2)

On Shaving My Head, a Poem for My Little Brother

The human realm is a house aflame, we cannot dwell here;
My own life is star-crossed, I have cried like the rain.
Mother died when I was only seven sui old,
And you, little brother, were still nursing.
I touched her coffin, seeking our mother, crying 'til my voice gave
    way.
Father and I consoled one another.
Mother was gone, but still you and I had father,
Someone we could lean on.
But one day father passed too.
Little brother, you and I clung together in this vacated world.
Our grief was boundless, our travails unrelenting.
Head in hand I beseeched the heavens, but heaven was silent.
Now, I reckon that I have you, little brother, to continue our
    family line,
And you agree I should learn Buddhism.
But I ask, how can one "leave home" if one has no home?
Alas, a human life is but lodging for a traveler.
I say this to my little brother, and he does not grieve.
I will practice my Dharma, he will continue our family.

(1873)

(l.3)

*Searching for the Early Flowering Plums
on Solitary Hill, West Lake*

Though a chrysanthemum may brave frost,
Only the plum blossom will burst through snow.
If one goes alone to Solitary Hill,
One may chance upon flowers in bloom.
Although the delicate fragrance has not yet peaked,
Those powder-dabbed butterflies have clustered.
I was about to step closer and write a poem for you,
Catching the wind, I wince at the limits of my talent.

(1876)

(I.4)

On Owing the Plum Blossom a Poetry Debt

Snow falling, I falter, my dull lines embarrass me.
I remember the words of old Su Dongpo, and crack a smile.
Though breeze and moonlight inspire me, my coffers are empty.
I still owe the plum blossom a poetry debt.

(1876)

(.5)
One of Three Verses I Added to My Painting of
a Wandering Monk Toiling at Poetry

A young man and a white-haired elder, humble ascetics,
Whistling at the moon, singing with the wind, feeling inspired
    again.
I reckon the plum blossoms laugh at me
Because I cannot fight off a single poetry demon!

(1880)

II

Smaller Collection of White Plums, a Complete Translation (1904)

(II.1)

White Plum

Cut off from all worldly concerns,
Where even Cold Mountain would find delight,
Dusk, a lone tendril of fog dims,
The new moon's glow is faint.
Space itself holds no shadows.
The perfume of the plum seems to carry feelings.
My simple heart is well at ease here,
And for a moment my whole being finds comfort.

(1897)

(II.2)

Mr. Infatuated with Plum Blossoms Asked Chen Shizeng
to Sketch the Likeness of White Plum Blossoms, I Added Three
Poems in Acclaim

Once I awaken from my dream of floral reverie,
What remains is this tranquil life.
Almost no trace of snow in my mind,
It seems there is no spring beyond these blossoms.
Cold, I enter a lonely meditative vision,
Pure, like one leaving the world behind.
Returning from where waters and mists meet,
I nurture these truths in solitude.

And I appreciate the weight of truth,
Solitary fragrance that carries only itself.
Unassuming in this frozen place,
A lofty branch stands above the rest.
Its blossoms can dispel all worldly dust
With the wonder of their pure color.
They smile knowingly at pines and cypress,
Those present, who do not wither.

Cold and snow suddenly stop,
And still no worldly dust arises.
By chance, across the brook
I spy a glimmer at the edge of the bamboo grove.
Blossoms, cold and capable of such clarity:
Perfume abundant and yet immaculate.
Who can explain the logic of their purity?
Plum blossoms echo this monk's sensibility.

(1898)

Translator's Notes: Mr. Infatuated with Plum Blossoms was a nickname for Li Ruiqing (1867–1920), a well-known calligrapher, painter,

and modern educator. Chen Shizeng is a renowned painter and the recipient of another poem below. He was also the son of Jichan's close friend Chen Sanli, who also received a poem, translated below.

(II.3)

On the White Plum Tree, for the Venerable Pure Karma

Secluded gully, a ground free of searching thoughts,
High and frozen, this is our home.
I labor toward the poetic words, and only then see the tree's
     bones;
Bosom cold, I almost resent these blossoms.
Karmic traces permeate its delicate undertaking:
So fine a fragrance—no use for bluster.
Once again I give proper respect to the great hermit Lin Bu
Shaken from reclusion to sing of the plum's "oblique lines."

(1898)

(II.4)

Mr. Infatuated with Plum Blossoms Illustrated a Plum for Venerable Huoran, Added Five of My White Plum Poems, but There Was Still Room on the Page, so I Wrote This New Poem

Though some look toward spring as to a heaving sea,
I am fond of mountain denizens, their silent stillness,
Those lightly resting against solitary mounds,
Who from their tallest branches cast winter into flowers.
Yes, from the beginning there is no form,
But where is it that these "oblique lines" take shape?
If we don't recognize the spring wind's intentions,
We chase spring down paths that turn and zag.

(1898)

(II.5)

Facing a Plum Tree and Recalling the Honorable Chen

Upstream the western river has begun to thaw,
Outside eastern hall buds sprout again.
Blossoms are friends to what is born from solitary Chan,
Roots come to life from the frozen earth.
Wind and frost take pity on the kalpas gone by;
Heaven and earth favor the solitary and pure.
I accidentally entered Master He's song,
Speechless, I didn't realize I'd started crying.

(1899)

Translator's Notes: "Administrator Chen" is Chen Sanli (1853–1937), the well-known poet from Hunan. His father was Chen Baozhen (1831–1900), reformist governor of Hunan. "Western river" is likely a reference to Jichan and Chen's Hunanese home along the middle reaches of the Yangtze River. "Eastern hall" is metonymy for an official's residence. "Master He" is He Xun, a poet of the Liang dynasty (502–557), well-known among Chinese poets for being among the first to admire the qualities of plum blossoms. Jichan also likely had in mind a couplet by Du Fu about He Xun, which similarly describes plums by an official's residence: "Outside eastern hall the officials' plums stirred poetic inspirations, / just as for He Xun at Yangzhou."

(II.6)

Facing a Plum Tree, Waking Up

Sundown, the sky clear after snowfall,
I face the wooded park in silence, my robes solemn.
The stream still, I compare myself to my reflection,
Looks like he is the one listening to the snow singing!
For winter's three months I've been without warmth,
At once I understand, I see this heart of spring.
Silence, silence—I yearn for someone to tell—
Wisps of cloud dot the distant hills.

(1899)

(1.7)

Facing a Plum Tree beneath the Moon

Such lofty cold does not suit people well.
This austere bearing seems to forsake companions.
A waning moon is above the four mountains,
It is spring by the small bridge of a lonesome station.
One moment, I turn to face flurries like snow,
But their pure aroma is not of this dusty world.
The immortal Lin Bu recognized them from their shadows.
Who else can discern their truth?

(1903)

(II.8)

Searching for Plum Trees after Snowfall

The sky is suddenly clear, heaps of snow are everywhere.
I grab my goosefoot staff and set off searching.
In cold repose the blossoms sprout from ancient cliffs,
In their quiet awakening a delicate aroma rises.
The fog stands, held by thin boughs' shadows;
Moonlight backs the blossoms' fine glow.
Is there a person who can match such solitary purity?
A single smile just so and filled with feeling.

(1903)

III

Poems from the Posthumous Complete Works (1919)

(III.1)

On a Painting of Fishing the Snowy River

He dangles his hook east from the plank bridge,
Snow presses cold into his straw cloak.
Below the frozen river's unmoving surface,
Fishes chew at the shadows of plum blossoms.

(1884)

(III.2)

Chastising Myself

I turn ten years into a single poem,
Use five characters to grasp the Great Wall.
Like this my thoughts churn—why does my mind toil so?
Then quietly I sing a poem—tears begin to flow
And in that moment I fret I've abandoned my Buddhist training,
Though perhaps I have not falsely earned my reputation:
With our Dharma I see the delusions of poetry.
That I can say this does not deserve praise.

(1897)

(III.3)

My Feelings as I Set Off from Young Master Chen

No use in breaking a willow branch in two
As the eastward wind sends me hiking.
Leave-taking sentiments are as intoxicating as sweet herbs;
Spring dreams as ephemeral as falling blossoms.
I have not yet realized the fruit of the Three Vehicles,
And merely work the realm of five-character poetic lines.
Could I one day deserve a legendary Lotus Society biography?
Sadly I am merely known as a poet.

(1898)

Translator's Notes: The young man addressed here is Chen Shizeng, a well-known artist. Jichan calls him "young master" (*gongsun*) because Shizeng was the eldest son of a prominent family. His grandfather was Chen Baozhen, the governor of Hunan. A Lotus Society biography would be written for a monk who devoted himself to leading a group of lay practitioners.

(III.4)
Tune of the Enlistees (One of Three)

Thirteen enlistees guard the frontier,
As five thousand cavalry flash by in an endless chain.
One battle at the Great Wall, the whole regiment gone.
How can we expect their portraits to hang in Frozen Cloud
    Pavilion?

(1898)

Translator's Notes: The poem is from the perspective of the thirteen enlistees guarding a military outpost who watched five thousand countrymen go to battle and not return. Frozen Cloud Pavilion was where Tang emperors hung portraits of those ministers whose exemplary service was to be honored. The poem implies that the Qing government is unlikely to honor the numerous ordinary people who died in war.

(III.5)

Writing about the Young Student Hu following
the Defense of Niuzhuang (Third of Five)

A sheet of paper, the treaty, lands on shore.
But our national humiliation not repaid, how shameful that the
    army is held back!
When I turn around, all are dead. Where have they gone?
Makeshift graves everywhere I look, where their tents once stood.

(1898)

(III.6)

First of Two Poems Written to Match the Rhymes of a Poem Written by the Talented Lu Yinqiu

We are doddering and yet still seek to become one-word poetic
   masters;
Dare we name the successes and failures known deep in our own
   hearts?
I do not desire to become a buddha, nor attain rebirth in some
   heaven.
I pray only that good poetry will exist among men.

(1903)

Translator's Notes: "One-word poetic master" refers to a deeply talented poet, one who can transform another poet's mediocre verse
into a great poem by replacing one word with the perfect alternative.

(II.7)

Unsleeping

When the Chan temple bells and Sanskrit intoning have ceased,
Unsleeping I hear a gibbon's song.
In my old age, wild inspiration grows harder to dispel;
In my sickness, the poetry demon trespasses upon me ever more.
I move my bedding into moonlight
And search for poetic lines as if they are gold.
I've long known the emptiness of frivolous fame,
Nevertheless, this is the mind I have in the night.

(1904)

(III.8)

Admonishment to the World, First of Two Poems

Listen, the entire world can be hidden in a single grain.

A cosmic Buddha's life is *immeasurable* and yet we speak of *three*
  bodies.

A flower was lifted and Mahākāśyapa delicately smiled.

With his mouth closed, Vimalakīrti spoke with silence.

Few can be called away from the clatter of beauty and sweet
  voices.

Even the rich and powerful have honeyed dreams only if they are
  asleep.

What a pity! Everywhere I see the ignorant acting like children;

While the six thieves, entering one home after the next, are
  welcomed like sons.

(1908)

Translator's Notes: The final line expands on images from the *Śūraṃgama Sūtra*. "The six thieves" refers to unwholesome perceptions
through our six senses—the five bodily senses plus the mind. The
senses are imagined as gates and windows through which perceptions pass. The ordinary manner of relating to our perceptions tends
to lead to desire and unwholesome behavior, and turns perceptions
into thieves that rob us of our connection to buddha-nature.

(III.9)

Thoughts about the Way

Stones turn to powder, pines wither away—don't bother to ask
  when;
Dragon asleep, tiger at rest—each so peaceful.
You ought to know a person of stillness has a heart coursing with
  marvels;
And do not think I, a mountain monk, am so strange, my words
  full of contradiction.
The great earth could sink into the sea—still we'd have delusion.
The open sky could crumble—that would not yet be Chan.
If you wish to practice the dharma of awakening in this lifetime,
Step forward from the top of that hundred-foot pole.

(1909)

(III.10)

Dreaming of Lake Dongting

Last night's dream decants Dongting Lake,
Pours the green of Mount Jun into a bottle,
Tips it to stew the full moon,
Swirls around to bathe a cluster of stars.
A crane comes to take the precepts,
A group of dragons arrives to hear a sutra.
Is there someone who can play a flute
To wake me from beneath the pines?

(1909)

Further Reading

Bingenheimer, Marcus, and Ting Shen. "The Portrayal of Women in the Poetry of Jing'an Eight-Fingers." *Studies in Chinese Religions* 6, no. 2 (2020): 119-40.

Egan, Ronald. "*Shi Poetry*: Ancient and Recent Styles (The Five Dynasties and the Song Dynasty)." In *How to Read Chinese Poetry: A Guided Anthology*, edited by Zong-qi Cai, 308-26. New York: Columbia University Press, 2007.

Goossaert, Vincent. "Republican Church Engineering: The National Religious Associations in 1912 China." In *Chinese Religiosities*, edited Mayfair Mei-hui Yang, 209-32. Berkeley: University of California Press, 2008.

Lai, Rongdao. "Praying for the Republic: Buddhist Education, Student-Monks, and Citizenship in Modern China (1911-1949)." PhD diss., McGill University, 2014.

Mazanec, Thomas. *Poet-Monks: The Invention of Buddhist Poetry in Late Medieval China*. Ithaca, NY: Cornell University Press, 2024.

Protass, Jason. *The Poetry Demon*. Honolulu: University of Hawai'i Press, 2021.

Notes

Introduction: Flowers in the Snow

1. Pung Kwang Yu, "Confucianism," in *The World's Parliament of Religions: An Illustrated and Popular Story of the World's First Parliament of Religions Held in Chicago in Connection with the Columbian Exposition of 1893*, by John Henry Barrows (Chicago: Parliament Publishing, 1893), 411.

2. The World's Congress of Religions, *The Addresses and Papers Delivered Before the Parliament* (Philadelphia: J. W. Keeler, 1894), 513.

3. William Remfry Hunt, *Heathenism Under the Searchlight: The Call of the Far East* (London: Morgan and Scott, 1908), 33-34.

4. D. T. Suzuki, "Review of H. Dumoulin: The Development of Chinese Zen after the Sixth Patriarch," *Review of Religion* 19, nos. 1/2 (1954): 52.

5. Vincent Goossaert, "1898: The Beginning of the End for Chinese Religion?" *Journal of Asian Studies* 65, no. 2 (2006): 308.

6. Mayfair Mei-hui Yang, ed. *Chinese Religiosities: Afflictions of Modernity and State Formation* (Berkeley: University of California Press, 2008), 19.

7. *Xuyun heshang nianpu* [Annals of the Monk Xuyun], in *Xuyun heshang fahui nianpu ji* (Nantou: Caituan faren Zhongtai shan Fojiao jijinhui, 1999), 216-17.

8. The Dharmaguptaka Vinaya is best known in China through the interpretations of the eminent monk Daoxuan (596-667), who is credited with establishing the Nanshan Vinaya tradition that still prevails in Chinese Buddhist traditions.

9. In a letter to Adolf Hitler recommending that the German people, "the most excellent scion of ancient Aryan stock," all convert to Buddhism, Taixu signed off as the "Leader of the Buddhists in China." Donald S. Lopez, *Buddhism and Science: A Guide for the Perplexed* (Chicago: University of Chicago Press, 2008), 73-74.

10. Vincent Goossaert and David A. Palmer, *The Religious Question in Modern China* (Chicago: University of Chicago Press, 2011), 160.

11. The National Committee of the Chinese People's Political Consultative Conference, "Using Socialism as the Core Value System for Guiding and Strengthening the Ideology of Our Nation's Religious Thought," November 1, 2023, http://www.cppcc.gov.cn/zxww/2023/11/01/ARTI1698824776531780. shtml.

About This Book

1. Yu Lingbo, *Zhongguo jindai Fomen renwu zhi* [Buddhists of Modern China] (Taipei: Huiju chuban she, 1993).

Chapter One: The Modern Reviver of Chan—Xuyun

1. For gong'an, see Guo Gu, *Passing through the Gateless Barrier: Koans for Real Life* (Boulder, CO: Shambhala Publications, 2016); Jimmy Yu, *Readings of the Gateless Barrier* (New York: Columbia University Press, 2024).

2. For a translation of Xuyun's autobiography, see Charles Luk, *Empty Cloud: The Autobiography of the Chinese Zen Master Xu Yun*, rev. ed. (Shaftesbury, UK: Element Books, 1988). For scholarly studies of Xuyun life, see Daniela Campo, *La construction de la sainteté dans la Chine moderne: La vie du maître bouddhiste Xuyun* (Paris: Belles Lettres, 2015), or her "Chan Master Xuyun: The Embodiment of an Ideal, the Transmission of a Model," in *Making Saints in Modern China*, ed. David Ownby, Vincent Goossaert, and Ji Zhe (New York: Oxford University Press, 2016), 99–136.

3. See Charles Luk, *Empty Cloud: The Autobiography of the Chinese Zen Master Xu Yun*, rev. ed. (Shaftesbury, UK: Element Books, 1988), 61.

4. Luk, *Empty Cloud*, 106–8.

5. For a detailed study of his life, see Jimmy Yu, *Reimagining Chan Buddhism: Sheng Yen and the Creation of the Dharma Drum Lineage of Chan* (Abingdon, UK: Routledge, 2021).

6. For this work, see Sheng Yen, *Chanmen xiuzheng zhiyao* [Essentials of practice and awakening in the Chan Gate] (Taipei: Fagu Wenhua, 1992), 234–47. Sheng Yen has written over a dozen books on Chan Buddhism. For a couple of examples, see the "Further Reading" section of this chapter.

7. See *Da foding rulai miyin xiuzheng liaoyi zhupusa wanxing shoulengyan jing*, T. no. 945, 19:147c9–10.

8. See *Da foding rulai miyin xiuzheng liaoyi zhupusa wanxing shoulengyan jing*, T. no. 945, 19:109c11.

9. *Da foding rulai miyin xiuzheng liaoyi zhupusa wanxing shoulengyan jing*, T. no. 945, 19:109c7–14.

10. An incense board is a wooden, sword-shaped board, a little over three feet long, that monitors in the Chan Hall use to strike sleeping meditators or

punish those who violate the disciplines of the hall. It is called "incense" because traditionally the duration of each sitting period is measured by the time it takes for an incense to burn.

11. This image of having one's "tongue pulled out for cows to plow on" is a Chinese Buddhist medieval conception of a particular hell reserved for those who deceive others. The tongue in this case is analogous to verbal transgression; hence, it becomes the object of punishment.

12. The "eighth consciousness," or *ālayavijñāna* in Yogācāra Consciousness-Only Buddhism, refers to the most fundamental region of one's consciousness, the storehouse or repository consciousness of all the karmic impressions from one's experiences. It is the locus of transmigration of birth and death in *samsara*. The other seven consciousnesses are the first five consciousnesses connected to the five senses, the sixth consciousness corresponding to the function of discrimination, and the seventh consciousness corresponding to self-referentiality or self-grasping.

13. This word *Wu*, or "No," refers to the first of forty-eight cases of gong'ans in the *Gateless Barrier* collection: "One day a monk asked Chan Master Zhaozhou Congshen, 'Does a dog have buddha-nature?' Zhaozhou replied, 'Wu.'" (English: No; Japanese: *Mu*). See Jimmy Yu, *Readings of the Gateless Barrier* (New York: Columbia University Press, 2024).

14. This is reference to a gong'an case in the *Transmission of the Lamp in the Jingde Era* in which an old lady burned down the hut of the monk whom she supported for twenty years. The story goes that one day, in order to test the monk, the old lady asked her daughter to hug the monk when she brings his meal. She did that, and the next day the old lady asked the monk how he felt when her daughter hugged him. He replied that it was like "a withered log leaning on a cold cliff." Upon hearing this, the old lady regretted that she has been supporting this monk and chased him out of the hut. After which she burned it down.

Chapter Two: A Formidable Chan Master—Laiguo

1. Laiguo Miaoshu, *Zixing lu* [Autobiography] (Shanghai: Daxiong Shuju, 1949), 12–13.

2. Laiguo's monastic code is titled *Chanlin siliao guiyue* [Regulations for the Four Departments of a Chan Monastery]. The four departments are the abbot's quarters (*fangzhang*), the meditation hall (*chantang*), the guest hall (*ketang*), and the business office (*kufang*).

3. Laiguo, *Chanlin siliao guiyue* (Shanghai: Shanghai guiji chubanshe, 2004), 3:47; Holmes Welch, *The Practice of Chinese Buddhism* (Cambridge, MA: Harvard University Press, 1967), 14–15.

4. Welch, *Practice*, 75–77. The current schedule for intensive meditation

retreats at Gaomin is somewhat more forgiving. The day begins at 4:30 a.m. and ends at 11:00 p.m. Chan meditation retreats have their Pure Land corollary in buddha recitation retreats, which can also last up to ten weeks. During recitation retreats, participants are directed to silently repeat Amitābha's name at all times. According to a monk who participated at one such retreat at Lingyan temple, "Mind and sound must be united; pure thoughts of Amitābha must succeed one another without interruption, like a son thinking back on his mother." Chen-hua, *In Search of the Dharma: Memoirs of a Modern Chinese Buddhist Pilgrim*, ed. Chün-Fang Yü, trans. Denis C. Mair (Albany: State University of New York Press, 1992), 151.

5. *Dahui Pujue Chanshi yulu* [The discourse record of Chan Master Dahui Pujue], T47, no. 1998a, 886a28.

6. Morten Schlütter, "'Who Is Reciting the Name of the Buddha?' as Gongan in Chinese Chan Buddhism," *Frontiers of History in China* 8, no. 3 (2013): 382.

7. Jeffrey L. Broughton, *The Recorded Sayings of Chan Master Zhongfeng Mingben* (New York: Oxford University Press, 2023), 36.

8. "Chanqi kaishi," in *Foyuan laoheshang kaishi lu*, 110. Campo, "Disclosing the Self."

9. Laiguo Miaoshu, *Laiguo chanshi quanji* [The complete works of Chan Master Laiguo] (Yangzhou: Gaomin Si, 2005), 360.

10. Incense boards are swordlike wooden sticks wielded by monastic officers. Very similar to the *kyosaku* found in Japanese Zen monasteries, incense boards were used to rouse sleepy monks and discipline those who broke the rules.

11. The civil service exams were rigorous, multiday tests that required complete mastery of the Confucian classics and specific forms of writing. The most successful candidates were ensured a coveted post in the imperial administration. Those who aspired to such positions would spend many years preparing for the exams.

12. The *Book of Hundreds of Surnames*, compiled sometime during the Song dynasty, consists of 507 Chinese surnames arranged in rhyming lines of eight characters. Used to teach children common Chinese characters, the text was intended to be memorized but had no semantic value. The English equivalent would be a text reading "Smith, Johnson, Williams, Brown, Jones..."

13. These are the consciousnesses associated with the five senses: eyes, ears, nose, tongue, and body. Since these precede the consciousness of the mind, they are referred to as "prior" consciousnesses.

14. On doubt in the context of Chan practice, see page 38-42 in this volume.

Chapter Three: The Great Reformer—Taixu

1. Unlike a traditional master with his disciples, Taixu held limited actual power over the students in his seminaries. This was a novel arrangement. As a result, he was held responsible for what they said and did by those who understood the relationship according to the traditional framework.

2. For a translation of Taixu's major work on this theme, see Charles B. Jones, *Taixu's "On the Establishment of the Pure Land in the Human Realm": A Translation and Study* (New York: Bloomsbury Academic, 2021).

3. For a translation of the Tibetan version of this text, see Asaṅga, *On Knowing Reality: The* Tattvārtha *Chapter of Asaṅga's* Bodhisattvabhūmi, trans. Janice Dean Willis (repr., Delhi: Motilal Banarsidass, 2002).

4. The term literally means "defeat" and refers to an offense so great as to have defeated the purpose of taking precepts in the first place. Thus, a monastic who commits a parajika offense is no longer a monastic.

5. That is, to observe proper decorum, avoiding behaviors that might cause them to doubt the Dharma.

6. Tang and Wu were the founders of the Shang and Zhou dynasties, respectively. They rose up against evil rulers and succeeded because their impeccable virtue had earned them the Mandate of Heaven. The Duke of Zhou ruled as regent following the death of his brother King Wu. These figures were the archetypes of virtuous rule that inspired Confucius and later thinkers in China and the rest of East Asia for over two thousand years.

7. Those of humans, gods, arhats, solitary buddhas, and bodhisattvas.

8. Those of arhats, solitary buddhas, and bodhisattvas.

9. Afflictive and cognitive.

10. This diagram, it must be said, is a bit opaque. The identification of the four goals arranged in the center with the emphases of Human Life Buddhism and prior Buddhism to the left and with the emphases of philosophy and science and higher religions tracks with the essay. The way these are mapped onto the Two Vehicles and the Great Vehicle, however, seems to deviate from it in counterintuitive ways. One suspects that there was some sort of mistake, but it has been carried over in subsequent printings. Regardless, the inclusion of a diagram represents the appeal of scientific discourse and its conventions.

11. Beings born in Tuṣita outside of Maitreya's Inner Court are simply devas who will enjoy a long and pleasurable life but remain within the ordinary course of samsara. The idea that rebirth within the Inner Court likewise left the aspirant trapped in samasara was a common charge made by advocates of the Western Pure Land in the Tang dynasty and again in the Republic in response to Taixu and his associates' promotion of Maitreya.

12. This is a somewhat odd misquotation in this context. The *Lotus* actually says, "When life reaches its end, the hands of a thousand Buddhas reach out to receive you, so that you are not afraid and do not fall into evil paths but are reborn in Tuṣita where Maitreya Bodhisattva resides." It seems Taixu is combining the passage from the *Lotus* with passages from other sutras such as the *Mahāratnakūṭa* that do promise rebirth in whatever buddha land one aspires to.

Chapter Four: A Peripatetic Bodhisattva-Artist—Hongyi

1. Scholars have taken numerous approaches to a translation of this highly compressed title, including such examples as *The Human Profile*, *Spiritual Guide*, *Manual for Man*, *On Human Morality*, *Human Schemata*. I often think of it as something like *How to Be a Human*. The text itself has not appeared in English translation.
2. Hongyi, "*Lü xue yao lue*" [Essentials of Vinaya studies], in *Hongyi dashi quanji* [Complete writings of Great Master Hongyi], vol. 1 (1935; Fuzhou: Fujian renmin chuban she, 1991), 199a.

Chapter Five: Pure Land Patriarch—Yinguang

1. The other three eminent monks are Taixu (1890-1947), Hongyi (1880-1942), and Xuyun (1839-1959).
2. For more on the patriarchs, see Charles B. Jones, *Chinese Pure Land Buddhism: Understanding a Tradition of Practice*. Pure Land Studies (Honolulu: University of Hawai'i Press, 2019), 172-77. See also Chen Chienhuang, "The Process of Establishing and Justifying the Thirteen Patriarchs of the Lotus School," trans. Charles B. Jones, *Pacific World: Journal of the Institute of Buddhist Studies*, 3rd ser., 19 (2017): 129-48.
3. This account was derived from the following sources: Chen Chienhuang, "Yinguang Dashi zai Fayusi qijian de xiuzheng jingyan" [Great Master Yinguang's experience of cultivation and attainment during his time in the Fayu Temple], in *Hanchuan fojiao zuting wenhua guoji xueshu yantaohui wenji* (Beijing: Zongjiao Wenhua Chubanshe, 2016), 2:1199-1212; Chen Chienhuang, *Yuantong zhengdao: Yinguang de jingtu qihua* [Thorough penetration, realizing the way: Yinguang's pure land innovations] (Taipei: Dongda tushu gongsi, 2002); and Shen Quji, ed., *Yinguang fashi nianpu* [A chronological biography of Dharma Master Yinguang] (Taipei: Fotuo Jiaoyu Jijinhui, 2012).
4. The proximity of this date to the lunar New Year has created some difficulty in determining which year this is in the Western calendar. Xianfeng

11 normally converts to 1861, and so many modern sources give this as his year of birth. However, this lunar year extended to January 29, 1862. Thus, the date January 11, 1862, appears most likely. See also Jiang Canteng, *Zhongguo jindai fojiao sixiang de zhengbian yu fazhan* [The struggles and development of modern Chinese Buddhist thought] (Taipei: Nantian Shuju, 1998), 417. Shen Quli's *Chronological Biography* (in Chinese) gives the year as 1861, while others, such as Chen Chienhuang's *Thorough Penetration* (in Chinese) leave the date in its original form without converting to the Western equivalent.

5. Shi Guangding, ed. *Zengding Yinguang dashi quanji* [The complete works of Great Master Yinguang, expanded] (Taipei: Fojiao shuju, 1991), 2:1257. Hereafter *Complete Works*.

6. Chinese ages are indicated by the word *sui*, which literally means "harvest." Children are automatically aged one sui at birth, but in some cases the number of sui might be two more than the age given in Western systems. Thus, Yinguang was either nineteen or eighteen years old at the time.

7. *Complete Works*, 5:2397.

8. Shen Quji, ed., Shen Quji, ed. *Yinguang fashi nianpu* [Chronological biography of Master Yinguang]. (Taipei: Fotuo jiaoyu jijinhui, 2012), 42-43. "Cash" refers to copper coins with a hole in the middle kept on strings.

9. The couplet refers to Yangqi Fanghui (995-1049), who, in making sandals for private sale, made sure he did not use any of the monastery's oil to light his work; and Baoshou (978-1054), who would not let even his own master take ginger from the common kitchen.

10. In elite Chinese society, a "courtesy name" or "style name" was bestowed upon reaching adulthood, and served as the name by which one was known outside the family. Buddhist monks adopted this practice, assigning new ordinands a courtesy name once fully ordained.

11. For more on Chewu, see Charles B. Jones, "Mentally Constructing What Already Exists: The Pure Land Thought of Chan Master Jixing Chewu (1741-1810)," in *Journal of the International Association of Buddhist Studies* 23, no. 1 (2000): 43-70.

12. *Complete Works*, 5:2400.

13. Jan Kiely, "The Charismatic Monk and the Chanting Masses: Master Yinguang and His Pure Land Revival Movement," in *Making Saints in Modern China*, ed. David Ownby, Vincent Goossaert, and Ji Zhe (New York: Oxford, 2017), 37.

14. Kiely, "Charismatic Monk and the Chanting Masses," 41.

15. Jiang, *Zhongguo jindai fojiao*, 423-24.

16. Cizhou, "The Great Master Taught me a Method of Nianfo" (*Dashi jiao wo nianfo fangfa*), *Complete Works*, 7:472-473.

17. Jones, *Chinese Pure Land Buddhism*, chap. 4.
18. See Jones, *Chinese Pure Land Buddhism*, 113-15. For an English translation of Yinguang's essay, see Yinguang, "Treatise Resolving Doubts about the Pure Land (*Jingtu jueyi lun*) by Master Yinguang (1861-1940)," trans. Charles B. Jones, in *Pacific World: Journal of the Institute of Buddhist Studies*, 3rd series, 14 (2012): 27-61.
19. Kiely, "Charismatic Monk and the Chanting Masses," 56.
20. Charles B. Jones, *Taixu's "On the Establishment of the Pure Land in the Human Realm": A Translation and Study* (New York: Bloomsbury Academic, 2021), 58.
21. *Fo shuo Amituo jing*, T12, no. 366, 346c13-c14. Translation mine.
22. *Complete Works*, 4:1938-1939.

Chapter Six: From Laywoman to Tiantai Master—Benkong

1. On May 30, thousands of workers and students, enraged at the unfair treatment meted out to workers by the owners of a Japanese-owned company, staged an anti-foreign and anti-Japanese demonstration in Shanghai during which thirteen demonstrators were killed and many others wounded by the British municipal police. This led in turn to three months of demonstrations, strikes, and boycotts all over the country.
2. Zhang Ruzhao, *Lutian yishici ji* [The verdant skies collection of poems and lyrics] (publisher unknown, 1925), 5a. There is a digitized version of this rare book available on the Ming Qing Women's Writings Digitalization Project, see https://digital.library.mcgill.ca/mingqing/search/detailswork.php?workID=433&language=ch.
3. Presbyterian missionaries Aimee Boddy Millican and her husband, Frank R. Millican (1883-1961), were very actively involved in educational and outreach activities in the Shanghai-Ningbo area during this period.
4. Benkong was so moved by the account of Jichan's untimely death in 1912 that she composed an inscription for his stupa at the Tiantong Monastery in Ningbo.
5. Normally conducted in a ritual setting overseen by a senior monastic or teacher, the Mahāyāna bodhisattva vow is an expression of one's aspiration to cultivate the six perfections of generosity, moral discipline, patience, effort, concentration, and wisdom to achieve full awakening for the sake of all sentient beings.
6. This essay, the full title of which is *Fahua sanmei zhi jiantao xian ji xiuxue zhi jingguo* [A study of the Lotus Samadhi and my experiences in its practice], was first printed in 1936 in the Buddhist journal *Haichao yin* (vol. 17, no. 3, pp. 70-88). It would later be reprinted several times, including more

recently, in Zhang Mantao, ed., *Tiantai dianji yanjiu* [Researches on Tiantai] (1979; Bejing: Beijing Library Press, 2005), 260-94. The excerpt translated here can be found on pp. 290-94.

7. While often the three refuges and the five precepts are taken together at the same time, Benkong appears to have been more cautious when it came to making a commitment to Buddhist belief and practice.

8. In 1922, Master Taixu founded the first Buddhist seminary for male monastics in Wuchang (a district of Wuhan, the capital city of Hubei Province). Two years later, he established the Wuchang Female Institute of Buddhist Studies (*Wuchang foxueyuan nüzhongyuan*), the first school for Buddhist nuns and laywomen.

9. T46, no. 1911, 13b11-12. See Paul L. Swanson, trans., *Clear Serenity, Quiet Insight: T'ien-Tai Chih-I's Mo-ho Chih-Kuan*, Nanzan Library of Asian Religion and Culture (Honolulu: University of Hawai'i Press, 2017), 2:290.

10. This is a genre of ancient Chinese poetry characterized primarily by its use of uniform line lengths of five or seven syllables that make paired couplets. Rhymes (not used in the English translation) generally appear at the end of each couplet.

11. Gaya Farm and Forest (Gaya nonglin in Cixi); see the section "Meeting Master Yinguang."

12. The Three Baskets refers to the Buddhist canon, or Tripitaka.

13. The ten schools of Chinese Buddhism, such as Pure Land, Chan, Tiantai, etc.

14. The interpretation of things as real or material as opposed to unreal or immaterial.

15. In other words, it often takes strict and difficult training for realization to be attained,

16. The sword of discriminating wisdom that slices through delusion.

17. The six senses, which give rise to afflictions and delusions.

18. The eight winds that can blow one off the path: prosperity, decline, disgrace, honor, praise, censure, suffering, and pleasure.

19. The Vinaya in Ten Recitations refers specifically to the code of rules and regulations adhered to primarily by monastics and recited communally on a regular basis. Although still a laywoman, Benkong aspires to a stricter monastic discipline.

20. This refers to the famous four-line verse recited to this day in many Mahāyāna Buddhist communities:

> Sentient beings are numberless; I vow to save them.
> Desires are inexhaustible; I vow to put an end to them.
> The dharmas are boundless; I vow to master them.
> The Buddha Way is unattainable; I vow to attain it.

21. The five traditional sciences or fields of knowledge in ancient India: language, logic, medicine, fine arts and crafts, and spirituality.

22. Literally, "my karmic-reward body," or the body that is the product of the karmic actions of this and previous lives.

23. The ritual begins with an extended veneration of the buddhas, followed by the expression of sincere repentance for all the sins committed throughout one's (many) lifetimes.

24. The notion of ten mentalities that lead to the continuous cyclic flow of birth and death (samsara) and the ten mentalities that counteract this flow was developed by Zhiyi as an aid to repentance. See Swanson, *Clear Serenity, Quiet Insight*, 618-26.

25. The sea of two deaths refer to the fragmentary (samsaric) death and the miraculous (enlightened) death. The shores of the tree virtues refer to the three aspects of the Buddha's virtue: that of compassion (*cide*) cutting off affliction (*duande*) and wisdom (*zhide*).

26. The wording that Benkong uses here is found in *Emended Procedures for the Lotus Samadhi Visualization* (*Fahua sanmei xingshi yunxiang buzhuyi*), T46, no. 1942, 956a13-15, by Zhanran (711-782), the ninth patriarch of Tiantai.

27. Benkong is referring here to her life of semi-seclusion at the Gaya nonglin.

28. Many of Benkong's early acquaintances, especially those fervently dedicated to the work of political and social reform, regarded her turn to Buddhism as both selfish and escapist.

29. Here, Benkong appears to be referring to herself as the (Buddhist) equivalent of a model Confucian wife or mother, one of whose primary duties was to keep her family on the straight and narrow path of moral behavior.

30. A central component of the Lotus Samadhi ritual involves a heartfelt repentance of sins committed throughout one's many lifetimes because of attachment to the objects of the six sense faculties.

31. In many schools of Chinese Buddhism, although perhaps especially in Pure Land, it was believed that to be born female was the result of negative karma.

32. Zhiyi, *Lotus Samadhi Penitence* (*Fahua sanmei chanyi*), T46, no. 1941, 952b10-12.

33. See Burton Watson, trans., *The Lotus Sutra* (New York: Columbia University Press, 1993), 12.

34. Watson, *Lotus Sutra*, 26.

35. These lines are from a poem the poet Lu You (1125-1210) wrote to his young son. It expresses the notion, often espoused by Confucians, that only persons of integrity who are able to resist the lure of fame or riches can engage in true learning and write good poetry.

36. There is an allusion here to a well-known poem by the great Tang poet Du Fu (712-770) composed in the wake of the calamitous An Lushan rebellion during which the capital of Chang'an was largely destroyed. The first two couplets of this poem read, "The nation in ruins, mountains and river remain / the city in spring, grass and trees burgeoning; / Feeling the times, the flowers elicit tears / hating separation, the birds startle the heart."

37. Here Benkong refers to the story of a certain Mr. Feng who was skilled at catching tigers and who, even after becoming educated, was unable to resist the temptation to go back to his former profession.

38. This line appears to actually be from the *Śūraṃgama Sūtra*, Chinese Buddhist Electronic Text Association (CBETA) T19, no. 945, 111c26-27.

39. To lay down the bamboo stand might be seen as the equivalent of laying down one's intellectual fixation on the words of the text and directly apprehending its deeper significance.

40. From Zhiyi's *Lotus Samadhi Penitence Ritual* (T46, no. 1941, p. 952c21-25.)

41. These two lines are from a verse in a series of mountain-dwelling poems (*shanju shi*) by the great tenth-century Chan master Yongming Yanshou (904-975).

42. The girl was a fellow retreat participant.

43. Watson, *Lotus Sutra*, 43.

44. Frank Millican, the husband of Benkong's friend, Aimee Boddy Millican.

45. Unfortunately, I've not been able to identify the two people mentioned here: the Chinese transliteration of British person's name is "Laisirui" (Royce?); the name of the person from India is transliterated as "Gantianshi." Benkong had always wanted to travel outside of China, and so this invitation must have been particularly difficult for her to turn down. She did finally make it to India after her ordination, although I've been unable to find any detailed information about this trip.

46. Watson, *Lotus Sutra*, 238.

47. According to the well-known story from *The Platform Sutra*, Shenxiu (606?-706), the senior student of Hongren (601-674), known as the Fifth Patriarch of Chan/Zen Buddhism, wrote this verse on the wall of Hongren's monastery as an expression of his understanding. It was refuted by the illiterate Huineng, who declared that since in actuality there was no such thing as a mirror, there was nowhere upon which dust could settle and thus no need for polishing. Huineng, who came to be known as the Sixth Ancestor of Chan/Zen Buddhism, is regarded as advocating the "sudden" as opposed to the "gradual" approach to awakening. Here, Benkong appears to be saying that, at certain stages of one's practice at least, a concerted effort to "polish the mirror" or control one's thoughts is necessary.

48. Zhiyi, *Procedure for the Lotus Samādhi Repentance* (*Fahua sanmei chanyi*), CBETA T46, no. 1941, 953a27–b01.

49. These two lines can be found in various sources, including a four-line gāthā sometimes ascribed simply to an "ancient patriarch." They reflect the basic notions of ineffability and emptiness (the moon's reflection in the water is often used as a metaphor for all that is illusory and unreal).

50. Zhiyi's *Procedure for the Lotus Samadhi Repentance* concludes with a detailed summary of the various signs that indicate a successful realization of the ritual. These are divided into the three categories of superior, intermediate, and inferior, with each of these being further subdivided into superior, intermediate, and inferior grades. The purification of the six sense faculties and the opening forth of the wise vision of the Buddha, neither of which Benkong claims to have realized, pertain to the very highest or superior category and grade.

51. The opening up of the heart of faith and the experience of dharma joy are listed among signs belonging to the highest grade within the third or inferior category.

52. According to Indian medicine, the four elements of material existence (earth, water, fire, and wind) in harmony is an indication of good physical health. According to Zhiyi's rankings, this, as well as strength and vigor, are signs that indicate the attainment of the lowest grade within the third or inferior category.

53. This is an idiom originally found in the *Analects* of Confucius.

54. These lines can be found in many sources, especially Chan/Zen sources.

55. The Dharma, for all its diversity, is said to have a single "flavor"—that of liberation from suffering.

56. These are lines from a verse by Chan master Wuzu Fayan (1024–1104). See *Discourse Records of Chan Master Fayan* (*Fayan chanshi yulu*, CBETA T47, no. 1995, 667c07).

Chapter Seven: Student and Huayan Master—Changxing

1. An English translation of this text, along with Chengguan commentary, can be found in Thomas Cleary, *Entry into the Inconceivable: An Introduction to Hua-yen Buddhism* (Honolulu: University of Hawai'i Press, 1983), 69–124.

2. The following is a translation of Changxing 常惺. "Foxue gailun 佛學概論 (An Outline of Buddhism)," *Haichaoyin* 海潮音 8, no. 11–12 (January 12, 1928): 1–25. MFQ 169.79–103.

3. Burton Watson, *Chuang-Tzu: Basic Writings* (New York: Columbia University Press, 1996), 35.

Chapter Eight: The Plum Blossom Monk—Jichan

1. The poems here were greatly benefited by discussions of them with Genine Lentine. The author also thanks Matt Zepelin at Shambhala for his excellent suggestions and feedback.

   Taixu composed the biography in 1914, entitled *Zhongxing Fojiao Jichan An hesheng zhuan*, published in *Haichaoyin* 2, no. 4 (1921).

2. A concerted effort to interpret Chan principles in Jichan's poetry is given in Ma Tianxiang 麻天祥, *Ershi shiji Zhongguo Foxue wenti* 20世紀中國佛學問題, 2nd rev. ed. (Wuhan: Wuhan daxue chubanshe, 2007), 38–61. See also work by Huang Ching-chia, cited below.

3. This section relies on the autonarratives given by Jichan in his 1888 piece *Shiji zishu* 詩集自述, which was published together with an edition of his collected poems to date; and in his 1909 piece *Lengxiangta zixu ming* 冷香塔自序銘, which Jichan wrote specifically to be inscribed near his own funerary pagoda at Mount Tiantong, where it can still be seen today.

4. The year of Jichan's birth has generated confusion because of differences between the traditional lunar and Gregorian calendar systems. He was born in the first year of the Xianfeng reign (which mostly corresponds to 1851). However, Jichan was born in the twelfth month of that lunar year, so it was 1852 when he was born. On top of this, Chinese scholarship calculates the timeline of his career using traditional Chinese sui, which are ordinal numbers: a person in their seventh sui is about six years old. Western scholars normally convert from traditional Chinese sui by subtracting one (e.g., seven sui is six years old). In the traditional Chinese counting method, people gained one sui at the lunar new year (not on their individual birthday). Jichan's case is confounding because he was born in the twelfth month of the lunar year. Like all people, he was one sui at the time of birth. When a new lunar year began a few weeks later, he turned two sui (he entered his second year), at which time he was only one month old. Therefore, Jichan's age in years is often two less than his traditional age in sui. In general, I follow the chronology given by Mei Ji in the appendix of *Bazhi toutsuo shiwen ji* (Changsha: Yuelu shushe, 1984).

5. Thomas Mazanec, *Poet-Monks: The Invention of Buddhist Poetry in Late Medieval China* (Ithaca, NY: Cornell University Press, 2024), 83.

6. My work in this section on plum blossoms is indebted to Huang Ching-chia 黃敬家, *Shichan, Kuangchan, Nüchan: Zhongguo Chanzong wenxue yu wenhua tanlun* 詩禪-狂禪-女禪--中國禪宗文學與文化探論 (Taipei: Taiwan xuesheng shuju, 2011).

7. He also published a collected works in 1888 or so, and his complete works were published posthumously. In addition, he coauthored *Yueyou changhe*

ji 嶽遊唱和集, published in 1888, about a visit to Mount Heng 衡山 of Hunan. It includes thirteen of his poems, and thirteen poems by Wu Jiaduan 吳嘉端, as well as finely produced illustrations of Mount Heng. A copy is available in Tōyō bunka kenkyūjo.

8. This translation was modified from that of Ronald Egan found in his full translation and analysis of Lin Bu's poem, given in Ronald Egan, "*Shi Poetry*: Ancient and Recent Styles (The Five Dynasties and the Song Dynasty)," in *How to Read Chinese Poetry: A Guided Anthology*, ed. Zong-qi Cai (New York: Columbia University Press, 2007).

9. Translation based on *Liandeng huiyao*, in *Shinsan Dainihon Zokuzōkyō*, vol. 79, p. 259, a7-10.

About the Contributors

RAOUL BIRNBAUM is Professor Emeritus of Buddhist Studies at the University of California, Santa Cruz. Across his career, his research has focused on three related areas: the great deity cults of Buddhist China, relations of religious conceptions and practices to mountain traditions in China, and the lives of individuals within this religious field, most especially figures active in China in the first half of the twentieth century. Birnbaum's first long publication, *The Healing Buddha*, was published by Shambhala in 1979 (2nd edition revised, 1989).

BENJAMIN BROSE is professor of Buddhist and Chinese Studies and chair of the department of Asian Languages and Cultures and the University of Michigan. He is the author of several books, including *Xuanzang: China's Legendary Pilgrim and Translator* (Shambhala, 2021).

BEATA GRANT, Professor Emerita of Chinese and Religious Studies (Washington University in St. Louis), lives in Santa Fe, NM. Her publications include *Daughters of Emptiness: Poetry of Buddhist Nuns of China* (Wisdom Publications, 2003); *Eminent Nuns: Female Chan Buddhist Masters of Seventeenth Century China* (University of Hawai'i Press, 2008); *Zen Echoes: Verse Commentaries by Three Female Chan Masters* (Wisdom Publications, 2017); and most recently, *An Anthology of Poetry by Buddhist Nuns of Late Imperial China* (Oxford University Press, 2023.)

GUO GU is a Chan teacher, author, and founder of Tallahassee Chan Center and Dharma Relief. As Jimmy Yu, he is also the Sheng Yen Professor of Chinese Buddhist Studies at Florida State University, and publishes academic works under that name.

ERIK HAMMERSTROM is Professor of East Asian Religion and History at Pacific Lutheran University, and has trained as a Buddhist chaplain. He has published two books on modern Chinese Buddhism with Columbia University Press.

CHARLES B. JONES is a retired scholar based in Washington DC whose research and practice focus on Pure Land Buddhism. He is the author of *Chinese Pure Land Buddhism: Understanding a Tradition of Practice* (University of Hawai'i Press, 2019), *Pure Land: History, Tradition, and Practice* (Shambhala, 2021), and *How Confucius Changed My Mind* (Shambhala, 2025).

JASON PROTASS is associate professor of religious studies at Brown University. He is the author of the book *The Poetry Demon* as well as essays such as "Buddhist Fund-Raising Poems and Other Lost Verse." He most recently co-edited a collection entitled *Countless Sands: Medieval Buddhists and their Environments*.

JUSTIN RITZINGER is an associate professor of religious studies at the University of Miami, whose research focuses on modern Buddhism in China and Taiwan. He spent almost a decade living, working, and traveling in the Chinese-speaking world, primarily Taiwan. The author of *Anarchy in the Pure Land: Reinventing the Cult of Maitreya in Modern Chinese Buddhism*, he is currently working on ethnographic study of a small blue-collar lay group in Taoyuan, Taiwan.

Index

Cover art: *Blossoming Plum*, ca. 1915, Li Ruiqing (Chinese, 1867–1920), hanging scroll; ink and color on paper, 70 1/2 x 18 7/8 in. (179.1 x 47.9 cm). The Metropolitan Museum of Art, gift of Robert Hatfield Ellsworth, in memory of La Ferne Hatfield Ellsworth, 1986 (1986.267.98). Image copyright © The Metropolitan Museum of Art. Image source: Art Resource, NY.